Law Enforcement and the INS

A Participant Observation Study of Control Agents

THIRD EDITION

George Weissinger

Hamilton Books

An Imprint of
Rowman & Littlefield
Lanham • Boulder • New York • Toronto • Plymouth, UK

Copyright © 2017 by George Weissinger

Hamilton Books
4501 Forbes Boulevard, Suite 200, Lanham, Maryland 20706
Hamilton Books Acquisitions Department (301) 459-3366

Unit A, Whitacre Mews, 26-34 Stannary Street,
London SE11 4AB, United Kingdom

Library of Congress Control Number: 2017932711
ISBN: 978-0-7618-6901-6 (pbk : alk. paper)—ISBN: 978-0-7618-6902-3 (electronic)

Dedication refers to the song *La Migra*, © 2005 George Weissinger, GWeissinger Publishing Co., BMI. Used by permission. All Rights reserved by the author. Recorded by the Kingston Trio on Born at the Right Time, Kingston Trio Music Publishing © 2012 BMI.

Cover photo: the author at Key West, Operation Boatlift.

♾™ The paper used in this publication meets the minimum requirements of American National Standard for Information Sciences Permanence of Paper for Printed Library Materials, ANSI/NISO Z39.48-1992.

For
La Migra

Contents

Preface

Earlier editions of this book focused on the perceptions of criminal investigators of the Immigration and Naturalization Service (INS) to describe the normative structure of the agency in its social context. The underlying theory explaining the control agents' perceptions treated norms as rules-in-use, and centered on the processes encountered by the participants in social interaction. As a dual-mandate agency, the legacy INS provided a service and a control function. Among INS investigators, problems of status and morale emerged from the dual mandate requirements of the agency. Problems also surfaced in the areas of organizational relations, as well as notions about professionalism that affect recruitment, retention, training, and worker expectations. On March 1, 2003, the Department of Homeland Security (DHS) combined INS enforcement with US Customs into Immigration Customs Enforcement (ICE), and the service function became US Citizenship and Immigration Services (USCIS). One might assume that this change might resolve the fundamental contradiction imposed by the dual-mandate structure. The updated material in this edition discusses these issues, and the processes contributing to the illegal alien problem.

As a criminal investigator with the INS between 1974 and 1985, the author utilized the participant observation method, as well as official statistics and focused interviews with other criminal investigators assigned to the New York District office (NYDO). The original interview guide included *verbal cues* covering investigative tasks, goals, policy directives, training, morale, and promotion. Factors affecting worker morale included liaison with other law enforcement agencies, and the role of the media in defining the illegal alien problem. These early interviews show a clear pattern of INS policy in the US, and may serve as a tool for future research on the immigration debate. A sample of illegal aliens apprehended in the NYDO was analyzed, and provided descriptive statistics relating to that database. In addition to DHS statistics, data from Number 2598, Survey of Inmates in State and Federal Correctional Facilities, Bureau of Justice Statistics provided information on foreign-born inmates in US correctional facilities.

I am indebted to the investigators that voluntarily participated in the original research process. I made careful efforts to protect their identity, and take full responsibility for the interpretation of their perceptions. A follow-up survey was administered in 2003, and some of the investigators who were previously interviewed in the original survey provided their perceptions on the current immigration problem. Agents in the DHS were also interviewed about the changes effecting interior enforcement, providing qualitative data on INS policies. Official statistics, reports, and statements also provide comparisons between the original perceptions and the current policies. I would like to thank the Author's Guild for their assistance. With limited resources and assistance I edited and formatted this work on my own, and even with careful attention to the process, I take full responsibility for the content, appearance, and any errors. A final note of appreciation to Bob Shane, and the Kingston Trio for recording my song, *La Migra*, on their recent CD, Born at the Right Time.

Chapter One

The Immigration Problem

A Study in Deviance

INTRODUCTION

The actions of participants in the system relating to the immigration problem may best be analyzed within the purview of the sociology of deviance. When control agency policies and mission conflict, implementing enforcement of the law becomes problematic. Other problems occur when a host society fails to deal adequately with migration, and the consequences can lead to chaos. Laws and control agencies to implement them exist in bureaucracies set up to promote efficient service, and fulfill tasks built into mission statements. The success of an agency in this environment is contingent on how well the stated mission is fulfilled. The immigration problem may also be defined in terms of how those in power sometimes interpret norms to satisfy their ideological preferences, instead of enforcing the law. Often, this reconstruction process ignores the true intent of legislation that created the norms, or redefines the underlying principles. When the social construction of reality occurs, it can take on a life of its own. The process can lead to a control agency that opts to promote ideologies, instead of fulfilling a mission.

Defining who the participants are, the costs and benefits of the stakeholders, and their perceptions, provides a more objective description of the schema. In sociology, norms determine which patterns of behavior are acceptable, or not. Sanctions, which include rewards as well as punishments for behavior, play a significant role in whether any rules are followed. However, the normative approach fails to acknowledge those that escape detection in the first place. The traditional reliance on official statistics as reported in the Federal Bureau of Investigation's Uniform Crime Report (UCR)[1], or the

New York Police Department's COMPSTAT[2] data are often used to describe the crime rate. The official statistics are defined and collected by law enforcement agencies, but labeling theory suggests that focusing on crime rates as indicators of deviance misses an important part of the deviance process. Official statistics can be used effectively to define the problem, and ignore other factors that contribute to understanding the total environment surrounding the data. The process is more important than the mere enumeration of offenses, and this process is the focus for this study.

Compliance to norms may take the form of full adherence through complete rejection, but the normative definition often ignores the environment that created the definition of deviance. The social constructionists[3] contributed to our understanding of labeling deviant behavior, and serve as the foundation for contemporary views about the sociological definitions surrounding deviance. Kitsuse[4] offered tertiary deviance as an alternative to this continuum, bringing attention to the outright rejection and reconstruction, or replacement of the definition. The idea of tertiary deviance is important in understanding the evolution of our perceptions about the illegal alien, and will be discussed later.

The *Whorfian* hypothesis that defines linguistic relativity suggests that one's worldview is perceived through the symbols that represent that world. For the most part, reality is shaped by language. In a study of color groupings, Davies[5] found *differences in color categorization associated with differences in the language,* suggesting that language does in fact contribute to our description of the world. Both Becker[6] and Bustamante[7] offered insights into the idea of *norms as rules in use,* and Hawkins and Tiedeman[8] offered the interpretive paradigm as an alternative to the normative definition of deviance. These, and other theories in the social constructionist model will be utilized to explain the illegal alien problem.

INS was a federal agency within the Department of Justice mandated to administer the Immigration and Nationality Act (INA), with sole jurisdiction to enforce the laws relating to aliens, or persons who are not citizens of the US. In a massive bureaucratic reorganization on March 1, 2003, the DHS took over the responsibilities formerly handled by INS[9]. The new agency blended former INS agents and US Customs agents into ICE. Although this new agency appeared to reconcile the dual function mandate found in the legacy INS, this partnership resulted in a division of power between two former control agencies. In addition, the conflicting mandate of service and control in the legacy INS carried over into ICE. US Customs agents, who previously had more resources and status in the law enforcement hierarchy, became dominant stakeholders in an organization where immigration priorities would be subordinated. Where service functions were prioritized in the legacy INS, ICE would downplay the enforcement of the immigration laws inside the US. As a result, morale issues regarding immigration enforcement would continue in this new agency. Even if the legacy INS agents were treated equally, the politics surrounding immigration enforcement would again play a role in the enforcement of the immigration laws.

Many take their citizenship for granted in the US, and societal perceptions about illegal aliens are similar to perceptions about crime. Although there is far more stability than instability in the social structure, societal perceptions about deviance are largely based on media descriptions, and stereotypes. To some extent, the media may be controlled by countervailing pressures between liberal vs. conservative bias to make a profit, and academics seem to vest their liberal and progressive yearnings in an effort to change the world. [10] It is no surprise that the national media leans to the left, and research and surveys support this finding. [11] In addition, the sociological fact that deviance is normal, and actually contributes to social solidarity [12] is not a common-sense notion in mass society. Similarly, inequality is universal and contributes to migration. Many illegal aliens are attempting to facilitate survival strategies by entering the US. Migration is also a universal pattern throughout history, and attempting to explain the illegal alien problem as uniquely American is shortsighted. Approaching the problem through a macrosociological lens offers a fuller understanding of the local issues. Analyzing the meanings behind social interactions will contribute to a better understanding of these issues, and make some sense out of the apparent confusion surrounding the illegal alien problem. As such, this book attempts to describe the normative structure surrounding the immigration problem, and the processes that create it.

The dual mandate is an apparent contradiction since it involves an attempt by one organization to provide a service to the public, while simultaneously attempting to enforce the law. Although DHS would break the chain between ICE and the service mandate, the needs of service to the participants in the system would continue. Interestingly, the program to deal with the service function would become an entity within the organizational structure with even more independence, and power. In a striking example, USCIS would cause some controversy when it barred DHS enforcement agents from investigating a lead related to a terrorist attack in San Bernardino, CA [13].

By focusing on the control agent, the original research analyzed the degree to which INS implemented the dual mandate. That study provides data that contributes to a better understanding of the evolution of present day ICE. Earlier editions of this work included direct observation of the agency at work, official statistics, and focused interviews with special agents assigned to the NYDO in 1981. INS enforcement policies were relatively consistent throughout the 1970's up until the passage of the Immigration Reform and Control Act (IRCA) in 1986. At that time, there was a shift toward locating and placing criminal aliens under deportation proceedings, but this was mostly symbolic since the agency failed to provide adequate resources to implement that change. Yet, millions of illegal aliens were apprehended and removed from the US, both through border and interior enforcement efforts. The enforcement of the immigration laws followed this approach until President Obama took office in 2008. The impact of executive orders, and agency policies in lieu of statutory law dramatically changed the enforcement of the immigration law, and will be discussed later.

This edition also includes an analysis of a sample of illegal aliens apprehended in the NYDO, a follow-up survey of agents who participated in the original study, and updated data on foreign nationals, including media reports and congressional testimony. The original research utilized a participant observation study, and the author was a criminal investigator at the NYDO from 1974 through 1985. Focusing on those who define the parameters of the illegal alien problem will provide more useful information than focusing solely on the illegal alien. As a corollary to this analysis, we may make certain inferences about the nature of the illegal alien population, the *raison d'être* of the immigration control agent.

Police departments routinely provide service, and control functions. Unlike police departments, the federal law enforcement establishment does not provide an alternative service role for their law enforcement personnel. The primary duty of federal special agents is law enforcement, and service functions are separate from their mission. On the other hand, police officers also help individuals, perform service functions such as delivering babies, aid accident victims, and resolve family disputes. Real police work means catching criminals, both for the police and the public, even though more than eighty percent of police work involves paperwork, and service functions. [14] Such role ambiguity creates a problem for the operator, and this appears to be a characteristic of dual mandate agencies where problems of status and morale surface at the operating level. In addition, problems of status and morale appear to be contingent on mission, dual task requirements of the agency, intra-organizational relations that develop as a result, and notions about professionalism among employees. All of these factors influence recruitment, training, and worker expectations.

As law enforcement officers, special agents view their status and morale in terms of how closely their tasks mirror the expected role previously alluded to as *real police work.* Among these agents, there is a hierarchy of tasks upon which they measure their status. Investigators consider criminal investigations to be the most important task, in which the length of sentence often determines the severity of the crime, and the worthiness of the investigation. Control agents consider only tasks directly related to law enforcement as worthy, and agents who routinely perform such tasks will exhibit the highest morale, and have the most status in the organization. The closer the task is to the top of this hierarchy, the higher the status and morale associated with it will be.

Special agents generally view managers as impediments to their *war on crime*. Control agents often place managers in the same category as judges. Generally, they view the courts as being soft on crime, and define good judges as those who are *tough on crime*. Managers must implement policies from above in order to facilitate political goals, and often without regard to the concerns of the field control agents. The terms manager and administrator are used interchangeably by control agents, who sometimes refer to these individuals as *suits*.

Focusing on the control agent will provide a better understanding of the structure and function of the bureaucracy under consideration.[15] One important work that deals with federal control agents is *The Investigators*.[16] Wilson uses Blau's *view from the bottom* perspective in his analysis of the Drug Enforcement Administration (DEA) and the Federal Bureau of Investigation (FBI). Interestingly, Wilson did not include INS criminal investigators in his sample even though they were also GS-1811 series criminal investigators. Furthermore, one should not underestimate the role of the environment in which the control agency operates, and where other groups help shape organizational structure, and contribute to change. As such, issues such as organizational effectiveness, and normative structure are far less important than interpreting the behavior of control agents.

> . . . the rates of deviant behavior produced by social control agencies or by sociological studies are not of interest to the ethnomethodologist as sources of substantive information. Ethnomethodologists choose rather to answer the questions: How are rates constructed? How do they come to be taken as real?[17]

INS AS A CONTROL AGENCY

After five years, a legal resident alien may apply for US citizenship. This process permits the alien to approach the *service* part of the DHS as a client, requesting DHS through USCIS as a professional, to provide the *service*— citizenship, or normalization to immigrant through adjustment of status, either permanent or temporary. Naturalization was originally a judicial process, but now USCIS may approve a naturalization petitions, adding additional power to that program in DHS's hierarchical structure.

> . . . Service organizations involve voluntary symmetrical relationships between professional and client, while control agencies involve asymmetrical, usually involuntary relationships between agency and clients.[18]

The illegal alien becomes the subject of an investigation when reported to INS by an informant. This relationship is asymmetrical, and usually involuntary. Until 1906, INS fell under the Department of the Treasury, was later consolidated into the Department of Commerce and Labor, and in 1913 returned to the Department of Labor. Under a Commissioner, INS moved to the Department of Justice on June 14, 1940.[19] In 2003, under the appointed Secretary of DHS, INS and US Customs agents merged into the DHS-ICE.

An important part of the mission of the DHS-ICE is administering and enforcing the immigration laws. This requires control activities such as inspection of persons who apply for admission into the US, patrolling the international borders to prevent the illegal entry of persons into the US, investigating the status of aliens, and processing and removing those aliens who are found to be in violation of the INA. The legacy INS also performed many service activities such as adjudicating applications for benefits conferred by the statutes, recommending to the courts persons eligible for naturalization, and the maintenance of records on all aliens who are in the US.[20]

As a result of the dual mandate, INS went from department to department in the federal bureaucracy. A complex web of underlying social and political issues blankets the administration of the INA, and creates an identity problem for those who administer it. Where should the administration of immigration law be placed? Does it belong in Commerce where commodities are the focal point? Does it belong in Labor where the workforce and the economy are an issue? As an agency in the Department of Justice, the legacy INS shared the company of the FBI and the DEA, which are enforcement agencies dealing primarily with criminal investigations. DEA went through a similar reorganization, beginning in 1930 as the Federal Bureau of Narcotics, taken out of the Treasury Department merging with the Bureau of Drug Abuse Control in 1968, then in the Department of Health, Education, and Welfare, and installed in the Department of Justice under a new name, the Bureau of Narcotics and Dangerous Drugs. Five years later it was renamed the Drug Enforcement Administration, taking over substantial parts of the Customs Service, and all of the Office of Drug Law Enforcement.[21] Wilson points out that such organizational changes may have very little impact on the nature of the control agent's work. However, the organizational shift from the legacy INS to DHS ICE appears to have exacerbated the problems relating to interior enforcement of the immigration laws, especially with regard to morale. Previously, agents advised that internal changes were occurring at the district level, especially in the New York-New Jersey district, and that these changes might be favorable. Since that time, media reports reflect an ongoing problem inside the DHS-ICE with regard to enforcement of the immigration laws. Prior to the 911 terrorist attacks, there were renewed efforts to promote an amnesty bill, but the attacks would delay such hopes. Yet, after less than two years the idea of amnesty resurfaced. Apparently, politicians have deferred consideration of comprehensive immigration reform until after the 2016 election of a new president. In the absence of speculation, one must remember that immigration reform should only take place through legislation. President Obama's executive orders took the form of a *de facto* amnesty for millions of aliens in, and entering the US. Except for an amnesty provision, surveys[22] suggest that most voters would like to see the immigration laws reformed, and allow the illegal aliens in the US to have a path to citizenship if certain requirements are met. However, partisan views on immigration reform may be placed along a continuum between open borders and mass deportations.

INS: SPECIAL AGENTS AND BORDER PATROL AGENTS

The special agents described in this study are commonly referred to as 1811 investigators, and the titles criminal investigator and special agent are used interchangeably throughout. DHS-ICE agents merged after March 1, 2003 into an agency with a mission unlike the legacy INS, and will also be discussed later. These control agents have the statutory power to arrest criminal law violators without a warrant, normally carry firearms, and are considered to be working under hazardous conditions. Other 1811 investigators in the Department of Justice include special agents of the FBI, and the DEA. Unlike the FBI and the DEA, which are composed almost exclusively of agents at the operating level, the legacy INS included special agents, border patrol agents, deportation officers, and immigration inspectors. Border patrol agents do not routinely conduct criminal investigations, and they are not in the same 1811 personnel classification as special agents. The legacy INS may be compared with a police department which has detectives and patrol officers. Unlike city patrol officers who deal with various crimes and services, the primary function of the border patrol agent is to prevent the illegal entry of aliens into the US. Both legacy and ICE special agents enforce the immigration laws inside the US.

Border patrol agents measure their productivity by the number of apprehensions they make during the fiscal year. On the other hand, special agents deal with more varied problems such as conducting complex criminal investigations, and their work often touches on more politically sensitive issues. Technically, the burden of proof and the rules of evidence are significantly more stringent for the special agents, who usually work in urban areas with large and diverse populations. As a result, investigative productivity is more difficult to measure.

Two examples include the Iranian student problem caused by the hostage crisis at the American Embassy in Iran during 1980, and the Cuban refugees who flocked to the US during *Operation Boatlift* when President Castro announced his plans to allow Cubans to leave Cuba. More recently, the debate on sanctuary cities in the US adds to the problems surrounding interior enforcement. Compared with interior enforcement, the mission of the US Customs and Border Patrol (CBP) would seem to be clear, however that too has become mired in controversy. Even the basic tasks of the CBP have been challenged by current enforcement policies, and their morale has suffered as a result. President Obama's executive orders relating to the Deferred Action for Childhood Arrivals (DACA), and Deferred Action for Parents of Americans (DAPA) essentially deferred any immigration actions against millions of illegal aliens, albeit a temporary deferment. Such executive actions often turn into permanent waivers of deportation. The border patrol union has voiced strong opposition to the executive orders that ultimately evolved into an enforcement policy of *catch and release*[23]. Under DACA and DAPA, illegal aliens that are caught by the border patrol attempting to enter the US are simply released inside the US.

The DHS will handle both border enforcement as well as interior enforcement under a Director of Border and Transportation Security (BTS). Both border patrol agents and investigators will be absorbed within BTS, and join U.S. Customs Service agents, Transportation Security Administration (TSA), and other enforcement personnel to protect the borders. This new mission includes enforcing the immigration laws, as well as narcotics enforcement, illegal commerce, and combating terrorism. The matter of locating and apprehending illegal aliens will continue to present problems in such a diverse country as the US, and reactions to any large-scale "round-up" to solve this problem will meet with both positive, and negative reactions from those concerned. Focusing on criminal groups and terrorists will distract the public and the media from critical review, but not entirely. Even after the terrorist attacks on 911, there were concerns about selective enforcement, or profiling certain groups over others. The official US policy includes objectivity and fairness, and excludes the singling out of any group or individual.

> This Bureau will bring together the enforcement and investigation arms of the Customs Service, the investigative and enforcement functions of Immigration and Naturalization Service and the Federal Protective Services. The reorganization involved approximately 14,000 employees, including 5,500 criminal investigators, 4,000 employees for immigration and deportation services and 1,500 Federal Protective Service personnel that will focus on the mission of enforcing the full range of immigration and customs laws within the interior of the US in addition to protecting specified federal buildings. The air and marine enforcement functions of the Customs Service will also be a part of this bureau.[24]

In analyzing police organizations, one often observes compartmentalization and exclusivity between sections. Homicide detectives may have higher status than other detective units since they conduct higher priority investigations, and the plainclothes detectives may be at odds with the uniformed division over who is doing a more important job. Similarly, we would expect such perceptions to surface between the investigators, and border patrol agents. However, legacy INS investigators did not consider the border patrol agents, or their mission, any less important than their own. The perceptions regarding the allocation of resources, and the failure to implement the interior enforcement mission were directed at management, not the border patrol agents. In this environment, the legacy INS used the border patrol the same way it did the investigations program. Now that the border patrol has merged with customs patrol into DHS-CBP, they too are beginning to experience morale problems due to manpower shortages. A rift existed between the investigations branch, and the border patrol within the legacy INS. The border patrol commanded a large part of INS budget, while interior enforcement worked with a relatively small part of the agency's overall budget. However, the border patrol was also experiencing morale problems throughout the legacy INS period. Investigators respected the border patrol mission, but also believed that investigations lacked similar support and resources. The role played by the border patrol and inspections is just as important as the role played by investigators in enforcing the immigration laws, and this perception was nearly universal among the investigators.

INVESTIGATING AND PROCESSING ILLEGAL ALIENS

The phrase illegal alien is a popular expression rather than a term defined in the INA. The DHS defines an illegal alien as a foreign national who (a) entered the US without inspection or with fraudulent documentation or (b) who, after entering legally as a nonimmigrant, violated status and remained in the US without authority.[25] It replaced the more colloquial term *wetback* that was widely used throughout the fifties and is now considered a derogatory term. In the past, opposing groups have debated the use of the terms *undocumented alien,* or *illegal alien.*[26] Those opposed to the use of the term illegal alien claim the term ignores sensitivity to the concerns of the Mexican government, or that it connotes criminality, while the opposing group maintain that the term illegal alien is a more accurate characterization of the offender.[27] Other labels used to describe the illegal alien include *illegal immigrant, undocumented worker, undocumented alien, unauthorized immigrant,* and *deportable alien.*[28]

An alien is any person not a citizen or national of the US (INA), and we may define an illegal alien as any alien in the US in violation of the INA. Illegal aliens are subject to arrest and deportation proceedings by INS, the only agency empowered to enforce the INA. As stated earlier, the border patrol had prime jurisdiction over enforcement of the INA along the border, while interior enforcement was the function of the investigations section.

Although legacy INS investigators were statutorily limited to enforcing the INA, the nature of their work involved possible encounters with other than immigration law violators. In these instances, an agent could take action by arresting a suspect. In states where federal agents have *peace officer* status (New York State identifies most special agents as peace officers), special agents can make citizen arrests for other than immigration violations. At the time, the policy of INS was to avoid encounters with such offenders, most likely tied to issues involving due process, and liability. Federal agents do not decide to arrest law violators casually, since the arresting officer is subject to judicial review, and civil action if the person arrested is subsequently vindicated. As we shall see, legacy INS agents did not perceive that managers would support them in such cases. It is the policy of the US Attorney's office to defend the action of officers acting within the scope of their employment, but the legacy INS agents believed that they would be excluded from such protection. Such perceptions can adversely impact on work performance, as well as morale.

The vast majority of legacy INS enforcement operations involved deportation proceedings, and were administrative in nature. Deportation has been defined as the removal of an alien out of the country simply because their presence is deemed inconsistent with the public welfare, without any punishment being contemplated or imposed. A crime is any violation of law punishable in a criminal proceeding.[29] In such proceedings, the illegal alien faces either deportation or adjustment of status to legal resident. Many illegal aliens are simply asked to voluntarily leave the US at their expense. Although deportation theoretically excludes punishment, some consider it an economic sanction. Since most illegal aliens come to the US to work, their removal could be considered a deprivation of economic needs, and aspirations.

Furthermore, one essential factor associated with illegal aliens as a group is their fear of being apprehended, and deported by INS. In labeling jargon, this factor alone creates a sizable hidden population that could be considered secondary, or career deviants.

Even if an agent encounters an illegal alien, equities may exist preventing removal. In some instances, there may be a rational justification for ignoring an alien's illegal status. The Romans rewarded foreigners with citizenship if they contributed to the military pursuits of the nation in any way. Similarly, if an illegal alien completes military service, that alien becomes eligible for permanent resident status.

> What, then happened to the culprit, the man who . . . was prosecuted in a criminal court and found to have been passing himself off falsely as a Roman citizen? His punishment, it seems, was very mild indeed; he was merely forbidden to continue to live in the city of Rome.[30]

Agents begin processing illegal aliens by advising them of their due process rights, even though deportation is an administrative proceeding. The constitutional provisions of *Miranda v. Arizona* (1966) apply to criminal, not administrative proceedings. Providing free legal representation to illegal aliens profoundly impedes the system, and would be both costly and time consuming. The legacy INS focused on locating and apprehending low-level visa abusers, or worksite apprehensions, and the majority of interior apprehensions were administrative law violations. Although there were special units in the legacy INS (Special Investigations, Frauds, Smuggling, Organized Crime Drug Enforcement Task Forces) they were a small part of enforcement operations in the legacy program where The Area Control Illegal Status (ACIS) unit made the majority of interior apprehensions. Since 2008, the priorities of the interior enforcement of the immigration laws shifted away from the low-level abuser (worksite enforcement) toward criminal aliens, and terrorist investigations.

During processing, aliens are asked about their entry into the US, and factors surrounding their activities that subject them to deportation. Also, attempts are made to determine if there are any favorable factors that would permit them to remain in the US. The source for most of this information is the Form I-213, Record of Deportable Alien. Some of the recommendations an agent can make after processing an alien are: (1) issuance of an order to show cause why the alien should not be deported with, or without an (2) issuance of a warrant of arrest to detain the alien; (3) voluntary departure of an alien by a certain date; (4) no action, alien in status, or, (5) further investigation to determine amenability of the alien to INS proceedings. Furthermore, certain events may cause entire categories of aliens to receive indefinite waivers from deportation, such as a natural disaster, or a civil disorder in their country of origin. A supervisory agent will then review the recommendations (primarily for accuracy), and either approve or refer the matter to the agent for further information as may be required. Most cases are routinely approved simply because they are similar in nature. When President Obama issued his executive orders on DACA and DAPA, this created an entire category of aliens that would be immune from immediate prosecution, or deportation proceedings.

Upon admission into the US, nonimmigrant or temporary aliens are issued a Form I-94, Arrival-Departure Record, which they are required to carry at all times, and present to an immigration officer on demand. An agent can readily classify an alien when he reads this form, since the admission stamp indicates the period of time for which the alien was admitted, and the type of visa. The Arrival-Departure Record begins the processing apparatus, and determines alienage and deportability. However, most illegal aliens do not have any travel documents at all because they simply walk across the southern border, or are smuggled into the US. If they are located by DHS, they will be interrogated and asked to provide a written statement about how they entered the US. The written statement then serves as the basis for the charges of deportability.

Routinization of work emerges from this process, with such actions as the issuance of orders to show cause, which are pre-typed forms with a blank space to insert the aliens name. In most cases, the charges and the disposition will be the same, and due to the enormous volume of cases, a typical funneling effect takes place. In lieu of actual deportation, many aliens are offered voluntary departure, another example of routinization.

Cases are *typified* through quick classification into standardized categories that elicit routine responses. The individuals dealt with by the organization are reacted to as instances of those *normal* types, and disposition of their cases . . . are made accordingly. The likelihood of this happening is heightened still further when, as so often occurs, work overload compels the organization to employ *assembly line* methods. [31]

ADMINISTRATIVE AND CRIMINAL LAW VIOLATIONS

Unlike the FBI and the DEA whose main tasks involve investigating crimes, the primary concern of the legacy INS Investigations Branch was the enforcement of administrative violations of the INA. The goals of criminal enforcement agencies are rarely questioned, although their methods have been questioned on legal, ethical, and moral grounds. In contrast with the INS, very few people in society would argue that what FBI and DEA agents do is not in their best interests.

> . . . while citizens will disagree as to what constitutes right and seemly conduct, they will usually agree that murder, robbery, burglary, and illicit trafficking in dangerous drugs are wrong, that they are worthwhile objects for investigative efforts, and that those responsible for these offenses deserve punishment. [32]

Even though the agent is enforcing the law, certain cultural values pose a dilemma for the control agent. It is difficult for the ordinary citizen to distinguish between illegal aliens, and immigrants, since many of them enter to work. The hard work ethic, sympathy for the underdog, and cultural diversity are core values in American culture. Similarly, the perception of most people about illegal aliens is that they are not dangerous deviants, or criminals. The media, pro-immigrant activists, and most in academia actively promote these perceptions, often ignoring data that contradicts such perceptions. Therefore, when the investigator arrests an illegal alien in the work place, citizens sometimes will remark that the alien *isn't really doing anything wrong,* or *he's just trying to earn a living. Why not go after real criminals?*

An official policy of the agency was to place a priority on criminal cases. Two of the most common types of violators of the INA are aliens who have entered without inspection (EWI), and alien crewmen that desert their vessels. Such cases are both administrative (the alien is subject to deportation proceedings), and criminal (the alien is subject to prosecution under the criminal statutes).

The majority of criminal violations (EWI) are not even presented to the US Attorney for prosecution. In 1977, the agency reported 13,726 convictions for aliens who entered illegally. However, there were an astounding 818,849 *direct departures under safeguards,* chiefly Mexican nationals who entered without inspection. In essence, these individuals were *caught in the act* and summarily required to depart at that time. As a result, only one percent of these violations were prosecuted. There is nothing unique about such policies, and they occur throughout the criminal justice system where many cases are not prosecuted simply because it is not in the best interests of society. Furthermore, criminal prosecutions are time consuming, costly, and require a system that can facilitate the processing of a massive number of cases. Sociologically, this amounts to a form of *de facto* decriminalization, and destigmatizes deviance as well.

In the sample of aliens processed in the NYDO, INS processed twice as many visitors as EWI's. The NYDO office is located near major ports of entry including JFK and Newark International Airports, where foreign applicants require passports and visas in order to enter the US. Aliens that commit visa fraud, or overstay the amount of time they were allowed to remain in the US, were the most common types of violations encountered by the agency. Twenty four percent of the illegal aliens processed by the NYDO were aliens that entered without inspection, and most of these cases involved aliens that successfully eluded the border patrol along the Mexico-US border. Their trek from the southwest border of the US to New York illustrates another important interior enforcement concern, that of transporting and harboring illegal aliens which are both felonies. The border patrol may legally inspect vehicles and persons within 100 miles of the US-Mexico border, however once the alien goes beyond this perimeter interior enforcement agents are bound by the restrictions mandated by due process. This makes interior enforcement of harboring and transporting illegal aliens far more difficult.

The majority of apprehensions by the legacy INS were Mexican nationals. Of the 1,062,279 deportable aliens located in 2002, 95.6% were from Mexico, and the majority of these apprehensions (97%) were classified as entry without inspection (ewi)[33]. Compared with more current apprehension data, there was a dramatic decrease in true interior apprehensions depending on how you interpret the new organizational priorities. DHS created the Enforcement Removal Operations (ERO) section that included CBP apprehensions along the Mexico-US border. According to DHS, the decrease in apprehensions reflected what they referred to as clearer and more refined civil INS strategies, which ICE began implementing in FY2015[34]. Shifting priorities presumably to *keeping our Nation safe and secure* did not include the sanctuary cities that release criminal aliens with immigration detainers, nor did the DHS policy that amounted to a catch-and-release program which resulted from President Obama's executive orders on DACA and DAPA. The enforcement priorities program also redefined criminal convictions which strangely excluded certain illegal aliens with felony convictions who were now deemed inappropriate for removal. Such policies hardly keep a nation safe and secure, but they do facilitate a *de facto* amnesty for illegal aliens.

In 2004, ICE apprehended 103,837 deportable aliens inside the US. In 2013, Homeland Security Investigations (HSI) the ICE special agents that conduct interior investigations apprehended only 11,996 aliens. In the NYDO sample analyzed later in this book, 10,843 illegal aliens were apprehended in one year in that district alone. During that same period, agents apprehended 204,193 deportable aliens, which reflects a dramatic decrease in interior enforcement apprehensions. Although there were 229,698 additional apprehensions by ICE-ERO in 2013, these additional apprehensions misrepresent the actual interior apprehensions because they include CBP apprehensions near the US-Mexico border. It is also interesting to note that there was a significant decrease in the apprehension of aliens from Mexico (424,978 in 2013 compared with 1,142,807 in 2004) and a dramatic increase in apprehensions of aliens from El Salvador (51,226 in 2013, 19,180 in 2004), Guatemala (73,208 in 2013, 14,288 in 2004), and Honduras (64,157 in 2013, 26,555 in 2004). The increases and decreases can best be explained as a result of policy changes implemented as a result of the aforementioned executive orders. Essentially, realignment of the interior program to include ERO makes it appear that DHS-ICE is actually enforcing the immigration laws inside the US. Even a casual observer would agree that the interior enforcement of the immigration laws is less than aggressive. DHS justifies this decrease in interior enforcement as a strategic plan meant to focus on criminal aliens, and use limited resources to enforce the INA. However, one might also conclude that policies that ignore the millions of illegal aliens in the US represents a *de facto* amnesty, bypassing the expected legislation necessitated by such a dramatic change.

THE RIGHTS OF ALIENS IN THE US

Illegal aliens are entitled to the rights afforded in the Fourteenth Amendment to the Constitution.

No state shall make or enforce any law which shall abridge the privileges or immunities of citizens of the US; nor shall any state deprive any person of life, liberty, or property, without due process of law; nor deny to any person within its jurisdiction the equal protection of the laws . . .

Aliens serving in diplomatic status are not considered to be under the jurisdiction of the US, however they are protected by diplomatic immunity from most administrative and criminal statutes. In fact, they may enjoy more rights than most others.

Legacy INS agents were bound by the rules of criminal procedure and evidence, even though most of what they did was administrative work. As previously stated, illegal aliens are now afforded the same rights as criminals, including legal counsel. Of course, in a criminal proceeding the individual may ultimately lose his freedom, whereas in a deportation proceeding, *no punishment is imposed, or contemplated.* Both the USA Patriot Act of 2001[35] and The Enhanced Border Security and Visa Entry Reform Act of 2002[36] focus on issues of national security and preventing terrorism. As such, the rights of aliens are still intact. Except for "enemy combatants," or those designated as the enemy by the commander-in-chief, aliens are afforded all due process provided in the Constitution. In general, it is easier to prevent an alien from entering the US (exclude) than it is to remove an alien from the US (deport). Recent legislation has also attempted to remove criminal aliens more expeditiously, but human rights groups are intent on maintaining the equilibrium between individual rights and social control. Humanitarian response to global crises have a profound impact on immigration law enforcement. The Mariel Boatlift, the Iranian hostage crisis, natural disasters in Central America, earthquakes in Haiti, hurricanes, and of course the refugee crisis in the Middle East will change the way immigration laws are enforced.

Immigration officers duly designated by the US Attorney General are authorized by statute to investigate, interrogate, and apprehend illegal aliens in the US, and most of these apprehensions are without a warrant. Arrest without a warrant was the routine rather than the exception among the legacy INS agents.

> . . . the great majority of arrests made by an FBI agent are made by executing an arrest warrant issued by a judicial officer . . . the *FBI Handbook* instructs agents that, whenever possible, prosecution should be authorized and a warrant issued prior to arrest. *An arrest without a warrant is acceptable only in emergency situations.*[37]

INS agents are bound by the same guidelines, but they rarely have the time to obtain an arrest warrant before the violator absconds. The majority of arrests made by legacy INS agents were without a warrant because the likelihood of an illegal alien absconding is very high. As a result, agents develop a *feel* for the kinds of people they encounter in the field. A great deal of *typing* goes on in the field, especially regarding suspected law violators.

Typing or categorizing both situations and individuals is understandably relied on as a means of sifting through an overwhelming body of observations and impressions to gain a sense of predictable patterns and some confidence in reacting to them.[38]

The conditions of this process are especially relevant in terms of negotiating situations as they occur. This typification process will be discussed later. In their daily activities, immigration officers may encounter any of the following:

An alien who is illegally in the US
An alien with fraudulent documents
An alien in police custody for a reason unrelated to his immigration status
An alien who is a member of a subversive/terrorist organization
An alien smuggled into the US

It is not uncommon for an alien to share the above characteristics simultaneously and to have equities muting the status altogether. As one can imagine, interior enforcement of the immigration law is both complex, and problematic. The nature of these problems will also be discussed later.

PROBLEMS OF STATUS AND MORALE AMONG AGENTS

Legacy agents were assigned to different sections in the Investigations Unit. In order to transfer to another section, an agent had to submit a memorandum through official channels requesting one. Agents were asked to discuss the differences between the sections, and why membership in one section might hold more status than another. Also, since INS is a large government bureaucracy and agents receive similar training, a small sample of elite interviews should accurately reflect the inner workings of the agency.

Grade level is another important status distinction among special agents. Legacy agents were hired at the General Schedule (GS) 5 level and promoted annually (if requirements are met, but generally automatically) to the GS-11 level. The promotion schedule is as follows: entry at GS-5; after one year promotion to G-7; after two years, promotion to G-9; after the third year, promotion to G-11. Promotions after the GS-11 grade level are supposed to be based upon competitive selection processes. However, agents distinguish between earned promotions and those based on factors such as nepotism, or *whom one knows* rather than *what one knows*. A GS-12 position is posted and applied for by agents. In the legacy INS, only seventeen percent of the agents were GS-12, and the prospects for promotion to GS-12 were nonexistent due to a promotion freeze beyond the career ladder. This factor had a significant impact on such variables as attitude, incentive, morale, and goals of the agents. In 1991, significant changes were made in the pay rates of federal law enforcement officers, which seemed to confirm that their salaries were below their counterparts in state and local governments. In addition, there were changes made to address the variable of differences in cost of living at different geographic areas in the US. Obviously, a GS-12 agent stationed in a rural area fares better economically than one stationed in New York City.

Salaries are a critical factor affecting the attitudes and self-concepts of employees. The average grade of the legacy INS agent was the lowest of all agents in the Department of Justice, including FBI and DEA agents, although all are 1811 investigators. In May 2004 DHS reportedly corrected this problem and gave competitive grades to the former legacy INS agents.

The following chapter discusses the major trends in the development of immigration law and policy, and can contribute to explaining some of the problems involved in interior immigration enforcement.

NOTES

1. FBI, *Uniform Crime Reporting*, https://ucr.FBI.gov/

2. NYPD. *Crime Prevention*, http://www.nyc.gov/html/nypd/html/crime_prevention/crime_statistics.shtml

3. Among others, the classic works include: Erving Goffman *The Presentation of Self in Everyday Life*. NY: Anchor Books, 1959; Howard Becker, Outsiders: *Studies in the Sociology of Deviance*. NY: Free Press, 1973; Edwin Lemert. *Social Pathology*. NY: McGraw Hill, 1951; and John Kitsuse, "Societal Reactions to Deviant Behavior: Problems of Theory and Method," *Social Problems*, 9:247-257.

4. J. W. Schneider and J. I. Kitsuse, *Studies in The Sociology of Social Problems* (1984).

5. I. R. Davies, "A study of colour grouping in three languages: A test of the linguistic relativity hypothesis," *British Journal of Psychology 89*(3) (1998): 433.

6. Howard Becker, (1989). "Moral Entrepreneurs: The Creation and Enforcement of Deviant Categories," in Delos H. Kelly, *Deviant Behavior: A Text Reader in the Sociology of Deviance*, edited by Delos H. Kelly, 24. New York: St. Martin's Press.

7. Jorge A. Bustamante, "The Wetback as Deviant: An Application of Labeling Theory," *American Journal of Sociology*, 77(4) (1972): 716.

8. Richard Hawkins, and Gary Tiedeman, The Creation of Deviance: Interpersonal and Organizational Determinants (Ohio: Merrill, 1975).

9. "Who We Are," DHS website, Accessed June16, 2016 https://www.ice.gov/

10. D. Sutter, "Mechanisms of Liberal Bias in the News Media versus the Academy," *Independent Review, 16*(3), (2012): 399-415.

11. T. J. Smith III, "The Media Elite Revisited. (Cover story)," *National Review*, 45(12), (1993): 34-37.

12. George B. Vold, and T. J. Bernard, *Theoretical Criminology, 3rd Edition* (New York: Oxford University Press, 1986), 146-150. Emile Durkheim considered crime a normal, inevitable and integral part of all societies. *The Rules of Sociological Method*, tr. by Sarah Solovay, and J. Mueller, ed. By G. E. G. Catlin, (New York: The Free Press, 1965).

13. Malia Zimmerman and M. Dean, "Feds Blocked from Person of Interest after San Bernardino Attack," Foxnews.com, 2016, March 15. http://www.foxnews.com/politics/2016/03/15/feds-blocked-from-person-interest-after-san-bernardino-attack-lawmakers-told.html.

14. Peter K. Manning, *Police Work: The Social Organization of Policing* (Massachusetts: MIT Press, 1977), 5.

15. Peter M Blau, *On the Nature of Organizations,* (New York: John Wiley and Sons, Inc., 1974), 15.

16. James Q. Wilson, The Investigators: Managing FBI and Narcotics Agents, (New York: Prentice Hall, Inc., 1978).

17. Richard Hawkins and Gary Tiedeman, *The Creation of Deviance: Interpersonal and Organizational Determinants,* (Ohio: Merrill Publishing Company, 1975), 24-25.

18. Ibid., 217.

19. *US Code Annotated,* (St. Paul, Minnesota: West Publishing Company, 1976), Section 1551.

20. *US Congress, Department of State, Justice, and Commerce, The Judiciary, and Related Agencies Appropriations For 1981,* Hearings Before a Subcommittee of the Committee on Appropriations House of Representatives, 96th Congress, 2nd Session, Washington, DC: U. S. Government Printing Office, p. 538.

21. James Q. Wilson, The Investigators: Managing FBI and Narcotics Agents, (New York: Prentice Hall, Inc., 1978), 6.

22. Daniel Cox, Juhem Navarro-Rivera, Robert P. Jones, "Citizenship, Values, and Cultural Concerns: What Americans Want from Immigration Reform," PRRI, March 21, 2013, http://www.prri.org/research/2013-religion-values-immigration-survey/

23. J. Kevin, (n.d). Border patrol catches, then releases, illegals. (USA Today).

24. *History of ICE,* DHS website, Accessed June 16, 2016, https://www.ice.gov/history

25. DHS website, Accessed June 16, 2016, https://e-verify.uscis.gov/esp/media/resources-Contents/Glossary/glossary.htm#i

26. Procon.org, Accessed June 16, 2016, http://immigration.procon.org/view.answers.php?questionID=000757

27. FAIRUS.org, Accessed June 16, 2016, http://www.fairus.org/DocServer/research-pub/Use_of_Illegal-Alien.pdf

28. Committee on the Judiciary, *U. S. Immigration Law and Policy: 1952-1979,* Washington, DC: U. S. Government Printing Office, 71.

29. *US Code Annotated,* St. Paul, Minnesota: West Publishing Company, 1976.

30. J. P. V. D. Balsdon, *Romans and Aliens,* (North Carolina: University of North Carolina Press, 1980), 101.

31. Edwin M, Schur, *Interpreting Deviance: A Sociological Introduction,* (New York: Harper and Row, 1979), 339.

32. James Q. Wilson, The Investigators: Managing FBI and Narcotics Agents, (New York: Prentice Hall, Inc., 1978), 20.

33. Abridged table, Source: Table 3, INS Statistical Yearbook, 2002

34. DHS website, Accessed June 16, 2016, https://www.ice.gov/removal-statistics

35. Rosemary Jenks, (December 2001). *The USA Patriot Act of 2001: A Summary of the Anti-Terrorism Law's Immigration-Related Provisions.* (Washington, DC: Center for Immigration Studies), The complete text of the law is available on line at: http://thomas.loc.gov

36. Rosemary Jenks, The Enhanced Border Security and Visa Entry Reform Act of 2002: A Summary of H.R. 3525. (Washington, DC: Center for Immigration Studies, June 2002).

37. James Q. Wilson, The Investigators: Managing FBI and Narcotics Agents, (New York: Prentice Hall, Inc., 1978), 20.

38. Edwin M, Schur, *Interpreting Deviance: A Sociological Introduction,* (New York: Harper and Row, 1979), 356.

Chapter Two

Immigration Laws

The Task of Social Control

A REVIEW OF IMMIGRATION LEGISLATION AND POLICIES

The US is often referred to as a nation of immigrants, with immigration legislation and policies tied to an expanding country. As this need was satisfied, newcomers met with resistance and discrimination. Some examples of restrictions on immigration policy included: the *Alien and Sedition* Acts (1798), nativist movements against Catholic immigration (1830's), the Chinese Exclusion Acts (1882), as well as limiting access to certain types of immigrants (southern and eastern Europeans, and Asians). The 1924 National Origins Act established immigration based on those groups already here, and the McCarran-Walter Act (1952) retained the national origins system, as well as unrestricted immigration from the Western Hemisphere. As a result, immigration law centered on reuniting families, protecting domestic labor, and recruiting needed skilled workers that were scarce. The Immigration Act of 1990 sought diversity in increasing the numbers of special skills workers, and replacing European immigration in large part by migrants from Africa and Asia.

The INA Amendments of 1965 imposed an annual ceiling of 120,000 immigrants on previously unrestricted migration from the Western Hemisphere. It also fixed an annual ceiling of 170,000 immigrants from Eastern Hemisphere countries, with a 20,000 visa limit on each Eastern Hemisphere country, and 120,000 visas for the Western Hemisphere. The 1976 Amendments extended the preference system to the Western Hemisphere, and the 20,000 per country limit to both hemispheres, with 170,000 visas for the Eastern Hemisphere, and 120,000 visas for the Western Hemisphere.

Legislation enacted by the 95th Congress, Public Law 95-412, continued the
reforms initiated by the 1965 amendments. The Act of October 5, 1978, established a single worldwide ceiling of 290,000 for the admission of immigrants,
combining the existing separate ceilings of 170,000 and 120,000 on the Eastern and Western Hemispheres, respectively. The preference system is applied
once under this single worldwide ceiling . . . [1]

Although the INS began collecting apprehension statistics in 1925, it is
difficult to trace the exact course of enforcement operations. The border
patrol program started in 1924, and INS investigations began operations in
1946. Initially, the investigations program concentrated on locating and de-
porting subversive and criminal aliens, and thereafter focused on the broad
task of locating and removing illegal aliens from the US. Thereafter, international issues created an environment in which the investigations program
played a more complex role. Governments often focus on aliens during a
war, but the 911 terrorist attacks immediately acknowledged the role that
immigration plays in national security. Both the USA Patriot Act, and the
creation of DHS-ICE were related to this reaction to a crisis.

In fulfilling its mandate, the legacy INS maintained that it did not discriminate against any groups. Some critics allege that the agency focused on
apprehending illegal aliens from Mexico. Phillip Smith, Assistant District
Director, INS Los Angeles District Office, stated, "our enforcement policy
relates the same, regardless of nationality. We apprehend aliens who are in
this country illegally from all nations."[2]

Like the war in Vietnam, some observers believed INS was waging a war
it could not win.

Our border patrol boggles our minds with its statistics—all about Mexicans. It
claims to arrest 3,000 Mexican illegals each day. But these figures are de-
signed to dazzle us and hide the truth, like the 'body count' in Vietnam. Over
90% of those arrested are recycled—that is, sent back to Mexico the same
day—and they appear in the statistics again and again.[3]

Such statistics seem to confirm that the legacy INS was attempting to
prevent the illegal entry of Mexicans into the US. In 1978, 97% of the aliens
apprehended by the Border patrol (870,640) were from Mexico, but a closer
look reveals something else. In that year, the investigations program apprehended 187,337 aliens, or 22% of total INS apprehensions (1,057,977)[4]. In a
previous study of illegal aliens apprehended by the NYDO, only 11.5% of
the aliens processed between December 1977 and October 1978 were from
Mexico. INS estimated that 58.3% of the illegal alien population in 1990 was
from Mexico, and that number increased to 68.7% in 2000.[5]

The Antiterrorism and Effective Death Penalty Act of April 24 1996
included procedures to expedite the removal of aliens who were classified as

terrorists. In addition, the law focused on excluding members of terrorist organizations from entering the US in the first place. The 1996 Act also attempted to deal with the criminal alien population by making certain crimes (alien smuggling) Racketeering Influence Corrupt Organization (RICO) offenses, increasing efforts to deport those involved in crimes of moral turpitude, and authorizing state and local law enforcement officials to arrest and detain certain illegal aliens. [6]

The Personal Responsibility and Work Opportunity Reconciliation Act of August 22, 1996 attempted to restrict aliens from receiving public assistance, including legal resident aliens with some exceptions from obtaining food stamps, and Supplemental Security Income. The Act attempted to increase the responsibility of alien sponsors by enforcing provisions of the affidavits of support, and extending the period of adjustment before an alien becomes eligible.

The Illegal Immigration Reform and Immigrant Responsibility Act of September 30, 1996 attempted to enhance border and workplace enforcement measures, limit issuance of driver's licenses to illegal aliens, and again focus on monitoring compliance of Social Security benefits, as well as higher educational assistance programs. The Act also changed certain INS regulations regarding asylum applicants, parole authority discretion, students, and collecting information on foreign students in the US.

A closer look at apprehension data from the NYDO sample provides a more accurate description of the illegal alien problem. Compared with national data, only 11.5% of the apprehensions were Mexican nationals, 8.3% Dominican Republic, 7.6% Ecuador, 7.5% Haiti, 7.1% Colombia, 5.9% El Salvador, 4.5% Jamaica, 3.6% Greece, 3.3% Guatemala, 2.6% Africa, and 38.1% other (less than 2% all other countries). Subsequently, President Obama's executive orders increased the number of aliens entering illegally from Central America.

The investigations program dealt with far more ethnic diversity than the border patrol, yet official statistics routinely presented broad category descriptions of operations combining the work of border, and interior enforcement. Perhaps, focusing on border enforcement supports the agency perception that illegal immigration is a Mexico-US problem. However, the immigration problem spills over the borders, and becomes an interior enforcement problem as well. Before INS special agents merged with Customs into ICE in 2003, INS statistical yearbooks began publishing previously excluded tables about the accomplishments of the investigations program. Apparently, the consequences of 911 caused the agency to officially acknowledge the efforts of the investigations program.

RECENT LEGISLATION AND POLICY

As previously noted, the 1976 Amendments to the INA attempted to normalize visa allocations to nationals of the Eastern and Western Hemispheres.
Generally, immigration legislation follows three principles: family, business,
and removing *undesirables*. The effects of the 1976 Act on enforcement took
the form of creating a new category of aliens in the US: Western Hemi-
sphere/Temporary Restraining Order aliens (WHTRO). These aliens became
eligible for preference visas, and received temporary legal status only after
INS processed them. Many voluntarily surrendered to INS for processing to
acquire this legal status. The processing allowed the WH-TRO alien to obtain
temporary legal residence with work authorization, and become eligible for
permanent resident visas under the preference system. The status of the alien
changes from control to service when they acquire such equities. In this
sense, INS provided a service to the alien by processing the application. At
the time, the INA restricted the admission of refugees under seventh preference visas to 17,400 annual admissions. However, the Attorney General of
the US often exercised discretionary power to admit aliens under a parole
provision.

> Since the fall of Vietnam and Cambodia in Spring 1975, approximately 200,000
> Indochinese refugees have entered the US as refugees . . . admitted under the
> parole provision . . . outside the numerical restrictions of the law . . . [7]

In *Operation Boatlift*, the large number of Cuban refugees into the US
created a problem for INS. Over 125,000 Cubans came to the US between
April 15, 1980 and October 31, 1980 from the port of Mariel, Cuba. Out of
the 23,000 refugees who admitted a prior criminal record to inspectors, only
2% of that number, or 2,746 Cubans, were considered criminals under US
law.[8] At the time, there were about 1,700 Mariel Cubans indefinitely detained in US prisons.[9] Cubans living in the US paid smugglers to travel to
Cuba, and return with their relatives. Even though the refugees would be
allowed to stay in the US, smuggling investigations were initiated. Since
smuggling involves illegal entries, it would be difficult to successfully prosecute such cases because the refugee would be legally admitted. As a result,
most of the indictments were vacated. The legacy INS responded to the
Mariel boatlift as if it were a crisis, and sent enforcement agents to Florida to
work on service related task forces. The purpose of this response was to clear
up the backlogs of applications that resulted from this massive influx of
aliens. The author volunteered for *Operation Boatlift* and conducted smuggling investigations both in Miami, and Key West, Florida. As indicated, the
agency did not prosecute many smugglers. Many more investigators were

assigned to adjudication task forces (service), and commented on *Operation Boatlift* later in this study.

> I was pleasantly surprised by the orientation when I arrived in Miami, Florida after volunteering to work in the anti-smuggling investigation, Operation Boatlift. An INS manager addressed the investigators, and promised the troops that they could have all the resources needed to complete the job. It was the first time at INS that I ever received a government car to use at my discretion, and I began to think that INS was finally going to do something useful. That euphoria quickly ended after my partner and I arrived at headquarters in Miami and we met our supervisor, a border patrol agent, with his boots up on the office desk. I remember him saying that he did not have too much experience in writing investigative reports and would be relying on the investigators to fill this void. The border patrol was running the show even though many investigators had the same, or higher, grade levels than the Border patrol supervisors. It turned out that INS was just spinning its wheels in Florida. It did not make much difference because nothing was ever accomplished except that thousands of refugees were allowed to enter the US. For a brief time, it was exhilarating to think that a task force might accomplish something with the resources and backing of the agency.

Essentially, INS shut down interior enforcement to support the Census Bureau's counting illegal aliens during the 1980 Census. The agency did this by creating a policy that prevented agents from conducting routine investigations at private residences. Apparently, INS believed that this policy directive would encourage illegal aliens to respond to the Census questionnaires and *be counted.* Such tactics are typical throughout the history of the investigations program, but the real intent is to obstruct interior enforcement of the INA. Such policies seek to create the perception that illegal aliens will become fearful, and therefore hesitate to cooperate with police, or report crimes. Policies that interfere with the rule of law may be explained as political efforts to pander to constituencies. Most likely, the intent of such policies is not to make society better, control abuse of power, corruption, or excessive use of force, but to help politicians get reelected.

EXECUTIVE ACTIONS AND REACTIONS TO CRISIS

With a majority of democrats in Congress, President Obama could have passed sweeping immigration reform when he took office in 2009. Some[10] believe the reticence to do so was a concern for the political fallout of an amnesty bill, and how that would impact on the reelection of its supporters. The presumption is that any such legislation would be liberal in terms of legal, and illegal immigration, and most voters would perceive this as an amnesty bill. If so, why did President Obama wait until the midnight hour to sign contentious executive orders that will most likely present the same problem in the 2016 presidential election? A brief overview of these executive orders, and their impact on immigration follows.

On November 20, 2014, President Obama initiated executive orders dealing with immigration. [11] Deferred Action for Childhood Arrivals (DACA), and Deferred Action for Parents of Americans and Lawful Permanent Residents (DAPA) were meant to deal with the millions of illegal aliens who have resided continuously in the US since January 1, 2010. Although these executive orders were a temporary reprieve from deportation for millions of illegal aliens, 26 states decided that the President overstepped his powers and decided to sue the US government. [12] A federal court in Texas blocked the executive orders with a preliminary injunction and the Texas federal appeals court upheld the preliminary injunction. On June 23, 2016 a divided Supreme Court continued the preliminary injunction and essentially confirmed that President Obama overstepped his authority by attempting to give amnesty to millions of illegal aliens. The executive orders imposed by President Obama applied to millions of illegal aliens currently residing in the US, and most likely would have encouraged hundreds of thousands of illegal entries, even though the orders had a cut-off date. In addition, verifying any applications submitted under these executive orders would become rubber-stamp details, as previously occurred in the legacy INS.

Aliens serve as excellent scapegoats for society's problems, and they can be blamed for unemployment, higher crime rates, and a general decline in the standard of living. It follows that INS might offer a solution to these problems. However, law enforcement agencies often prioritize their efforts based on various reasons. Inevitable crises take the form of natural disasters, increased crime rates, and the incidences arising out of the current threat of global terrorism. In the past, the investigations program apprehended a substantial number of illegal aliens, but this needs to be understood in context.

With only 2000 legacy agents, it was remarkable that so many aliens could be apprehended inside the US. Justifying their actions by limited resources, the investigations program focused on the mission of locating and apprehending illegal aliens inside the US who were in violation of the INA. Agents were reminded that their mission was to focus on enforcing the INA. Although illegal aliens are also involved in other criminal activity including narcotics, organized crime, firearms, vice, and just about every other criminal activity, the investigations program concentrated on locating and apprehending low-level visa abusers. Investigators essentially mirrored the efforts of the border patrol, and served as their backup. While the statutory powers of law enforcement agents should facilitate their mission, management can reshape the mission simply by changing policies. Even so, if the policy changes are broad enough, the control agent might still be able to successfully complete tasks. However, civil rights activists, and due process concerns trigger efforts to suppress the power of control agents in concert with the ideal to maintain a balanced, and civil society. This process may have a profound impact on the way law enforcement is administered. For example, when the mayor of New Orleans requested that the Department of Justice (DOJ) look into the New Orleans Police Department (NOPD) with regard to corruption and discrimination, it ultimately resulted in a consent decree between the NOPD and DOJ.[13] Part of this consent decree mandated that New Orleans actually become a *sanctuary city,* because officers were instructed not to assist ICE, or question criminals about their immigration status. Since this is a violation of 8 USC 1373, which states in part that no person or agency may prohibit or restrict a federal, state, or local agency form sending, requesting, receiving, or exchanging information about an individual's immigration status with ICE, the decree resulted in Congressional inquiries, and a letter from the New Orleans District Attorney's Office requesting a response, and clarification from the US Attorney General.[14]

In this context, it is interesting that the enforcement policies regarding immigration currently in place seem to focus more on civil rights, and due process rather than public safety. From the immigration agent's perspective, it is incomprehensible to justify ignoring an entire group of law violators (such as murderers, robbers, or drug dealers) by creating policies that surrender a mission due to lack of resources. One may accept the belief that the typical illegal alien (the low-level visa abuser illegally employed in the US) is not a serious problem, or may be ignored without serious consequences. However, doing so is more ideological than rational-legal, because the INA interior enforcement statutes is all about locating, apprehending, and removing illegal aliens. Ignoring the interior enforcement of the INA only exacerbates the problem, encourages illegal entries, and fails to address the mandates legislated in the INA. There is no doubt that individuals involved in violent predatory crimes pose a more serious threat to the public safety than the typical INA law violator. However, such a policy erases the deterrent effect of the law, and ignores the statutory mandates of the INA. Policies that essentially obstruct statutory enforcement efforts, including consent decrees that mandate sanctuary cities, should cause one to question the true intent of the policies.

Crises are events that require immediate response, and they are examples of how control agencies *muster the troops* to designate priorities. An example of this reaction to crisis occurred after Iranian militants took over the US Embassy in Tehran. One response involved an official inquiry about the status of Iranian students in the US, however INS could not provide reliable information about Iranian students, or any other group of aliens in this country. The legacy INS management ramped up the investigations program and started the *Iranian Project*. All Iranian nationals in the US with nonimmigrant visas (mostly students) were instructed to appear for processing. Iranian nationals that were in status, or officially registered as students, were validated as *bona fide* nonimmigrants, and could continue in their status. Iranians that were out of status were placed under deportation proceedings. This traditional reaction to crisis serves as an example of the law enforcement response to political pressure. It is reactive enforcement, and far less effective than proactive efforts to complete tasks. In order to be successful, a law enforcement agency needs to combine proactive efforts such as a robust intelligence program, with reactive efforts.

In addition to the *Operation Boatlift*, the *Haitian Project* in 1980 also serves as an example of a reaction to crisis. As a result of the economic problems in Haiti, the exodus of Haitians to Miami is a recurrent problem. If one considers the presence of over 11 million illegal aliens inside the US as a crisis, interior enforcement of the immigration laws might also be considered a continuing crisis.

The investigators shared their perceptions about such projects as *Operation Boatlift*, the Census and automobile restrictions, as well as the various task forces such as the highly criticized *Citizenship USA* project. Neil Jacobs, a former investigator in the NYDO subsequently was promoted to the Assistant District Director for Investigations in Dallas, Texas. Jacobs testified before Congress, and stated publicly that there was possible fraud, and other abuses in the *Citizenship USA* program. Essentially, many aliens were being naturalized that should not be naturalized, or investigated further. As a result of his testimony, INS retaliated by suspending Mr. Jacobs for 21 days, and reassigning him to a non-supervisory position. The Office of Special Counsel, and a Chief Administrative Law Judge finally settled arbitration in Mr. Jacobs favor. He was reassigned to Hawaii with all expenses paid to an equivalent grade and pay, his leave and pension benefits were restored, his attorney fees were paid, he received back pay with interest, and he received an additional $30,000 lump sum payment. [15] For those not familiar with the way the government deals with whistleblowers, this was an extraordinary confirmation as to the merits of Agent Jacobs' claims. In 1998, Mr. Jacobs initiated *Operation Last Call* in Dallas, Texas in an attempt to remove deportable aliens convicted of driving under the influence of alcohol. INS attempted to prevent this initiative by having the District Director of the Dallas office review cases of detained aliens swept up in the operation, and possibly release them through a process known as deferred action. [16]

More recently, the Obama Administration initiated a Task Force on New Americans and allocated $19 million into a program to register new voters that Judicial Watch [17] suggests will likely support Democrats in the 2016 presidential election. As Judicial Watch points out, the chair of the Task Force appointed by President Obama is Cecilia Munoz, the former vice president of the National Council of La Raza that Judicial Watch described as a powerful open-borders group. In light of the Jacobs case, the matter of concern may well be whether there are sufficient resources to conduct adequate background investigations on these potential citizens. Will the applicants be screened properly, or will the process become a rubber-stamp ritual conducted by USCIS, which has displayed an apparent conflict of interest with the enforcement side of the immigration system equation? In order for a bureaucracy the size of DHS to function properly, all parts of the bureaucracy should be working together effectively. However, service and enforcement functions generally clash, and this is especially true with regard to the administration of the immigration laws. In the legacy INS, the service branch included adjudications, citizenship, adjustment of status, and other service programs for individuals seeking to adjust their status, apply for legal permanent residence, or become citizens of the US. Service personnel administered these functions, and they were not criminal investigators. Inevitably, conflicts would arise if a field agent came in contact with an alien who had an equity based on an immediate relative who was a US citizen, or legal resident alien. When this occurred, the alien often received a waiver of deportation pending the outcome of the application for adjustment of status if one existed, and the agent was expected to inform the alien about this benefit. Although legacy agents had some discretion in executing their duties, policies were generally adhered to. In both the legacy INS, and the current DHS there is a distinct separation between service and enforcement, although both programs may be enforcement related. The incident that occurred at the San Bernardino USCIS headquarters after the terrorist attack in San Bernardino, suggests that the conflict between enforcement and service continues, and has actually worsened.

> Sen. Grassley said, "This is a classic example of the left hand not knowing what the right hand is doing in the Obama Administration's Department of Homeland Security. Agents we depend on to keep us safe, especially hours after a terrorist attack in San Bernardino, were blocked by officials within their own agency from conducting a routine law enforcement action to prevent a potentially dangerous situation at a federal building. This incident shows the disturbing lack of collaboration between the USCIS and ICE—two agencies tasked with enforcing our immigration laws. Thanks to whistleblowers and the Justice Department Inspector General's report, these agencies can better understand their own policies, what went wrong and the need to prevent future breakdowns." [18]

One might conclude that the confirmed error of the USCIS director, Irene Martin, after the San Bernardino terrorist attack was simply the misguided efforts of an administration sycophant seeking favor from the powers that be. But, subsequent to the OIG report that confirmed the absence of any official policy regarding her actions, DHS nominated Martin for the Secretary's

Award for Valor, which is either twisted logic, or simply the affirmation that DHS condoned the error.[19]

Crises may also be used to implement objectionable programs and priorities. As President Obama's former chief of staff stated: "You never want a serious crisis to go to waste."[20] Executive actions are used in response to events deemed to be in need of critical, or immediate attention, and they are reactions to a crisis. Law enforcement strategies may be enhanced, or muted when critical events occur. Active shooters turn domestic police agencies into armed combat personnel, and attacks on the homeland create an atmosphere of fear, and increased police activity. Most would approve of these tactics, because such strategies would allow the police to protect us more effectively. Gun control activists attempt to convince the public that the police can protect them when danger strikes, and the proliferation of guns is the cause of violence. However, this belief is illusory at best. A much quicker response to an armed offender might be an armed citizen that could at best remove the threat, or at least minimize casualties. The 2nd Amendment guarantees Americans the right to bear arms, and a trained citizenry could be a strong deterrent against the terrorists that plan to attack the homeland. Gun rights activists believe that strict gun control laws will only restrict law-abiding citizens, and that criminals will ignore them. Terrorists can attack soft targets where they will meet minimal resistance, and be able to successfully instill fear in the population. Gun-free zones are a perfect example of this, and offer the terrorist an exclusive opportunity to achieve their goals. Terrorists also seek harder targets, but these require more planning, and resources. Terrorists will most likely applaud efforts at strict gun control, with the ultimate goal to disarm the citizenry. The social contract that individuals in society enter into with governments posit that giving up liberties such as the right to bear arms, or taking the law into your own hands in exchange for the government (through the justice system) will offer the best arrangement for all parties concerned. The founding fathers had a different view when they included the 2nd Amendment in the Bill of Rights. Although citizens should acknowledge that vigilantism, and taking the law into your own hands leads to dysfunction, individuals should have the right to defend themselves against an attack.

DHS policies are derived from the executive branch of government. Although a law enforcement agency is theoretically independent from political influence, by nature they are still top-down bureaucracies. The President of the US (POTUS) appoints directors and Secretaries, and although the Senate confirms them, the POTUS has tremendous influence in shaping how laws are implemented, or not implemented. Congress may question policies, but it is difficult to change them once they are in place. When incidents with negative consequences occur as a result of policies, Congress may request the respective Office of the Inspector General (OIG) to investigate said incidents. The goal of such investigations is usually to insure the negative incident is not repeated, rather than to punish, or remove those who mandated the policy. Statements made by managers at Congressional hearings are placed in the official record, and usually filed with the agency's reports, or on agency websites. However, the Q&A after the official statement is often very telling about what is actually going on, and a good description of norms as rules in use. The heads of ICE and CBP were interviewed by Senator Jeff Sessions in 2016, and one could readily understand from their testimony that although they disagreed with the policy regarding enforcement of the INA based on the executive orders relating to DACA and DAPA, they complied with them.[21]

At times, incidents reach the level of national outrage. Two cases that are representative of this were Kate Steinle[22] and Casey Chadwick[23], both murdered by illegal aliens who had criminal records. The murderers were either deported, or supposed to be deported, but released from custody due to the immigration policies in place at the time, or they illegally entered the US after being deported. Unfortunately, these are not isolated examples.

A recent expose on how political correctness can impact on priorities, and policies suggest that reactions to crises can skew the mission of law enforcement in unusual directions. A key to successful proactive law enforcement is the use of intelligence data to plan enforcement strategies. Both the military and local police agencies employ intelligence agents to fulfill their missions, and such information is invaluable in terms of solving crimes, protecting the public, and preventing crimes. Even when law enforcement makes concerted efforts that go well beyond protecting civil liberties, the political arm of the systems network will ultimately influence the operation of intelligence gathering operatives. There is a negative correlation between public safety and due process, and the balance between the two is of utmost importance. After the 911 terrorist attacks, one could observe a heightened police presence with officers wearing combat gear, and carrying automatic weapons. A society in which the police presence is viewed as an occupation is no longer a free society, but the potential for such a condition becomes more a reality as domestic violence increases. One way to stop attacks such as San Bernardino[24] and Orlando, Florida,[25] would be to proactively implement effective intelligence gathering in order to identify suspects. Since radical Islamic terrorists offer intelligence agencies the opportunity to discover their terrorist plots, it would seem prudent to allow these intelligence agents to gather information that could prevent the acts from taking place.[26]

Philip Haney is a retired DHS employee who asserted that the Civil Rights and Civil Liberties division of DHS, and State Department pressure, shut down the investigation program he worked in because it was *politically incorrect*. Haney's unit was investigating travel related activities of suspected terrorists such as the *Tablighi Jamaat* (a Salafist Muslim fundamentalist group with 50 million members) looking for information suggesting terroristic activity. Such intelligence could prevent terrorist acts such as San Bernardino from taking place if agents can detect patterns that suggest them.[27] Haney also believes that the DHS cannot properly conduct background investigations on refugees from the Middle East and elsewhere, and failing to do so places the American public at risk. More importantly, Haney suggests that terrorist attacks might be prevented if the intelligence collected was utilized, and acted upon.

Executive orders and policies that flow from them have caused DHS to release illegal aliens with criminal records, and essentially create a *de facto* amnesty for low-level visa-abusers in the US. All of this is exacerbated by the failure of the State Department to insist that foreign countries accept deportable aliens, which could be accomplished by implementing a simple proviso that their nationals will not be legally admitted into the US if they do not cooperate with this international agreement. In addition, the lack of cooperation from so-called sanctuary cities that fail to notify DHS when they release deportable aliens from state custody for other than immigration crimes contribute to the overall problem. There are reported to be more than 300 sanctuary cities in the US that refuse to honor immigration detainers, or do not notify DHS when an illegal alien is released from their custody.[28]

Such policies cannot be in the best interest of the public safety, nor can they be excused as due process concerns since the aliens receive all the available due process, both before and after their alleged law breaking. More likely, these policies evolve out of ideological principles that tend to ignore the rule of law, as well as the legislative process. In my dissertation proposal, my mentor Professor Edwin Schur correctly suggested that law enforcement, and immigration research should focus more on the control agency rather than the illegal alien. The control agency has evolved into something quite unique, and more accurately describes reality, far better than the deviants in question.

Wadhia[29] traces the history of prosecutorial discretion in immigration law and suggests that President Obama's executive orders fall within acceptable parameters that include economic (insufficient resources to deport the illegal alien population in the US), humanitarian (that compelling equities exist that should exempt illegal aliens from deportation), and Congressional inaction (the failure of Congress to pass comprehensive immigration reform), citing prior decisions that support the executive orders. Wadhia affirms these executive orders as legally sound, but also notes the emotional aspect connected with immigration. The article utilizes official statistics obtained through Freedom of Information requests (FOIA) that represent the agency's policies rather than the agent's perceptions, and they accept the ideological yearnings of those who create them, or are unaware that such yearnings exist. These decisions run counter to the statutes that serve as the fundamental core of our legal system, and they are not found in the historical/traditional applications of deferred action, or executive orders. Wadhia's article also cites the sarcasm from US Congressman Luis Gutierrez (a staunch pro-immigrant advocate) who dramatized the idea of mass deportation, and blamed Republicans for failure to pass immigration reform legislation. Such partisan concerns reflect the impasse in constructing comprehensive immigration reform. The legislative efforts often turn into a tug of war between democrats and republicans on these issues, as well as an inherent bias in the justification of liberal, ideologically based policies by pro-immigrant activists.

AMNESTY & SCIRP

In 1978, the Select Commission on Immigration and Refugee Policy (SCIRP) set out to:

> (1) conduct a study and analysis of the effect of the provisions of the INA . . .
> (2) conduct a study and analysis of whether and to what extent the INA would apply to . . . Puerto Rico, the Virgin Islands, Guam, American Samoa, the Northern Mariana Islands, and the other territories and possessions of the US.
> (3) review and make recommendations with respect to the numerical limitations (and exemptions therefrom) of the INA . . . (4) assess the social, economic, political, and demographic impact of previous refugee programs . . . (5) conduct a comprehensive review of the provisions of the INA . . . (6) make semiannual reports to each House of Congress . . . (7) make a final report not later than September 30, 1980.[30]

The Carter Administration sought amnesty for illegal aliens, and Congress recommended establishing a study panel. As a result, the SCIRP began its study of the illegal alien problem. The report of the SCIRP came out in March 1981 following President Reagan assuming the office of President. President Reagan convened a Presidential Task Force on Immigration and Refugee Policy chaired by his Attorney General, William French Smith. President Reagan rejected the recommendations of his Task Force, because the more the Task Force looked at the problem, the more it realized that tighter immigration controls were needed, not increasing legal immigration as the Administration seemed to want.[31]

Critics argue that the SCIRP was set up to delay making decisions on a politically sensitive problem.[32] This argument would appear to be justified since the final recommendations presented by the Commission were less than aggressive. The major recommendations included amnesty, issuance of a worker identity card, and employer sanctions on hiring illegal aliens.[33] The recommendations of the Commission were presented to a new Administration, and subject to review once again by that Administration. SCIRP echoed the policy statements made by President Jimmy Carter, and the anti-restrictionist school of thought.

> Briefly, the President proposed injunctions and fines for employers who knowingly hired illegal aliens, intensified border enforcement, a three tier adjustment of status, and increased foreign aid to those countries from which most illegals come. In spite of the fact that the Administration's proposals died a quick death in Congress, their major provisions merit attention because they will reappear in one form or another when legislation is reintroduced. [34]

The Immigration Reform and Control Act (IRCA) of 1986 included amnesty for illegal aliens that resided in the US prior to 1982, employer sanctions against those employing illegal aliens, and a special agricultural worker program to accommodate seasonal agricultural needs in the US. That law permitted 1.7 million illegal aliens who came to the US before 1982 to apply for amnesty from deportation.[35] The law intended to curtail the flow of illegal aliens into the US. The Triennial Comprehensive Report on Immigration indicated that 2,675,990 IRCA immigrants were admitted into the US between 1989 and 1994.[36] Unfortunately, apprehensions along the Mexican border soon broke old records.[37] By the year 2000, total apprehensions of deportable aliens by INS rose to 1,814,729. Throughout the history of immigration legislation, the border patrol continued to receive a large part of INS budget including more personnel. The investigations program remained a small part of the agency.

Enforcing the employer sanctions is difficult without a secure identity document, and the so-called employer sanctions in the 1986 Act reportedly caused widespread discrimination against foreigners, according to the General Accounting Office.

> Based on sample surveys, the watchdog agency said 10 percent of an estimated 4.6 million employers nationwide had engaged in practices that amounted to illegal discrimination against job applicants on the basis of national origin. Nine percent of the surveyed employers said that the law had caused them to begin hiring only persons born in the US.[38]

THE IMMIGRATION ACT OF 1990

The 1990 Commission for Immigration Reform echoed the earlier recommendations of its predecessors, but the proposal to reduce legal immigration by one third was viewed as *radical* by some experts in the field.[39] On the other hand, the INA of 1990 (IMMACT90) signed by President George Bush on November 29, 1990 did not follow the recommendations of the Commission. The major sections of the law will:

(1) raise total annual immigration levels from 540,000 to 700,000 in 1992-94, then drop them to a minimum of 675,000. (2) Besides more than doubling employment-based immigration for mostly highly skilled workers, set aside 10,000 employment visas for those who invest at least $1 million in a new enterprise in the US that employs 10 or more workers. (3) Swiftly deport aliens who have committed violent or drug-related crimes—offenders who currently account for nearly one quarter of the federal prison population. (4) clarify the authority of Immigration and Naturalization Service enforcement officers to make arrests and carry firearms. (5) Increase the size of the Border patrol and create new civil penalties for those involved who deal in fraudulent immigration documents. (6) Refine provisions of the 1986 Immigration Reform and Control Act to deter discrimination resulting from sanctions against employers of illegal aliens. (7) Provide temporary protected status to certain categories of foreign nationals facing dangerous circumstances in their homeland, specifically singling out those from El Salvador.[40]

President Bush said that the new law "is good for families, good for business, good for crime fighting, and good for America." According to the DHS,

> The Immigration Act of 1990 (IMMACT 90) retooled the immigrant selection system once again. IMMACT 90 increased the number of available immigrant visas and revised the preference categories governing permanent legal immigration. Immigrant visas were divided into 3 separate categories: family-sponsored, employment-based, and "diversity" immigrants selected by lottery from countries with low immigration volumes.[41]

A good deal of discussion was generated by legal scholars and academics regarding IMMACT 90, and most of the concerns centered on the need to increase the number of special skills immigrants, supported by the belief that the US was falling behind the rest of the world in attracting these individuals of "extraordinary ability."[42] The concerns voiced about the way INS processed the applications centered on the discretionary nature of decisions made by the examiners. Recommendations from scholars included developing a point system based on education, age, English language proficiency, work experience, and employment assignment so that applications could be facilitated and expedited, and overall numbers could be increased. The added points for younger applicants seem interesting since they discriminate against older applicants, and some even suggest that all foreign students who complete a college degree should automatically be granted legal permanent resident status. The push for increased legal immigration based on these ideas fail to take into account other factors such as the brain-drain caused by the extraordinary immigrants who leave their country of origin where they might have improved conditions, by contributing their knowledge to the developing country. In essence, these calls to increase immigration of the special skills classes are selfish ideologies that ignore the need of the sending countries, and they create academic, and technological wastelands. Countries such as China and India recognize the impact of the brain drain, and create programs in order to attract the needed workers, and to encourage the return of those who left.[43] Whether it is for special skills workers or any other benefit, in the processing of these applications it is imperative that the control agencies also address the ever-growing concerns about national security.

ANTI-TERRORISM & EFFECTIVE DEATH PENALTY (AEDPA) ACT AND IIRIRA

President Clinton signed into law AEDPA on April 24, 1996 in response to the Oklahoma City bombing, and the first World Trade Center attack. This law mandated detention for certain classes of criminal aliens including aggravated felons, firearms, and narcotics convictions. The provisions of AEDPA required that any alien with such a conviction(s) shall be taken into custody and expeditiously removed from the US. Regarding aliens convicted prior to the passage of the law, immigrant advocates considered the law unconstitutional.

NOTES

1. Committee on the Judiciary. (1979). *U. S. Immigration Law and Policy: 1952-1979,* Washington, DC: U. S. Government Printing Office, p. 66.
2. US Commission on Civil Rights, *A Study of Federal Immigration Policies and Practices In southern California,* Washington, DC: U. S. Government Printing Office, p. 15.
3. Grace Halsell, *The Illegals,* (New York: Stein and Day, 1978) 5.
4. INS, *INS Annual Report,* (1978) Tables 6-7.
5. INS, INS Estimates of the Top 15 countries-INS Data—Mexico continued to be the leading source of unauthorized immigration to the US.
6. DHS website, Accessed June 16, 2016, http://www.immigration.gov/graphics/shared/aboutus/statistics/legishist/act140.htm
7. Committee on the Judiciary, 1979, p. 77.
8. Global Security, *Mariel Boatlift.* GlobalSecurity.org, Accessed June 16, 2016, http://www.globalsecurity.org/military/ops/mariel-boatlift.htm
9. Mark Dow. (October 21, 2003). *Scarface and Mariel's Forgotten Prisoners.* Miami, FL: Miami Herald. Retrieved from http://www.cubanet.org/CNews/y03/oct03/22e9.htm
10. Byron York, "Why didn't Obama and the Dems pass immigration reform whey they could have in 2009," Washington Examiner, (September 9, 2014), Accessed June 20, 2016, http://washingtonexaminer.com.
11. DHS website, "Executive Actions on Immigration," Accessed June 20, 2016, https://www.uscis.gov/immigrationaction
12. Huffington Post, "Over Half the States Are Suing Obama For Immigration Actions," Accessed June 20, 2016. http://www.huffingtonpost.com/2015/01/26/states-lawsuit-immigration_n_6550840.html
13. City of New Orleans website, Accessed June 16, 2016, http://www.nola.gov/nopd/nopd-consent-decree/

14. Judiciary.house.gov, "Goodlatte and Gowdy demand answers on DOJ's efforts to coerce New Orleans to adopt sanctuary policies, Accessed on June 16, 2016, https://judiciary.house.gov/press-release/goodlatte-gowdy-demand-answers-dojs-efforts-coerce-new-orleans-adopt-sanctuary-policies/.

15. Retrieved from http://www.osc.gov/documents/press/2000/pr00_09.htm

16. William Branigin. (Dec. 22, 1998). INS Reviews DWI Deportations; Texas Offices' Program Angers Immigrants' Rights Groups, The Washington Post, p. A21.

17. JudicialWatch.org, Accessed June 16, 2016, http://www.judicialwatch.org/blog/2016/04/obama-allots-19-mil-to-register-immigrant-voters/

18. US Senate, "Grassley Johnson Comment on DHS Inspector General Report Revealing Lack of Cooperation Between DHS Entities in Aftermath of San Bernardino Terror Attack," Accessed June 17, 2016, https://www.hsgac.senate.gov/media/majority-media/johnson-grassley-comment-on-dhs-inspector-general-report-revealing-lack-of-cooperation-between-dhs-entities-in-aftermath-of-san-bernardino-terror-attack

19. Michael Cutler, Frontpage magazine, "Terror Investigation Obstructer Nominated for Secretary's Award for Valor: DHS manager gets honored for thwarting the San Bernardino Investigation," (June 27, 2016) Accessed on June 27, 2016, http://www.frontpagemag.com/fpm/263313/terror-investigation-obstructer-nominated-michael-cutler

20. WallStreetJournal.com, Accessed June 16, 2016, http://www.wsj.com/articles/SB122721278056345271

21. Senate.gov, Accessed June 16, 2016, https://www.judiciary.senate.gov/imo/media/doc/05-19-16%20Homan%20Testimony.pdf

22. Senate.gov, Accessed June 16, 2016, https://www.judiciary.senate.gov/imo/media/doc/07-21-15%20Steinle%20Testimony.pdf

23. Norwichbulletin.com, Accessed June 16, 2016, http://www.norwichbulletin.com/article/20160411/NEWS/160419919

24. NYTimes.com, Accessed June 16, 2016, http://www.nytimes.com/2015/12/05/us/tashfeen-malik-islamic-state.html?_r=0

25. USAtoday.com, Accessed June 16, 2016, http://www.usatoday.com/story/news/nation/2016/06/13/orlando-shooting-what-we-know/85815500/

26. Vladtepesblog.com, Accessed June 16, 2016, http://vladtepesblog.com/2015/12/16/dhs-whistleblower-philip-haney-in-open-letter-to-congress-no-confidence-in-administrations-vetting-process/

27. John Hayward, "DHS Whistleblower: PC killed investigation that might have stopped San Bernardino Attack," Breitbart, (December 11, 2015), Accessed June 21, 2016, http://www.breitbart.com/big-government/2015/12/11/dhs-whistleblower-philip-haney-p-c-killed-investigation-might-stopped-san-bernardino-attack/

28. CIS.org, Accessed June 16, 2016, http://cis.org/Sanctuary-Cities-Map

29. S. S. Wadhia, "The History of Prosecutorial Discretion in Immigration Law." *American University Law Review, 64*(5) (2015). 1285-1302.

30. Committee on the Judiciary. (1979). *U. S. Immigration Law and Policy: 1952-1979,* Washington, DC: U. S. Government Printing Office, p. 82.

31. Sylvia Ann Hewlett, *Coping with Illegal Immigrants,* Foreign Affairs, (Winter 1981-1982) 358-378.

32. Otis Graham, "Illegal Immigration and the New Restrictionism," *The Center Magazine,* (1979), 12(3) 54-64.

33. John M. Crewdson, "Legalized Status for Most Aliens in U. S. Proposed," *New York Times,* (Dec. 5, 1980), A20.

34. Eugene Sofer, "Illegal Immigration: Background to the Current Debate," (1980) *CO-NEG Policy Research Center, Inc.*

35. Russell Snyder, "Bush Signs Sweeping Immigration Bill," *United Press International* (November 30, 1990).

36. USINS, "The Triennial Comprehensive Report on Immigration," (May 1999), Accessed June 16, 2016, https://www.uscis.gov/sites/default/files/USCIS/Resources/Reports%20and%20Studies/tri3fullreport.pdf

37. David Johnston, "Border Crossings Near Old Record: U. S. to Crack Down," *New York Times,* February 9, 1992, 1, 34.

38. Jack Sirica, "Audit Finds Immigration-Law Backlash," *Newsday*, March 30, 1990, 15.

39. Thomas Muller, "Missing the Boat on Immigration," *Newsday*, June 18, 1995, A39.

40. Ronald J Ostrow, "Bush Signs Law Boosting Immigration Quotas by 40%," *Los Angeles Times*, Nov. 30, 1990, 39.

41. DHS, "Late Twentieth Century," Accessed on July 18, 2016, https://www.uscis.gov/history-and-genealogy/our-history/agency-history/late-twentieth-century

42. Chris Gafner and Stephen Yale-Loehr. "Attracting the best and the brightest: a critique of the current U.S. immigration system." *Fordham Urban Law Journal* 38, no. 1 (November 2010): 183-215. *Legal Source*, EBSCOhost (accessed July 18, 2016).

43. Ismail, Maimunah, Mageswari Kunasegaran, and Roziah Mohd Rasdi. 2014. "Evidence of Reverse Brain Drain in Selected Asian Countries: Human Resource Management Lessons for Malaysia." *Organizations & Markets in Emerging Economies* 5, no. 1: 31-48. *Business Source Complete*, EBSCOhost (accessed July 18, 2016).

Chapter Three

The Illegal Alien Environment

Norms as Rules in Use

INTRODUCTION

An organizational analysis based on norms-as-rules-in-use is most effective in understanding the immigration problem. Considering the total environment, including political factors, interest groups, and the media, permits a better understanding of the perceptions about the tasks of control agents. These tasks include: discretion, the working personality, status, morale, role conflict, and strain. The underlying theory is grounded in the assumption that actors work in a dynamic environment which determines the rules of the game.

The underlying processes that create deviance offer an alternative to understanding the behavior we call deviance. Relying on official statistics will describe only the behavior that those who create the label want us to see. Comprehending the illegal alien phenomenon goes beyond the enumeration of interior, and border apprehensions. The total environment surrounding the illegal alien problem exists as a network in which multiple factors contribute to the perceptions about it. Since official statistics are prepared by those who have the power to define the deviance, analyzing the statistics alone will fall short of a comprehensive understanding of the problem.

DEALING WITH THE DANGEROUS CLASSES

To effectively deal with the dangerous classes made up of " . . . an unmanageable, volatile, and convulsively criminal class . . . "[1] society created the police. The Hobbesian notion of social order and a social contract to provide it, form the basis for the relationship between the community and the police.

> . . . was designed not to deny men a life of competition and acquisition, but to ensure that they could have it . . . The price they would have to pay did not seem to Hobbes to be too high: they would have to acknowledge, as if they had contracted to do so, an obligation to obey the laws of the sovereign as long as the sovereign was able to protect them.[2]

Logic suggests a need for an efficient means of dealing with the daily problems of social life. Accordingly, the use of local police forces seems more appropriate than a standing army in a civil society, while the idea of a national police force suggests a threat to the sovereignty of the states.

> . . . it was ill equipped to meet the enduring needs of a policed society. It was largely officered by an agrarian class which sometimes did not distinguish itself for zeal in protecting the property of manufacturers. More fundamentally, however, it was difficult for the army to act continuously in small dispersed units in civilian society.[3]

The objections to a national police force contributed to the creation of what is now referred to as the *crime control establishment.* According to Silver, it is

> . . . a specific combination of men and agencies (mostly concerned with the subject of *crime control*) whose activities—most often, for the worse—substantially shape public attitudes toward crime. Also, these agencies have the political capability to transform their views about *crime* and *crime control* into law and, more importantly, into law enforcement.[4]

Specialists evolved out of the industrial revolution to maintain post-industrial society, and this phenomenon manifests itself throughout the various institutions created to implement such maintenance. The crime control establishment includes various specialists at the macrosociological, and microsociological levels. For example, the INA specifies that only immigration officers can enforce the laws relating to illegal aliens in the US.

Public attitudes towards the police appear to be a function of community relations, public relations, press relations, and human relations.

> Community relations is the everyday relationship between the police and the public . . . Public relations is the attempt to improve the image of the agency as opposed to community relations which attempts to actually improve the agency . . . Press relations is mostly a staff function and consists of giving information to the public through the media to which they are entitled. Human relations . . . the least formalized of all . . . insight into human nature.[5]

A mutual understanding between the police, and the public determines the success of the former. As the police become more like an army of occupation, members of society become disadvantaged in the relationship. The media magnify this role, and the public expects a great deal from organizations saddled with the dual roles of service, and control. In most contexts, the police are responsible for maintaining the equilibrium, and insuring mutual understanding between them and the community. When the equilibrium falters, as it has with regard to the illegal alien problem, different reactions occur from the participants in the environment. Chaos and instability occur when the social contract fails, and either the control agents or the community fail to fulfill their parts of the contract. Police shootings of unarmed African-Americans, and riots that follow are examples of this tenuous balance. With regard to the immigration problem continuum, responses occur from the civil libertarians who demand an open border, through the isolationists that want to seal the border. In Arizona, armed patrols of citizens classifying themselves as part of a militia movement have begun patrolling the border in response to the apparent breakdown in enforcement there.[6] If the community perceives that the control agency is not following the rule of law and the deviant ignores the law itself, the Hobbesian prophecy is fulfilled.

THE INTERPRETIVE FRAMEWORK AND THE ORGANIZATIONAL CONTEXT

INS, police, as well as most formal organizations are integrated internally by *loose coupling.*

> The degree of coupling between persons, roles or units within organizations depends upon the activity of their common variables. If two elements have few variables in common, or if variables common to both are weak compared to other variables influencing the elements, then they are relatively independent of each other and thus loosely coupled . . .[7]

Considering the service priority, the legacy INS should be tightly coupled. In fact, the legacy INS was more loosely coupled than one might expect, and the view from the bottom-up underscores this belief. The service and control mandates arising out of the INA are not complementary. At DHS-ICE, one might expect a shift toward a tightly coupled arrangement in which ICE agents control the enforcement of the immigration laws, and USCIS the service function. As a result, ICE should be able to concentrate on enforcement matters, and USCIS would provide services to the immigrants applying for admission, adjustment of status, or naturalization. In this ideal arrangement, both parts would work tightly coupled to fulfill the dual mandate. Based on a preliminary analysis of the administration of DHS, it appears that ICE is downplaying interior enforcement with regard to low level visa abusers. Rather than attempt to deal with the millions of low level visa abusers already inside the US, the current enforcement policies are supposed to focus on criminal aliens, terrorism, and job-site enforcement (concentrating on the employer, rather than the employee). Even the latter becomes problematic, because it concentrates on employers that fall under the umbrella priorities. The stakeholders concerned with comprehensive immigration reform generally accept the idea of increased immigration, provided that secure borders and interior enforcement are included in any new legislation. The former is relatively easy to implement, but the latter is doomed to failure. Once again, the problem of the illegal alien inside the US is perceived as impossible to deal with, or that meaningful strategies to implement solutions are unacceptable.

The DHS website lists 20,000 employees in ICE, but only about 6,500 of these employees are HSI agents. The rest are ERO (deportation officers) and support personnel. DHS has a staggering annual budget (2015) of $60.9 billion, but only $5.4 billion is allocated for ICE. CBP has $12.8 billion, and USCIS has $3.3 billion.[8] The incident[9] that occurred at the USCIS headquarters in San Bernardino, in which a USCIS director reportedly obstructed the investigation of HSI agents who were looking into terrorist activities, suggests that the rift between the two sections continues. Perhaps the apparent understanding of the official, that policies existed to allow the obstruction when no such policies in fact exist, more accurately reflects the loose coupling that continues in the DHS. As expected, DHS denied that any obstruction occurred, and explained the incident as a misunderstanding, or lack of communication that was corrected as soon as it was discovered. However, one must remember that such lapses in life and death situations can have dire consequences in law enforcement operations.

Codified laws, rules, and policies guided the legacy INS investigators where the control agent's daily activities were based on handbooks, statutes, policies, and guidelines. Even though INS kept accurate records of the number of annual apprehensions, critics accused them of having unreliable data about the alien population. However, official rates of deviance are social facts *par excellence,* and the way in which the control agency publishes rates of deviance is a concern for the sociologist. Creating policies and annual reports that conclude the successful implementation of these priorities do not reflect the view from the bottom-up, nor do they accurately document whether the organization is fulfilling its mission, except in the Becker's *eyes of the beholder*. There is ample evidence in congressional testimony, media reports, blogs, whistleblower statements, and other sources touched upon in this study.

. . . the forms that must be explained are those which not only are defined as deviant by members of such structures but those which also activate the unofficial and/or *official* processes of social control. By directing attention to such processes, the behavior and rate producing processes may be investigated and compared within a single framework. [10]

Normative behavior, or organizational analysis offer reliable ways to analyze such data. For example, if one determines just what rules and laws an investigator must enforce, it is relatively easy to measure productivity. The researcher can accomplish this by analyzing official statistics, enumerating case closings, and determining how operators accomplish tasks. Such a strategy does not consider critical parameters, or what Weber called the meaningful relatedness (*sinnhafte Bezogenheit*) of social acts. With such an understanding " . . . we are able to understand, quite apart from objective development, the subjective meaning which a social relationship holds for man and by which he is guided in his social conduct." [11] Taking this into account, this study views the normative structure in the social context.

Such an interpretation of the normative structure includes the ongoing processes encountered in social interaction, and treats norms as *rules-in-use*. [12] This approach also focuses on unraveling the meanings behind the complex web of interaction that occurs in everyday life, and goes beyond a mere codification of behavior.

. . . it does little good to start at the top and inquire into the ability, motives, or policies of high-ranking managers, for that will only lead to the observation that sometimes agents do what is asked of them and sometimes they do not, thus implying that perhaps there is something wrong with the abilities or motives of the agents. In short, sorting out, from the top down, the effects of administrative arrangements does not solve many puzzles, it only uncovers new ones. [13]

Norms as rules in use is derived from the labeling approach, and relies on the definitions of those who create the label in the first place. The general environment contributes to the overall definition of the situation, and although the illegal alien is defined by statute, the labeling approach is concerned with how the definition is constructed, and who constructs it. The control agency relies on the codified law in attempting to accomplish its mission, but the various players in the general environment contribute to the overall definition. Furthermore, definitions of mission and goals become problematic if they are not analyzed in the wider context. In the last eight years, the DHS-ICE has dramatically decreased the number of apprehensions both on the border, as well as inside the US. The way this data is presented creates the impression that the agency is focusing on protecting the public, but even these strategies have been criticized by the public, as well as politicians. On the other hand, creating such self-serving caricatures justifies the underlying ideological beliefs through policies that are manifested by the outcomes they cause.

An organizational analysis invites the perception that the organization defines the acts of individuals. The interpretive framework views the actor as an integral part of the way in which an organization operates. In this approach, the focus becomes the way members interpret the operation, and the actor's perceptions become the most reliable data for the participant observer. For this reason, the interpretive framework becomes the appropriate methodology to study the apparent contradiction inherent in the dual mandate found in such control agencies. Traditionally, the illegal alien problem was defined by enumerating the millions of apprehensions made by the legacy INS. However, it is far more important to focus on the ways in which these *deviants* come to the attention of the control agency, rather than merely counting those who happen to be caught up in the process. In addition, careful scrutiny beyond the official statistics could provide insights into a more complete description of the problem. This may allow us to discover why certain individuals either escape detection, or are rarely caught. Executive orders, and the policies created to implement them, allowed the control agency to relabel the deviant in such a way that their original deviantness disappears.[14] The interpretive framework does not accept the consensus model of society, and views the interaction process as problematic. The organizational structure of the control agency contributed to intraorganizational conflict, which was evident among the control agents directly interacting with the *deviants*. This methodology aims at unraveling what actual *rules in use* exist between the control agency, the control agent, the illegal alien, and the wider environment.

Once we have established what the rules-in-use are for a given situation, then the question of violations of these rules becomes meaningful . . . The impact of sanctioning attempts on the future occurrence of the behavior is a central question which labeling theory attempts to answer.[15] The interpretive framework, and rules-in-use coding more accurately reflect the actions that occur in a control agent's environment. In his testimony before the House Immigration and Border Security Subcommittee, Sheriff Charles Jenkins, Frederick County, Maryland, stated that the Obama Administration "has weakened INS by dismissing deportation cases, rescinding 287(g) agreements, encouraging sanctuary policies, and watering down detainer policies."[16] In referring to the "real victims of a reckless and lawless immigration policy," Sheriff Jenkins presented statistics on significant numbers of unaccompanied minors (DACA cases) who subsequently join gangs such as MS 13, and that when police are able to cooperate with ICE under the 287(g) program, it helps protect the community by removing potential criminal aliens from committing cries of violence. According to Jenkins, 64% of the alien gang members in 2015 were DACA, who are now adults committing crimes in the community. In the interpretive framework, this would seem to contradict the official policies of the control agency.

According to the Center for Immigration Studies (CIS),[17] DHS recorded 722,000 encounters with deportable aliens, most who come to the attention of ICE after incarceration for a local arrest. This resulted in charges of against 195,000, or only 25%. 68,000 aliens with criminal convictions were released, or only 35% of all criminal aliens encountered. Since the policy of prosecutorial discretion was implemented in 2011, interior enforcement activity has declined 40%. Basically, prosecutorial discretion is a euphemism for interior enforcement. It ignores the majority of illegal aliens in the US, and even waters down those who have committed crimes by redefining what actually constitutes a criminal alien. The entire policy mystifies logic since the illegal alien encountered is deportable even without a criminal charge, or conviction.

Directives come from the top down in a government agency, and managers rarely question them, nor do control agents have discretion in the process that unfolds. We expect that such an arrangement can affect the relationships between managers and operators, especially when the policies contradict the field agent's perceptions of what the mission should be.

> . . . operator tasks do not strongly shape managerial strategies. In consequence of this, tensions between operators and managers, between *the field* and *headquarters* are especially acute.[18]

The organizational charts for DHS show the leaders as directors of the different units. Through indelibly marked chains of command, ICE is under the Secretary, Deputy Secretary, Director, Executive Associate Director to Operations. Below the Executive Associate Director level are the lower level managers, such as section Chiefs and unit Supervisors that in varying degrees have direct contact with the control agents. Most field agents have direct contact with their immediate supervisor, but rarely interact with upper level managers. In this analysis, the operators are the field level special agents.

> Executives are responsible for the maintenance of the organization, managers for coordinating the activities of persons within the organization, operators for performing the critical or central tasks of the organization.[19]

One of the main problems within the legacy INS was the futile attempt to combine a service function with an enforcement mandate. Within the environment, the agency was administered from headquarters through the political apparatus. Service took a priority, and interior enforcement became secondary. The DHS seemed to acknowledge this dilemma by attempting to separate the service from the control function. The chain of command for

ICE is directly to the Secretary-Deputy Secretary, unlike the legacy INS where a Commissioner through Regional Commissioners, and District Directors governed the operations of both service and control. In 2005, DHS had over 180,000 employees, and a budget request of $40.2 billion. This has grown to a budget of $60.9 billion with over 240,000 employees, and a stated mission to secure the nation, and protect the citizenry from terrorism and natural disasters. Internal and external demands that counterbalance service and control complicate how this mission can be successfully accomplished.

Rules govern functions in bureaucratic organizations with a hierarchical chain of command, a division of labor, with each unit in the bureaucracy having specific duties and powers. Bureaucrats must be competent, and the organization is codified and recorded in writing.[20] Weber describes an ideal type since " . . . no empirical organization corresponds exactly to the scientific construct."[21] That is, " . . . the developing social structure inevitably does not completely coincide with the pre-established forms."[22] One focus of this study is how control agents respond to the bureaucratic model (ideal type) in an attempt to implement official mandates, and methodological concerns surface as a result of this focus.

As stated previously, organizations do not implement formal rules and procedures *exactly* as they should be. Control agents could attempt to create ways to circumvent rules that contradict their perceived notions of task. Furthermore, administrators in dual mandate agencies were sensitive to public responses to agency directives, which do not always receive a favorable response. Effective and efficient enforcement activity may be considered antagonistic in a free civil society. These issues also foster an interest in interpreting formal organizations in their environment, and this theoretical framework evolves from the ideas of reform social Darwinism where the individual controls the environment.

> . . . a more open model treats structure as partially a response to organizations' adaptations to their environments . . . how, under what conditions, in which specific ways are environments, as opposed to individuals, the driving force underlying organizational change.[23]

Democratic governments react to their environments, and political constraints shape the dynamics of these reactions. The Commissioner of INS was, and the Secretary of DHS is, a cabinet level appointee. Executive level positions include the Attorney General down to District Directors. In turn, these individuals control the selection of lower level managers, who in turn set priorities, and manage operators. Furthermore, they control operating resources that are critically important in determining the direction of enforcement operations. As we shall see, the legacy INS placed a priority on service to the public, while prioritizing administrative interior law enforcement, such as apprehending low level visa abusers in the workplace. The legacy INS chose not to prioritize the investigation of aliens involved in drug trafficking, and organized crime, although in 1982 it became part of a joint task force, the Organized Crime Drug Task Force (OCDETF). [24] Although INS agents assigned to this task force were promoted to a higher GS-level in the NYDO, very few of these positions were available. The FBI has primary jurisdiction over most federal investigations, especially those dealing with national security, and although organized crime continues to be one of their priorities, Director James Comey described the top priority as preventing terrorist attacks. [25] In the law enforcement community, most would agree that the FBI commands jurisdictional power, and other agencies will defer or cooperate with them, albeit sometimes begrudgingly. In the law enforcement community, the FBI will ultimately receive the credit for solving some crimes knowing that the success came with the exhaustive efforts of other law enforcement agencies. Whenever immigration agents are placed in any such hierarchy, they usually find themselves in the lower rungs of the hierarchical ladder. In addition, the service mandate was perceived by agents to supersede interior enforcement, which coupled with limited resources, the perceived border patrol mentality, and interior strategies that implemented such perceptions, contributed to low morale. Essentially, investigators had to accommodate service related priorities in the form of staffing adjudication task forces. Also, since the border patrol enforcement strategy had primacy, interior enforcement revolved around the strategies more appropriate to border patrol operations. This resulted in the overall apprehension of low-level visa abusers in large numbers, but mostly along the Mexico-US border. Currently, DHS counts a significant number of border apprehensions as part of the interior workload through ICE ERO operations, but these apprehensions occur on the border, where they are taken over by ERO for processing. Doing so inflates the number of apprehensions designated as ICE apprehension, or interior enforcement. Such efforts are in line with practice of inflating statistics, or relabeling priorities to convince the auditors that the organization is succeeding in implementing its mission (enforcing the immigration laws). Some suggest that under President Obama, more illegal aliens have been deported than any other President, but relabeling deportations as described above indicate that this is an erroneous conclusion.

Managers relay policy operations to control agents who have to carry them out. Refusal to follow policy directives could lead to disciplinary action, reassignment, and even dismissal. Except for a manager possibly acknowledging a disagreement, the opinions of control agents rarely impact on directives. Sometimes, investigators officially disagree with policy directives by filing union grievances. Control agents might even submit official memorandums to their superiors in an attempt to voice disagreement with such directives. Such official actions create tension between managers and agents.

Control agents may react to the environment and attempt to shape it, but they are rarely successful in doing so. The cost of rebellion is quite high, and whistleblowers usually surface only after they retire, or leave the agency. Immigration agents are now required to carry a card that lists the three priorities created by President Obama's executive orders on immigration. These priorities include national security threats, aliens convicted of multiple misdemeanor offenses, or a significant misdemeanor, and aliens who have been issued final removal orders. Failure to conform to these policies has consequences according to Director Sarah Saldana including termination.[26] In reality, this means that HSI agents do not have discretion to enforce the applicable statutes of the INA. They must strictly follow the edicts in the policy directives, and this translates into ignoring the majority of illegal aliens who are in the US in violation of the INA.

An example of this occurred on November 4, 1979, after followers of the Iranian anti-American cleric, Ayatollah Khomeini, seized the American embassy in Tehran, Iran, and took 52 diplomats and citizens hostage.[27] Afterwards, a group of Iranian students staged a protest in Washington, D. C. resulting in their arrest by local police. The police referred the Iranians to INS for a determination of their immigration status, and INS subsequently released the Iranian nationals even though agents stated that some were in the US in violation of the INA.

> Newspaper accounts revealed that criminal investigators assigned to the New York district office of INS staged a protest on the premature release of illegal Iranian aliens. The Iranian nationals were arrested in Washington, DC, on July 27, 1980 (by the police, not INS) and subsequently dumped into the laps of INS in order to determine their status . . . The protest by the investigators was in the form of an alleged sick-out. The alleged sickout was also referred to as evidence of generally bad morale among INS investigators. In response to the alleged sick-out, investigators received official telegrams from their district director indicating that they were taking part in an illegal work stoppage . . . INS investigators who processed the detained aliens were called in by INS and asked whether they spoke with the press, and to sign statements stating that they conducted a thorough investigation in the processing and release of Iranian nationals.[28]

INS accused the investigators of leaking information to the press in an attempt to gain public support. This action is highlighted by the fact that agents cannot make unauthorized public statements, and such behavior surfaces when you utilize the norms-as-rules-in-use approach.

> Rather than divert resources to correcting organizational deficiencies, authorities might calculate that a cheaper strategy is simply to expel discontented members, stop serving complaining customers, and control or suppress voice.[29]

Along these lines, managers often appeal to employee loyalty to maintain order. Such inducements, coupled with pleas to accept the inevitable, are highly effective when applied to law enforcement personnel. If all else fails, managers can retaliate, or attempt to co-opt the most vocal protester.[30]

When there are few career alternatives for the control agent, managers become even less concerned about officer morale. A government employee might express dissatisfaction over working conditions, and seriously consider *exiting* the organization. Such considerations depend on the availability of other federal law enforcement positions. Other agencies generally prefer to hire recruits, rather than seasoned officers with *attitude problems.* It is noteworthy that federal law enforcement agencies generally promote from within the organization. In addition, transferring to another agency often depends on *connections.*

An officer shared his experience with the INS exiting process:

> I decided to leave INS because I was disgusted with the way the agency operated. No one in management asked me why I was leaving. I do not believe that anyone in management cared. I went down to the basement at 26 Federal Plaza, and turned in my shield, handcuffs, and blackjack to the supply clerk. It was quite sad to see this person take the shield and throw it into a box. Somehow, it felt as if a ceremony, or ritual was taking place, but only I was aware of it.

According to the General Accounting Office (GAO), the NYDO lost forty-three investigators through retirement, separation, removal, resignation, and disability termination. The attrition rate is the highest of all district offices in the Eastern Region of INS. The GAO interviewed managers, and investigators to determine why the attrition rate was so high. According to the GAO report, managers considered the forty-three investigators generally experienced, good-performing investigators. The GAO also interviewed thirty-three of the forty-three investigators that left INS. Each investigator had at least five years of experience as a criminal investigator, and about fifty-eight percent had at least ten years of experience. Most of these investigators received at least one performance award during their tenure at INS.

> Of the 33, six retired mandatorily, or because of disability. Another seven retired voluntarily; three of these stated that at least one reason for retiring involved age discrimination. Eighteen of the 33 transferred to other agencies or jobs, two at pay higher than they were receiving at INS. Fourteen of these 18 told us that their primary reason for leaving NYDO involved friction with management, such as disagreement with management's methods of operating the district office, or the belief that management did not place enough emphasis on enforcement activities. Two of the 33 were fired.[31]

The problem of attrition of special agents continues through the present time. Even though the GAO revisited the problem of attrition in its 1999 report on criminal aliens,[32] INS still failed to correct the problem of high attrition among special agents. In 1997, the GAO reported that there was a 30-percent attrition rate for immigration agents, while the average attrition rate of all INS staff was only 11%. And the creation of DHS ICE did not seem to improve the morale problem. Immigration agents from ICE HIS, and ERO filed a lawsuit against the Obama administration regarding the Administration's enforcement policies. Agents advised that they were forced to ignore the law by releasing illegal aliens, who were in violation of the INA, and criminal laws at the state or local level, without even verifying the facts of the cases.[33]

EXTERNAL RELATIONS: POLITICS, INTEREST GROUPS AND THE MEDIA

The traditional analysis of organizations focused on internal structures, and task differentiation. Later, sociologists acknowledged the importance of external factors in shaping the analysis. In line with this, the network of relationships tied to INS becomes important. In this sense, INS is very much like other law enforcement operations.

> . . . the police have as their fundamental task the creation and maintenance of
> and their participation in, external relationships. Indeed, the central meaning of
> police authority itself is its significance as a mechanism for managing relation-
> ships.[34]

Although immigration agents are the units of analysis for this study, it is important to consider the levels connected above, and below them in the organization. Doing so allows the observer to avoid stereotypical thinking about behavior.[35] Considering the wider environment in which the organization operates further enhances intraorganizational analysis which in turn may provide insights into mission, goals, morale, training, and media relations. At the legacy INS, the Commissioner of the agency was a cabinet-level appointment. As such, it is expected that the Commissioner will represent the views of the Office of the President. Similarly, this applies to the Secretary of DHS, who is also a cabinet-level appointee. The role of the Commissioner will be discussed later as part of the internal relations in INS, but these managers stridently enforce the official mission, and policy of the agency. Executive level appointees impose a model that investigators easily understand, and in most instances the official policy did not correspond to the control agent's perceptions of how the mission should be implemented.

Viewing INS as an organization set assists in understanding the wider environment of the agency. "An organization set is composed of organizations in interaction with a focal organization. They provide inputs and receive outputs."[36] The organization set includes the general environment, INS, other agencies, interest groups, the media, and political factors. INS is accountable to the public in various ways. Interpreting how the agency operates requires a discussion of the relations between the agency, and the groups that help shape it. These external relations have an important impact on the way the agency operates.

> . . . direct sources of funding and general support as seen through *public opinion* and *good community relations* will almost always be two key orienting themes in this regard . . . . there will usually be some significant relationship to or concern for the legislature, judicial, and law enforcement systems; the local political and party system; and the local media of mass communication. Depending on a control agency's specific focus, any number of private organizations, groups, and lobbies can come into the picture—be they educational, religious, philanthropic, or *political* in nature.[37]

Hall[38] discussed the conditions of the general environment, which include: technological, political, demographic, ecological, legal, economic, and cultural components. At INS, the external relationships were somewhat different than the DHS (for example service vs. enforcement), and included local and state agencies (police, welfare, medical, etc.), local and national media, the Office of the President, where policy decisions are made and disseminated through the Office of the US Attorney General (DOJ), interest groups which are pro or anti-immigrant such as La Raza, the Catholic Church, Federation of Immigration Reform (FAIR), Center for Immigration Studies (CIS), social media, and the control agents themselves, who sometimes speak out as whistleblowers.

These connections reflect local input, as well as external national relationship, and contribute to formulating a national policy. For example, a US District Court decision has an impact on enforcement operations nationally, such as the aforementioned US v. Texas decision. In such cases, the Central Office applies the decision to *all* district offices to avoid potential conflict. Although this practice is not unusual, it reflects the impact of predicted external relations.

Input from district offices will be forwarded to the Central Office, where final decisions regarding policy are made. Although local managers have the discretion to make decisions regarding local operations, doing so is usually from a top-down perspective. Managers will routinely minimize risk to their own personal position, and they are aware of the consequences of making the *wrong* decision. As previously discussed, as long as the decision is in line with the top-down perspective it most likely will be supported even if the decision is incorrect, or causes problems. In a government agency, directives come from the top-down, and policies, either directly or implied through memoranda, will be implemented as such. In the aforementioned San Bernardino fiasco, where service personnel temporarily prevented enforcement agents from completing their mission, had the agents forced entry into the building to gain access to the required information, they most likely would have been sanctioned for their actions, even though the actions would have been lawful.

The following scenario describes how such external relations impact on immigration enforcement. The local news could report an increase in the number of illegal aliens applying for public assistance, information that tends to appeal to overburdened taxpayers, who in turn demand an immediate response. A local politician refers to the welfare applicants as *mostly poor people who are economic refugees*, pointing out that most are not criminals trying to evade the law, or commit fraud. Both advocates and critics of the illegal alien plan rallies, and the media insures prime time coverage of the event. As a result, the Central Office of the agency issues a policy memorandum to deal with the anticipated coverage, which often leads to pandering to the various participants. Obviously, it is not simply an issue of locating, and apprehending illegal aliens.

> . . . it is a rare bureaucrat who does not bear the fact constantly in mind. Once he has found a pattern of action which is not disturbing to these constituents and lets them turn their attentions elsewhere, he will vigorously resist any change in the pattern, for he knows where survival lies . . . [39]

Congressional liaison units received, and monitored Congressional inquiries about investigations, such as aliens that request intercession on behalf of their pending permanent resident visa applications. The politician merely sends a letter to the agency, or in some instances, a legislator informs the agency that there is a situation in his district requiring attention. An agency will place a high priority on all such inquiries, knowing that the long arm of the administration through Congressional leaders impact directly on both agency budgets, as well as personal ambitions. Like the legacy INS, DHS has an office of legislative affairs that maintains liaison with members of Congress. [40] Under the Obama Administration, there has been a consistent round of hearings both in the House, and the Senate regarding issues stemming from the executive policies, and directives to DHS ICE. The tone of most of these hearings follows partisan politics, and generally highlights the ineptitude, and failure of liberal policies with special regard to public safety issues, and enforcement of the INA.

> News, like beauty, is in the eyes of the beholder. News, to strip the point of euphemism, is what the press—publishers, broadcasters, editors, reporters—

say it is . . . The public sees what the searchlight sees, but is itself poorly equipped to pierce the surrounding darkness.[41]

The press is sensitive to issues relating to immigration, and illegal aliens. For example, California and Texas newspapers routinely print articles about illegal immigration due to the proximity of the Mexican border. In the past, illegal aliens from Cuba and Haiti also caused national press coverage. The press tends to focus on the emotional aspects of reunited families, increased crime, the phenomenon of a *tent city*, a temporary city to house the *refugees, sanctuary cities,* and other newsworthy items. In fact, the media creates images about a largely hidden population that most people rarely see. The images and stereotypes created in the media serve to socialize the wider population about illegal aliens, often pandering to the pro-immigrant biases they hold. As a result, agencies are susceptible to media coverage and have rules about how to deal with the press. Generally, control agents cannot make official statements to the press without the permission of their agency, which designates a public information officer to make official statements, or respond to press inquiries. This is especially true concerning highly sensitive issues, and most of the incidences involving the apprehension, or removal of illegal aliens fall into that category.

Since the illegal alien population is largely hidden, it is important to discuss the manner in which the media gathers information relating to it. Such information is suspect because illegal aliens do not normally lend themselves to media coverage (or research for that matter). As such, the analysis of media descriptions becomes problematic. With the proliferation of the internet, and social media such as Facebook, Twitter, conservative talk shows, and independent blogs and forums, both sides of the immigration debate can be observed. The mainstream media is no longer the sole proprietor and definer of reality, but still controls a large portion of it.

> The rules governing newswork are not simply given and available, but actually constructed, interpreted, and elaborated upon in the actual settings of news-work . . . accounts of newsworthiness render newsworkers' own work routines as rational, sensible, and competent . . . generating newsworthiness has a direct bearing on what appears or fails to appear in the newspaper.[42]

The media's description contributes to the public's perception of the illegal alien problem. Lester believes that the media gets information about illegal aliens primarily from the control agency, and illegal alien informants, which constitutes the background for the media's creation of *newsworthiness*. Of course, agency press releases are from the top-down and, as such, define the parameters of the illegal alien population reported by the media. In such a context, there is a symbiosis of sorts wherein the needs of one group shapes the output of the other. During a PBS Newshour interview,[43] Doris

Meissner, the former INS Commissioner responds to the concerns of mass deportations created by the media. Although the interviewer states that people seem to be worried about mass deportations, one could suggest that people also seem to be worried about the failure to remove large numbers of illegal aliens.

> ELIZABETH FARNSWORTH: Let's go through some other things people seem to be worried about. Will there be a huge rise in deportations which some people are saying they're worried about when they come into INS offices?
> DORIS MEISSNER: Well, INS will not be engaging in any mass deportations of any kind. We will not be taking--we will not be doing sweeps. We will not be doing round-ups, and we certainly will not be targeting specific nationalities. We will continue to deport people in accordance with what our priorities have been, which is to focus first on criminal aliens, focus on people who are employed illegally. People who are here illegally are always subject to deportation and they will continue to be, but the cases that you just cited where people are trying--are claiming hardship, people that have been here for long periods of time, the rules have changed for those people, and judges will be operating according to different standards.

We can derive a limited definition of the concept of the illegal alien from the carefully constructed INS press releases, and official statements. The relationship between INS and the press is mostly symbiotic. The media receives what INS thinks the media wants. In most instances, press releases are a function of media acceptance, or belief. This relates to the official releases by the agency, and are meant to insure the public that the agency in addressing both public safety, and humanitarian (service) concerns.

On the other hand, most of the media is pro-immigrant and selectively reports on matters that are aligned with this bias. Even when illegals come forward and inform the public about their situation,[44] their accounts are subject to the same limitations. The illegal alien surfaces to reveal interesting items about their life that is also newsworthy. Newsworthiness is draped in media bias.

INVESTIGATORS' PERCEIVED NOTIONS OF OVERLOAD

Law enforcement officers perceive the *war on crime* as a losing battle fought with insufficient resources, and the lack of public support contributes to their frustration. "The consequence of this perspective is that over time officers develop a sense of overload."[45] There was *real* overload at the legacy INS, and the participants generally agreed that it existed. The presence of millions of illegal aliens in the environment serves as a constant reminder that this sense of overload continues, but sheer volume alone does not necessarily induce burnout. DEA agents are similarly aware that illegal drugs seem to be everywhere, and most in society generally agree with the mission of the DEA. Besides overload, role conflict contributes to burnout.[46] The impact of real overload, as well as role conflict, may create a numbing effect on a control agent. This numbing effect directly impacts on officer morale, and career aspirations. One way to cope with this problem is to accept the inevitability of the staggering number of illegal aliens inside the US, and it appears that DHS selected this perception as part of its enforcement strategy. However, some politicians are not acquiescing to this conclusion, because they too perceive social unrest about lawlessness. At the US Senate Subcommittee Hearings on Immigration, Senator Jon Kyl from Arizona stated his concern about citizen's perceptions of lawlessness with regard to interior enforcement of the immigration laws. These hearings were in preparation of new legislation that might include a guest worker program, as well as recent congressional concerns.

> . . . I hope that . . . we begin to convince our citizens that their government is serious about enforcing the law so that when Congress considers a new law they will be receptive and open-minded to the changes that we're going to have to make. Frankly, a lot of them don't want to accept the fact that we accept a lot of illegal aliens in the country. They are going to do that I think reluctantly, grudgingly perhaps, but I think they'll do it if they know we are committed to enforcing the new law that we pass and that comes from a commitment to enforcing existing laws . . .[47]

Policy makers through the INS essentially paid lip service to the fact that there were millions of illegal aliens living in the US, and DHS through its priority enforcement program is vigorously following suit. The excuse that there were limited resources served as the justification for decreasing interior enforcement efforts, and this occurred both at INS and DHS. At this time, the special agents assigned to ICE include those assigned to immigration matters, and those assigned to other priorities (such as prior Customs type cases). Furthermore, except for criminal aliens, ICE appears to be ignoring interior enforcement altogether. As stated previously, ERO, or deportation officers, also take CBP apprehensions into custody, and these are counted as ICE apprehensions.

DISCRETION AND POLICE WORK IN A CIVIL SOCIETY

Members of a civil society and the organizations they create share a responsibility, and concern for one another, further requiring mutual trust between the police (legal system), and the citizenry.

... it is their willingness to live up to an obligation to mobilize the police for violations of the law, whether against themselves, others, or the public order, that is a major element in maintaining a civil society ... A police force that works mainly by responding to citizen requests for police service is more consistent with a civil society than is one that relies mainly on police initiative.[48]

Discretion involves the ability to act, or not to act as situations arise, and impacts on the maintenance of a civil society. Enforcing every rule is impossible in a democratic society, and priorities are constructed to achieve order. Scientific positivism, and social determinism developed in the nineteenth century and contributed to our current thinking about the causes of crime.

The regularity and stability of crime rates over time was to be sought for and found in the relatively stable and predictable nature of social forces, forces grounded in society itself. The same social forces operating over time produce predictable amounts of crime. This *discovery* was a forerunner of the essential sociological insight that was to be more clearly and definitively articulated by Emile Durkheim at the turn of the century, but without its class struggle implications which were to be outlined by Marx in the intervening years.[49]

Some believe that enforcing the immigration laws is in conflict with fundamental values of compassion, and freedom. As such, a dilemma arises when we attempt to remove restraints.

In a totalitarian state, the task of the police is relatively simple, because the maintenance of the social order takes priority over individual freedom and justice. In a democracy, however, the job of the police is regulated by the need to reconcile their objective of preserving order and safety with the democratic imperative of personal freedom. Ultimately, the resolution of this dilemma is left up to the individual police officer, whose authority allows him to make on-the-spot decisions affecting the lives of citizens.[50]

Technically, all law violators are subject to arrest, and the police can arrest anyone if they have probable cause to believe that person committed a crime. However, the criminal justice system does not operate in this manner. The amount of discretion increases as one moves down the chain of command in the law enforcement agencies, and the use of prosecutorial discretion has become a tool for the DHS in dealing with the incomprehensible number of immigration law violators. It is an excellent way to make the impossible, manageable. In addition, prosecutorial discretion can be effectively employed to redefine deviance, and to do so officially. Only legislation can truly relieve the stigma associated with being undocumented. Unfortunately, the policy decisions and prosecutorial discretion have only deferred the consequences of deviant behavior.

Wilson offers four examples of police discretion considering managers, police officers, and their contacts on the streets.[51] The first type includes so called victimless crimes such as vice, gambling and traffic offenses that are police invoked. Depending on departmental policy, the police officer has a great deal of discretion in dealing with such offenses. The second type involves citizen-invoked situations such as larceny, auto theft and burglary in which the citizen is the victim of a crime, and the police officer has the least amount of discretion in handling the case. With regard to juveniles, police administrators can establish appropriate guidelines on how to handle cases, and determine which resources, if any, are needed. The third example involves police invoked order maintenance situations such as drunkenness, disorderly conduct, or disturbing the peace. In such cases, the police initiate the encounter, and the patrol officer has a great deal of discretion. The last example includes citizen invoked order maintenance situations such as public or private disorders. The way police handle these situations will vary, and depend on the personalities of the actors rather than policy.

Legacy INS investigators had routine involvement in citizen invoked actions, but involvement in maintenance of order situations was rare. Some order maintenance situations could arise such as police encounters that lead questions about the immigration status of the suspects. Considering Wilson's model, most INS investigator actions require either little discretion, or discretion tempered by departmental control. In immigration, related encounters, the investigator has the authority to stop and question *anyone* believed to be an alien regarding their right to be in the US, and this involves a great deal of *typing* of individuals. In urban areas, an experienced investigator can usually *identify* illegal aliens, but questioning such individuals involves certain discretionary strategies. Court decisions require that investigators articulate the reasons for stopping anyone, and this means that merely stating that a person *looks* like an illegal alien is unacceptable. Investigators use such factors as dress and demeanor to satisfy the requirement, and as such, being able to properly articulate an action determines the use of discretion.

An example of controlled discretion involves agency policies that limit resources. Most of the agents perceived an arrest encounter with an illegal alien as inconsequential. However, an arrest encounter is potentially dangerous, and requires special skills. On the other hand, conducting a criminal investigation requires special skills, technical equipment, and resources. Investigations usually involve gathering evidence, locating and interviewing witnesses, using electronic equipment, as well as developing *confidential* informants. As such, managers exercise a great deal of controlled discretion regarding the allocation of resources in these areas. At DHS, agents are restricted in routine encounters with undocumented aliens, and even suggesting one could lead to disciplinary action against the agent. The executive priorities regarding immigration enforcement address public safety, national security matters, and aliens who have been convicted of serious crimes. Unless they are serious, even misdemeanor convictions are ignored, including multiple misdemeanor convictions. Since most of the illegal alien violations are administrative, the burden of proof is *preponderance of evidence,* not *beyond a reasonable doubt.* As such, processing such cases should be easier, not more difficult. However, given the current policies DHS created an environment that leaves the control agent confused. Agents are required to carry a card that lists the types of deportable aliens that are subject to arrest, but this process has essentially created a *de facto* amnesty for most of the illegal aliens in the US.

The relationship between operators and managers adds another dimension to the use of discretion, and the administration of justice. The police perceive their tasks as *craftworker,* and view policy makers, and the judiciary, as essentially hostile to their mission. "The policeman, as a tactical matter, recognizes an obligation to appear to be obeying the letter of procedural law, while often disregarding its spirit."[52]

The organizational structure in which a control agent operates assists in understanding police discretion. Three important factors emerge in considering this discretion: the processing apparatus, the common view held by control agents that they stand on the line between chaos and order, and the belief that the criminal justice system actually contributes to the crime problem.

EDUCATION, PROFESSIONALIZATION, AND THE POLICE

In police departments, education separates the professionals from the conservatives, but it also constitutes a movement toward professionalization.

> The middle-class college men who became policemen formed the nucleus of the future elite groups . . . It was not long before this select group sought to raise the prestige of the police occupation to match their middle-class ideologies and attainments. Only by professionalization could this be accomplished.[53]

Most of the NYDO investigators had college degrees, and this factor contributed to their attitudes about career advancement, and tasks. In law enforcement, the professional seeks recognition based on merit, while the conservatives rely on influence and patronage. "The police local zealously seeks a *rabbi* (an influential patron) and schemes how and when to use *clout* (pull or influence) to best advantage."[54] Where most of the operators have advanced degrees, one might assume that merit is the most important criteria in achieving advancement. However, reliance on the *rabbi,* and *schemes* seems to surface as the most reliable method. The federal civil service work philosophy suggests that merit determines advancement, and further minimizes *favoritism* or *cronyism*. Nonetheless, it appears that whom you know often means more than what you know. This is especially true for the legacy investigators whose career ladder stopped at the GS-11 grade. Individuals with similar educational levels compete for a minimum number of promotional opportunities.

> It is most clearly revealed when a man without education succeeds in being promoted. With what triumph in his demeanor does he constantly call to the attention of his college trained subordinates that he is their boss even though he never went beyond sixth grade or elementary school?[55]

The organizational structure of INS was not conducive to the professional status of the investigator. Investigators derived recognition through peer review, and peer evaluations offer important insights about organizational analysis. For professionals, the best way to operate is as participants in a *self-regulating company of equals.*[56]

Law enforcement personnel are sensitive to peer review, and seek the approval of their peers. Police share solidarity, and view their position in society as *we* against *them.* If investigators view their professional goal as law enforcement, then service related activities are inappropriate. Even if the organization prefers the service activities, the enforcers hold a negative view towards anything service related. The goals of the investigator will then compete with the goals of the agency. In such a setting, the investigator often has to choose between peer approval and promotion.

Investigators viewed *paperwork* and service activities as *dirty work,* and avoided places where this work is completed. This accounts for the normally empty offices of most police and investigative units. Law enforcement officers believe that their work is *on the street.* If the agency desires, the investigator can spend most of his career inside the office doing paperwork. Such a *threat* is an obvious way of controlling the investigator.

When the reality of police work is on the street, then all other forms of reality assume a lesser significance. Further, this means that the primary code into which all other events will be transformed, and in a way retained as reality, will be the code of the street.[57]

POLICE MORALE AND PRODUCTIVITY

The research on assembly line workers forms the basis of most of our knowledge about productivity and morale, where such variables are relatively easy to measure. Counting arrests reflects the crime rate, but says little about police productivity, or morale. The annual arrest rates continued to soar at INS, but officer morale continued to plummet. The dual mandate mission contributed to an understanding of this dilemma.

> A desirable organizational climate includes high levels of morale . . . We also
> know—or think we know—that disgruntlement breeds poor performance . . .
> productivity as it is usually recorded is not reflective of quality policing.[58]

The locus of control is a strong determinant of job satisfaction among law enforcement officers. Control agents will exhibit higher morale and job satisfaction if they believe that their behavior has a direct impact on the outcome of events. We refer to this as internal control.[59] Seasoned officers experience more feelings of internal control than police recruits, and such feelings contribute to enhanced job satisfaction. Although INS investigators exhibited discretion on the street, policy directives guided most of their tasks. Unlike the police, their routine tasks did not include order, or peace keeping, which usually manifests perceptions of internal control. Generally, federal law enforcement officers have perceptions of internal control, but to a lesser degree than the police.

ROLE CONFLICT AND ROLE STRAIN

Patrol officers usually respond in a special way to danger, authority, and efficiency, and the term *working personality* refers to this response mechanism.

> So far as exposure to danger is concerned, the policeman may be likened to a
> soldier. His problems as an authority bear a certain similarity to those of the
> schoolteacher, and the pressures he feels to prove himself efficient are not
> unlike those felt by the industrial worker.[60]

The *working personality* shared by police officers contributes to their isolation from the rest of society, and as length of service increases, police officers tend to cope with stress by becoming emotionally detached.[61] Stress is defined as " . . . a physical, chemical, or emotional factor that causes bodily or mental tension that may result in disease. A stressor is defined as a stimulus that causes stress."[62] Police officers experience higher than average rates of premature death and rank third among occupations in suicide rate.[63] As a possible example, an ICE ERO agent shot and killed himself in New York City, and DHS officially stated that "Tragically, a U.S. ICE deportation officer from the New York field office suffered a self-inflicted gunshot wound and has passed away."[64]

The single most disturbing contributor to police officer stress is the element of danger. Although police officers fear the dangerous elements of their work, it also adds excitement to the otherwise routine tasks they prefer not to handle. In addition to the element of danger, some policemen respond to the conflicts inherent in a service, or enforcement mandate, by developing *func-*

tional specialization.[65] Since police organizations share the dual mandate it is possible for police officers to *specialize* in one or the other. For example, juvenile work, or community relations, satisfy the police officer role in a service area, even though *real* police work involves law enforcement. As specialists, the primary function of federal investigators is law enforcement, and the criminal investigator does not have the option of specializing in service work. Doing so would stigmatize the agent as other than a law enforcer. Interestingly, the INS investigator is often involved in service work, involving the adjudication of immigrant visa applications. The investigation of the application often facilitates the processing (service) function. In addition, due to the backlog of applications in the service part of the agency, investigators are often detailed to "task forces" in attempts to clear them up. It is expected that investigators will experience conflict when working in service areas, and under service managers. Agents view such details as temporary, and they still consider themselves as part of the enforcement mission. Sometimes, agents will volunteer for these service duties just to take a temporary break from investigations.

The dual mandate priorities coupled with conflicting attitudes about the seriousness of the illegal alien problem also contribute to role strain. The attention paid to *human rights* is a further consideration in creating perceptions about criminals in general, and illegal aliens in particular. Such problems might cause agents to avoid participation in activities that contribute to this role strain.

> . . . Through the use of a technique such as *attention deployment*, an individual may successfully be able to manage contradictory role expectations by ignoring inputs which are fundamentally incompatible with the primary but conflicting role expectation.[66]

Schaefer's study of role behavior reveals that most police officers consider themselves *peacekeepers,* rather than *enforcers,* or *servicers.*

> Peace keepers embody the contradictory elements of support and control . . . were more desirous of authority and more willing to use force than Servicers, but less so than law enforcers.[67]

With regard to the illegal alien problem, considering the perceptions of the agent can better facilitate understanding their role.

> Deviance interpretation must proceed on several different levels, focusing on collective forces at the level of societies, on individuals, and on *people processing* organizations.[68]

It is expected that most illegal aliens will view themselves as victims rather than as criminals, and rationalize their deviance as a normal response to being poor and trying to survive. Third world governments most likely condone the mass migration of a portion of their population as a form of relief to their overburdened economies, and this hegira serves as a release valve. Illegals view incarceration as the fate of the poor, and the reason they are penalized is because they are powerless and impoverished, not because they are immoral. [69] This may also be viewed as a denial of responsibility for all participants in the interactions.

Immigration enforcement may also have its roots in *moral crusades.* The INA of 1921 necessitated the creation of the border patrol to enforce that law, and the investigations branch evolved out of the desire to eradicate communism in the US. Afterwards, the investigations unit expanded its mission to include all violators of the INA inside the US, and its evolving mission perpetuated its existence in an environment where organizations seek to do just that. 911 triggered an avalanche of law enforcement strategies, goals, task forces, revised missions, and other mandates to combat terrorism. In organizational analysis, this represents an ideal mission objective that can never be reached, and enables perpetual life for the goal seekers.

> The most obvious consequence of a successful crusade is the creation of a new set of rules. With the creation of a new set of rules we often find that a new set of enforcement agencies and officials is established. Sometimes, of course, existing agencies take over the administration of the new rule, but more frequently a new set of rule enforcers is created. [70]

The creation of the label *illegal alien* by various groups is somewhat self-serving, and the enormous population of illegals benefits certain groups. The illegal alien population represents a *subclass* in society that serves as a source of cheap labor, and economic exploitation discourages their assimilation, and full participation in the wider society. These societal contradictions create what Bustamante refers to as the *antilaw entrepreneur,* and they are not considered deviant.

> . . . it shows that a violation of law can also become the goal of an enterprise in the same sense that the creation of a law may be the goal of an enterprise. Both crusades to be successful, require leaders holding legitimate power, although in one case they have the added legitimization of answering to a moral imperative, whereas in the other, they answer to the economic interests of a specialized group. [71]

The public view of the illegal alien problem varies. Some individuals take a restrictionist stance, and consider illegal immigration a threat to organized society. Others feel that illegal aliens can be assimilated into mainstream society, and that most illegals are simply *economic refugees* entering the US only to work.[72] Some are unaware of the issues concerning nationality and immigration altogether. The continuous growth of the illegal alien population contributes to widespread restrictionist, *and* antirestrictionist views.

Society's mixed feelings about immigration law enforcement pose a dilemma for the immigration agent. The working personality of agents is similar to the police, yet the contradictions about enforcement of the INA lower their morale, and increase their feelings of role conflict, strain, and stress.

Since the original interviews, the legacy INS investigators transferred to DHS, but the same issues and problems seemed to carry over with them. The field agents continue to disagree with the policies, suggesting a continuing spiral toward low morale. In essence, millions of illegal aliens inside the US represent complete lawlessness, and society may find this lawlessness unacceptable. As a result, the problem will have to be revisited, and DHS-ICE, HSI, ERO, and CBP will be called upon to offer solutions. Focused interviews with legacy INS investigators provided most of the substantive data in this study, which concentrated on issues concerning the perceptions of the control agents about their agency. They were based on six major areas: task, goals, policy directives, training, morale, and promotion. We now turn to the methodological concerns surrounding the illegal alien problem.

NOTES

1. Allan Silver, "The Demand for Order in Civil Society: A Review of Some Themes in the History of Urban Crime, Police, and Riot," in David Bordua, *The Police: Six Sociological Essays*, New York: John Wiley and Sons, Inc. (1967) 3.

2. C. B. Macpherson, ed., "Introduction," in Thomas Hobbes, *Leviathan,* Maryland: Penguin Books, (1968) 53.

3. Silver, (1967). p. 12.

4. Isidore Silver, ed., (1974). The Crime Control Establishment, New Jersey: Prentice-Hall, Inc., p. 1.

5. John T. O'Brien, (1978). "Public Attitudes Toward Police," *Journal of Police Science and Administration*, 6: 303-310.

6. Jon Dougherty. (2003). "Border Militia Critic gets cold feet." World Net Daily. Retrieved from http://www.worldnetdaily.com/news/article.asp?ARTICLE_ID=32782

7. Howard E. Aldrich, (1979). *Organizations and Environments*, New Jersey: Prentice-Hall, Inc., p. 77.

8. DHS Budget Data, "Annual Yearbook," 2015.

9. Malia Zimmerman and M. Dean. "Feds Blocked from Person of Interest after San Bernardino Attack," Foxnews.com, 2016, March 15. http://www.foxnews.com/politics/2016/03/15/feds-blocked-from-person-interest-after-san-bernardino-attack-lawmakers-told.html.

10. John Kitsuse, and A. V. Cicourel. (1963). "A Note on the Use of Official Statistics," *Social Problems,* 11: 131-139.

11. Julien Freund, *The Sociology of Max Weber,* New York: Pantheon Books, p. 89.

12. Richard Hawkins and Gary Tiedeman. (1975). *The Creation of Deviance: Interpersonal and Organizational Determinants*, Ohio: Merrill Publishing Company.

13. James Q. Wilson, (1978). The Investigators: Managing FBI and Narcotics Agents, New York: Basic Books, Inc., p. 7.

14. DHS, "Consideration of Deferred Action for Childhood Arrivals (DACA)," Accessed on June 24, 2016, https://www.uscis.gov/humanitarian/consideration-deferred-action-childhood-arrivals-daca#guidelines

15. Hawkins and Tiedeman. (1975). p. 37.

16. Sheriff Charles Jenkins, Frederick County, Maryland, House website, (April 19, 2016), Accessed on June 22, 2016, https://judiciary.house.gov/wp-content/uploads/2016/04/Judicial-Testimony-2016-Sheriff-CJ.pdf

17. Jessica Vaughn, "Catch and Release," CIS, (March 2014), Accessed on June 22, 2016, http://cis.org/catch-and-release

18. Wilson. (1978). p. 15.

19. Wilson. (1978). p. 9.

20. Max Weber. (1947). *The Theory of Social and Economic Organization*, New York: The Free Press.

21. Peter M. Blau and M. W. Meyer. (1971). Bureaucracy in Modern Society, New York: Random House, p. 23.

22. Peter, M. Blau, *On the Nature of Organizations*, New York: John Wiley and Sons, Inc., p. 29.

23. Aldrich, 1979, pp. 22-23.

24. Department of Justice, "Organized Crime Drug Enforcement Task Forces," Accessed on June 23, 2016, https://www.justice.gov/criminal/organized-crime-drug-enforcement-task-forces

25. James M. Comey, FBI.gov, "Testimony: FBI Budget Requests for Fiscal Year 2016," (March 12, 2015) Accessed on June 23, 2016) https://www.fbi.gov/news/testimony/fbi-budget-request-for-fiscal-year-2016

26. Brittany M. Hughes, CNSnews.com, "ICE Director: Agents Risk 'Termination' For not Enforcing Obama's Immigration Policy, (April 14, 2005) Accessed on June 23, 2016, http://www.cnsnews.com/news/article/brittany-m-hughes/ice-director-agents-risk-termination-not-enforcing-obama-s

27. History.com Staff, "Iran Hostage Crisis," Accessed on October 16, 2016 http://www.history.com/topics/iran-hostage-crisis.

28. George J Weissinger, "Release of Iranians Brings Protest from INS Investigators," (1980). New York: Federal Law Enforcement Officers Association Newsletter.

29. Aldrich, 1979, p. 240.

30. Aldrich, 1979.

31. US General Accounting Office, "Briefing Report to the Honorable Alfonse M. D'Amato US Senate, Criminal Aliens: INS' Investigative Efforts in the New York City Area," (March, 1986) Maryland: U. S. General Accounting Office, GAO/GGD-86-58BR.

32. US General Accounting Office, "Criminal Aliens: INS' Efforts to Identify and Remove Imprisoned Aliens Continue to Need Improvement." (February 1999). GAO/T-GGD-99-47.

33. Stephen Dinan, The Washington Times, "Immigration agents sue to stop Obama's non-deportation policy," (August 23, 2012) Accessed on June 23, 2016, http://www.washingtontimes.com/news/2012/aug/23/immigration-agents-sue-stop-obamas-non-deportation/#pagebreak

34. Albert J. Reiss and D. J. Bordua. (1967). "Environment and Organization: A Perspective on the Police," in David Bordua, *The Police: Six Sociological Essays*, pp. 25-26.

35. Charles Perrow. (1979). *Complex Organizations: A Critical Essay, 2nd edition*, Illinois: Scott, Foresman and Company.

36. Richard H. Hall, *Organizations: Structure and Process*, New Jersey: Prentice-Hall, Inc., p. 322.

37. Edwin M. Schur, *Interpreting Deviance: A Sociological Introduction*, New York: Harper and Row, p. 370.

38. R. Hall, "Organizations: Structure ad Process, 2nd ed.," NJ: Prentice Hall, (1977) 303-312.

39. Murray Edelman, "Power and Symbol in Administrative Regulation," in Social Problems and Public Policy: Inequality and Justice, ed., by L. Rainwater, Chicago: Aldine Publishing Company, p. 317.

40. DHS, "Office of Legislative Affairs," Accessed on July 20, 2016, https://www.dhs.gov/about-office-legislative-affairs

41. Morton Mintz and Jerry Cohen, Power, Inc.: Public and Private Rulers and How to Make Them Accountable, New York: The Viking Press, p. 329.

42. Marilyn Lester, "Generating Newsworthiness: The Interpretive Construction of Public Events," American Sociological Review, 45(December): 984-994.

43. Doris Meissner, PBS Newshour, "Politics," (April 1, 1997), Accessed on June 24, 2016, http://www.pbs.org/newshour/bb/law-jan-june97-meissner_4-1/

44. Central Broadcasting System. (August 28, 1977). Undocumented Aliens, New York: CBS, Inc. Keely, Charles B., P. J. Elwell, et al., (1978). Profiles of Undocumented Aliens in New York City: Haitian and Dominicans, New York: Center for Migration Studies.

45. Peter K. Manning, (1980). The Narc's Game: Organizational and Informational Limits on Drug Law Enforcement, Massachusetts: MIT Press, p. 99.

46. John T. Whitehead, (1989). Burnout in Probation and Corrections, New York: Praeger Publishers.

47. Statement by Senator Jon Kyl, Arizona. (12/12/2004) Senate Subcommittee on Immigration, Washington, D.C. Senator Kyl was responding to Steven Law, the Deputy Labor Secretary's comments.

48. Albert J. Reiss, Jr. (1971). The Police and the Public, New Haven: Yale University Press, p. 173.

49. Richard Quinney and John Wildeman, The Problem of Crime: A Peace and Social Justice Perspective, California: Mayfield Publishing Company, pp. 48-49.

50. Alan E. Bent, (1974). The Politics of Law Enforcement: Conflict and Power in Urban Communities, Massachusetts: D. C. Heath and Company, p. 1.

51. James Q. Wilson, (1968). Varieties of Police Behavior: The Management of Law and Order in Eight Communities, Massachusetts: Harvard University Press.

52. Jerome H. Skolnick, (1966). Justice Without Trial: Law Enforcement in Democratic Society, New York: John Wiley and Sons, p. 228.

53. Arthur Neiderhoffer. (1963). A Study of Police Cynicism, New York University, Ph. D. Dissertation, p. 41.

54. Arthur Neiderhoffer. (1967). Behind the Shield: The Police in Urban Society, New York: Doubleday, p.58.

55. Neiderhoffer, 1963, p. 60.

56. Eliot Friedson and J. Lorber, editors. (1972). Medical Men and Their Work: A Sociological Reader, New York: Aldine-Atherton, Inc., 185.

57. Manning, 1980, pp. 220-221.

58. Hans Toch. (1978). "Police Morale: Living with Discontent," Journal of Police Science and Administration. 6:249-252.

59. David Lester and J. L. Genz. (1978). "Internal and External Locus of Control, Experience as a Police Officer, and Job Satisfaction in Municipal Police Officers," Journal of Police Science and Administration, 6(4): 479-481.

60. Skolnick, 1966, p. 228.

61. M. J. C. Hageman, (1977). "Occupational Stress of Law Enforcement Officers and Marital and Familial Relationships," Doctoral Dissertation, Pullman, Washington: Washington State University.

62. T. H. Walrod, (1978). "Causes of Stress to Police Officers Detailed," National Sheriff, 30 (October)12-29.

63. W. C. Richard and R. D. Fell. (1975). "Health Factors in Police Job Stress," in W. H. Kroes, and J. J. Hurrell, editors, Job Stress and the Police Officer: Identifying Stress Reduction Techniques, Proceedings of Symposium, Washington, DC: U. S. Government Printing Office.

64. Bob Price, Breithart.com, "ICE Agent shot and killed himself on Friday just blocks from his lower Manhattan office," (May 9,2016) Accessed on June 23, 2016, http://www.breitbart.com/texas/2016/05/09/ice-agent-shoots-blocks-new-york-city-office/

65. Roger Schaefer. (1978). "Law Enforcer, Peace Keeper, Servicer: Role Alternatives for Policemen," Journal of Police Science and Administration, 6:325.

66. Schaefer, 1978, p. 325.

67. Schaefer, 1978, p. 392.

68. Schur, 1979, p. 16.

69. Samora, Julian. (1971). Los Mojados: The Wetback Story, Indiana: University of Notre Dame Press.

70. Howard Becker, (1989). "Moral Entrepreneurs: The Creation and Enforcement of Deviant Categories," in Delos H. Kelly, Deviant Behavior: A Text Reader in the Sociology of Deviance, New York: St. Martin's Press, p. 24.

71. Jorge A. Bustamante, (1972). "The Wetback as Deviant: An Application of Labeling Theory," American Journal of Sociology, 77(4):716.

72. Austin T. Fragomen, Jr., (1973). The Illegal alien: Criminal or Economic Refugee, New York: Center for Migration Studies.

Chapter Four

Methodological Overview

INTRODUCTION

The ways agencies create and implement policies may confuse and frustrate operators. Immigration agents experience such reactions in their efforts to balance statutory powers with agency policies, which are often created by external forces. Mills considered reason and truth as basic methodological tools, and the sociological imagination may offer a way of dealing with such inconsistencies.

> . . . a quality of mind that will help them to use information and to develop reason in order to achieve lucid summations of what is going on in the world and of what may be happening within themselves. [1]

In part, sociology offered a means to explain the observed perceptions of the control agents in this analysis. Law enforcement officers develop close bonds, but this does not preclude an analytic discussion of their behavior when the observer is also one of the agents. Reporting accurate observations in the context where they occur become important methodological concerns, especially in participant observation research. Hopefully, I separated my role as law enforcer from the analysis in offering the descriptions of reality by the participants about how they completed their tasks.

Official statistics provide the analyst with information about whether the agency is fulfilling its mission statement, but official statistics are often self-serving. One must also consider the fact that manipulating official statistics, even a simple truncation of a few years instead of a more complete time series, can reinforce these official statements. Often, these summaries imply that the agency has exceeded all expectations, and met its goals. The North and Houston Report,[2] as well as Congressional hearings and Commissions, offer other reliable sources of information about the economic impact of illegal aliens on society. However, such data rarely provides information about illegal aliens that escape detection, or more importantly those that are intentionally ignored. The actual description of tasks by operators offers insights into such areas of concern, and the interpretive framework allows for a more direct way to explore how a control agency operates. Furthermore, it adds a valuable dimension to the research data on the illegal alien. Hopefully, such methods will provide awareness of the heretofore missing data about how operators complete their tasks in a bureaucracy. Perhaps, that is why agencies avoid publishing certain data, and why self-descriptions of what they do are so stringently controlled by the agency they work for. For example, operator's congressional testimony during Q&A sessions, after official (prepared) statements are placed in the record, provide more accurate descriptions of behavior, and often state more important information than the official statistics.

SELECTION OF TOPIC FOR RESEARCH

When I took the oath as a criminal investigator with INS, I was still a doctoral student at New York University, and there were two reasons I decided to select immigration as my research topic. I had relative ease of access to data about the illegal alien population, and most of the data on the illegal alien problem came from popular sources, or official statistics indicating a need for more research in this area. Although this is a participant observation study, I did not become a criminal investigator to study INS.

It is inevitable that critics of this study will insert their own biases, especially academics and the media who tend to be politically left of center regarding immigration matters. Others might sense an overall pessimism in the operator's statements, but that misconception fails to recognize the justified frustration of the participants. The original work commenced ten years after I decided to leave INS, and the preparation of the second edition allowed me to distance myself even further from the subject matter. This edition provides another level of objectivity, coupled with the historical record that sustains earlier conclusions. My primary interest in revising this account is to clarify and enhance the original work, what is occurring, and what is likely to occur in immigration law enforcement.

In 1985, I transferred to the Administrative Office of the US Courts, and worked there until 1998 when I decided to retire from federal law enforcement. This was short-lived, since I immediately began working as a special investigator, and independent contractor conducting investigations, for the FBI Background Investigation Contract Services (BICS). Although this had little to do with immigration enforcement, the experience highlighted the critical role that background investigations play in national security. That experience contributed to my concerns about policy decisions to admit thousands of refugees, who will most likely avoid necessary full background checks. As evidenced by the hundreds of individuals who were improperly naturalized by the USCIS, allowing thousands of refugees to enter the US from countries where we have little, if any, documentary evidence about their backgrounds, it is logical to assume that terrorists will gain lawful admission into the US.

> If a set of data . . . would make an agency uncomfortable, that agency does not seek those data . . . one must wonder, given the lethargic output of research results from the Immigration Service how enthusiastically it is pursuing knowledge in this area.[3]

UNIT OF STUDY

The units of study for this analysis were series 1811 criminal investigators of the INS NYDO. Shortly after they are hired, criminal investigators undergo intensive training including twelve weeks at the Federal Law Enforcement Training Center (FLETC) studying topics such as immigration law, investigative techniques, police practice, criminal law, Spanish language, and firearms training. The training continues after FLETC and the investigator must satisfactorily pass a nine-and-a-half-month comprehensive examination to retain the position. Afterwards, the investigator must attend a basic review course before achieving journeyman status. After the DHS reorganization, legacy customs agents underwent cross training to learn the immigration laws so that they could effectively conduct such investigations, and the legacy INS investigators received cross training in the areas of criminal investigation that were neglected in their previous positions.

At the time of the original data collection, there were 162 investigators at the NYDO, working in three investigative sections, and a processing group:

> (1) General Investigations Unit—primarily miscellaneous investigations not covered in the other sections, including character investigations, locate investigations, status determination investigations, government motor vehicle accident investigations involving INS personnel, and application/accreditation investigations. The Area Control Illegal Status (ACIS) Section, also a part of General Investigations, focuses on the location and apprehension of illegal aliens mostly at employments, and relies on complaints from the general public for information. Thirty-six investigators were assigned to this unit and ten were interviewed.
> (2) The Frauds Unit—focuses on investigating individuals involved in schemes to fraudulently obtain immigration benefits such as immediate rela-

tive applications and sham marriages. Thirty-five investigators were assigned to this unit, and eleven were interviewed.

(3) Special Investigations Unit—actually includes three squads: the Subversives Unit—investigates subversive aliens such as terrorists, or members of subversive organizations; Criminal, Immoral, Narcotic Squad—investigates aliens arrested or detained by local police or other agencies who are deportable because of the arrest or detention; and the Anti-Smuggling Unit—investigates the smuggling of aliens into the US. Forty-one investigators were assigned to this unit, and eleven were interviewed.

(4) The Alien Processing Group—includes agents detailed for ninety days who complete mostly paperwork, such as processing deportable aliens. Eight investigators were assigned to this unit, and all were interviewed. A total of fifty investigators were interviewed for the original study.

SAMPLE SIZE

Originally, I planned on interviewing half the members of each section in the NYDO, and planned to interview each member in units with less than ten members. However, several factors required a reduction in sample size, including time constraints of interviewees, and the unavailability of investigators who were detailed to other district offices. Since the interviewees are considered specialized, or elite participants, the small difference in numbers should not alter the validity of the data. Investigators were randomly, and proportionately selected from each section in the investigations branch. At least ten of the investigators were at the GS-12 grade level, (20%) of the sample.

SPECIALIZED INTERVIEWING

... an elite interview ... is an interview with any interviewee ... who in terms of the current purposes of the interviewer is given special, nonstandardized treatment . . . (1) stressing the interviewee's definition of the situation, (2) encouraging the interviewee to structure the account of the situation, (3) let the interviewee introduce to a considerable extent . . . his notions of what he regards as relevant, instead of relying upon the investigator's notions of relevance.[4]

The interviewer seeks to elicit the elite's definition of the situation, and uses the focused interview in an interpretive framework, and unlike standard or typical survey responses, offers a better definition of reality. During the focused interviews, I concentrated on eliciting the perceptions of the elite interviewee. Interviewing criminal investigators, who are trained interviewers themselves, requires special attention since skilled interrogators are capable of answering questions without revealing a true intent, or personal knowledge of how the agency operates. Investigators are reluctant to make statements, since doing so can lead to retaliation by the agency. As indicated earlier, investigators cannot officially speak to the press, and press releases come from a public relations officer, or some other designated officer. Sometimes, the agency allows the media to accompany agents on strictly controlled operations.

In my opinion, the investigators were very open in their responses, and freely provided reliable data. The fact that I knew them personally may have uniquely aided in establishing a rapport, which otherwise might not have occurred. Law enforcement officers are generally guarded in interview situations, and the nature of their work prevents them from discussing certain topics that might be deemed classified. In addition, investigators are skeptical of the media, and interviewees may view the interviewer as part of the media. Generally, law enforcement agents perceive the media as hostile to law enforcement or, in this case, hostile to immigration enforcement.

Such issues did not pose serious obstacles to this study, and concerted efforts were made to maintain a professional distance between the dual roles of participant observer, and investigator. I could elicit important information not usually available to the researcher without deception, and was ever mindful of avoiding *overrapport.*

> The researcher should not become a mere machine, but in situations involving overt and covert controversy, he should be wary of identifying himself symbolically and emotionally with a particular group . . . that his research activities are his prime reasons for being present.[5]

During the interview process, it was important to maintain a neutral position and avoid overrapport, but the preconceived notions of interviewees about the researcher could not be controlled, or even known.

CORRUPTION: A METHODOLOGICAL ISSUE

As a methodological concern, questions regarding corruption were not discussed with the interviewees. Because of the sense of solidarity peculiar to the working personality of law enforcement personnel, it is unlikely that investigators would care to answer such questions. As a methodological concern, such matters would have immediately broken rapport, and detracted from the core issues of concern. In my experience, corruption was not a significant problem among the *officer corps* at INS. Regarding immigration enforcement, one of the main concerns surrounding corruption of the officer corps is the influence of the drug cartels along the southwest US border. Cartels can offer an agent more money for participating in drug trafficking than the officer might earn in an entire year. The cartels can also threaten the agent, and his family if the agent rejects the offer. [6]

Allegations concerning corruption do surface, and one would be naive to assert that it does not exist. It would be more accurate to state that many of the allegations of corruption, and misconduct are directed towards the border patrol, and service operations. Border patrol agents have much more *discretion* than investigators, and discretion seems to precipitate more allegations of corruption. The service mandate of the agency is also concerned with *giving things away,* and the agency service priority creates a large group of employees that are susceptible to corrupt practices. Furthermore, the enormous backlog of cases creates a system wherein *expediting* applications attracts corrupt practices. Finally, higher education is correlated with lower levels of corruption, and investigators generally had more education that other officers. Corruption is not a core issue in this study, however its research significance in organizational analysis is noted.

FOCUSED INTERVIEWS

The intent of using focused interviews was to elicit operator perceptions about their agency, and how tasks were completed. Sharing the work experiences of the participants, and utilizing an interview guide, aided in the formulation of hypotheses. To elicit self-definitions of the work situation, data collection included unstructured interviews when needed, and included questions about operator tasks. To elicit accurate retrospective descriptions of incidents, the researcher employed supplementary probing with *verbal cues.* Individual, and group interviews with investigators took place during *other than normal duty hours* at the NYDO, which was an agency condition specified in the approval of my request to conduct the research. To elicit information without the fear of reprisal, protecting the identity of the interviewees was imperative.

Each interview lasted approximately one hour, was tape-recorded, and later transcribed and edited. In a few cases, participants requested that the interview not be taped, and notes were taken. Each participant also provided basic biographical data, completed a questionnaire, and were also asked if there were any areas that were not covered during the interviews. After the original data collection, legacy agents who were willing to participate in a follow-up study were contacted and interviewed. Recently retired agents spoke freely, and agreed to in-depth interviews, or the completion of survey questionnaires. Other qualitative data sources included official published statements about the interior enforcement of the immigration laws. A few current agents provided confidential information about the ICE transition, and operations in that agency. Methodologically, these sources are credible, and focused interviews with elites consistently provide reliable accounts.

This study also includes official statistics, as well as my original research on the NYDO apprehension data collected in 1977-1978, which supplemented the interview data. The research data, and information gleaned from the interviews were often in contrast to the official statistics. Through a Freedom of Information (FOIA) request, DHS provided statistics on interior enforcement. The underlying theme of this research stresses the basic rules of sociology regarding normative behavior, and I know of no other work that relies on the perceptions of control agents to explain the underlying problems surrounding immigration.

INFORMANTS

The fact that I was conducting interviews with investigators quickly spread throughout the investigations unit. Thus, the interviewees became active participants in the research process, and, over time they continued to supply anecdotal material. This data took the form of statements such as, "make sure you put *that* in your paper . . . " As a result, other important experiences began to surface that were missed during the formal interviews. Information about DHS-ICE came from survey responses received from current and former employees of the agency, and were supplemented with research, especially congressional committee testimony published on government websites, and media reports.

INTERVIEW GUIDE

The interview guide employed in this study focused on six major areas, and utilized *verbal cues* to elicit a possible range of responses from the interviewees. These open-ended cues allowed respondents to be more flexible in their responses, and unanticipated responses were encouraged and expected. When such responses surfaced, they were discussed in more depth.[7] The major areas and verbal cues used in each are as follows:

(1)Task—What kind of work does a criminal investigator do? The author asked investigators to describe their everyday activities, and used the official job description as a verbal cue:

Criminal investigators plan and conduct investigations relating to alleged or suspected violations of federal laws. The duties typically performed include those such as the following: obtaining physical and documentary evidence; interviewing witnesses; applying for and serving warrants for arrests, searches and seizures; seizing contraband, equipment and vehicles; examining files and records; maintaining surveillance; performing undercover assignments; preparing investigative reports; testifying in hearings and trials; assisting the U. S. Attorney's in the prosecution of court cases. Most criminal investigators are required to carry firearms and to be proficient in their use. The work may occasionally involve noncriminal investigations. Performance of these duties frequently requires irregular unscheduled hours, personal risks, exposure to all kinds of weather, considerable travel, and arduous exertion, under adverse environmental conditions. Criminal investigators may also be required to operate motor vehicles. [8]

The interviewer used this verbal cue to elicit the investigator's description of their tasks. Obviously, investigators do not always do all the activities described in the Personnel Manual. To compare the tasks performed in each section, investigators were asked to describe their everyday activities.

Investigators present a case to the U. S. Attorney's Office to initiate criminal prosecution, and the Assistant U. S. Attorney (AUSA) then decides whether to prosecute the case, or not. Sometimes, the AUSA will recommend that the investigator obtain more evidence before accepting the case. The interviewer asked the participants about their dealings with the U. S. Attorney's Office.

The author asked investigators about case assignments, and completions. The use of *informants* is an integral part of criminal law enforcement work, and the interviewer asked about the role they played in immigration law enforcement.

(2) Goals—What are the goals of INS? The author used two verbal cues to elicit responses about the dual mandate of INS. The first cue was former INS Commissioner L. Castillo's response to the question, "Do you agree with the general assessment that the illegals are more contributors than drainers on the public resources?" Castillo responded, "No question about it. Immigrants, with or without papers, are net contributors to this economy, to this society."[9]

Castillo placed a high priority on adjudicating backlogs of petitions, and set up task forces throughout the country to accomplish this. It was expected that investigators would have strong feelings about Castillo's statements. Although clearing backlogs is an appropriate organizational strategy, commandeering control agents to do such *dirty work* can only contribute to lowering morale. On the other hand, the statement could reflect an overall agreement with policy. Either way, the statement clearly offered an opportunity to trigger a strong response.

Another cue focused on the goals of INS, and took the form of a statement made in an INS publication. In commenting on the adjudication task force,

... at the same time, we want to also develop an expertise among our officers which will allow them to effectively interdict the escalating and evermore

sophisticated forms of fraud being perpetrated by those who would gain benefits to which they are not entitled.[10]

Since the Commissioner dictates policy, both cues reflect important aspects of the agency's interpretation of its mission. The interviewer used these
cues to elicit the perceptions of the investigators that are tasked to implement
the Commissioner's policies.

(3) Policy Directives—What are some of the policy directives issued by INS,
and how do they reflect, and effect the agency's mission? The interviewer
asked the agents to discuss some of INS policies regarding everyday tasks, and
whether such policies agreed with their perceptions of mission.

Normally, the policies of law enforcement agencies specify what control
agents cannot do, rather than what they can, or ought to do. The *Investigator's Handbook* offers basic guidelines on officer conduct. It is impossible to
delineate how an investigator should act in every circumstance, and investigative duties seem to produce uncertainty and stress due to the nature of the
tasks. Often, such tasks require unprecedented decision-making skills, and
the investigator must decide in an environment where no clear guidelines
exist. Usually, only the investigator suffers the consequences of *wrong* decisions. Errors can be avoided if the investigator can plan the investigation,
however locating and apprehending illegal aliens does not lend itself to planning, and usually occur routinely, and randomly. Although they are routine
and may occur randomly, the circumstances surrounding these encounters
can become problematic.

Another example might serve to illustrate this point. INS policy dictates
that an investigator can use a firearm (deadly force) in *only* three instances:
self-defense, defense of partner, and defense of an innocent third party. Although this policy appears to be clearly stated, self-defense is not easily
defined. Is the agent justified in using deadly force if someone appears intent
on causing bodily harm, or threatens to do so? Should an investigator display
the weapon when an arrest is made? This is standard procedure when a
criminal arrest is made. However, most INS arrests are administrative (even
though many illegal aliens have committed a crime by entering without inspection). Often, this dilemma is compounded by the fact that an agent cannot be sure whether an arrest will be administrative, or criminal.

(4)Training—The author asked investigators about training, and whether it
was relevant to their tasks. The investigator should receive appropriate training
to function effectively in his assigned tasks. The agency often reflects its
priorities through the kind of training it offers. For example, criminal investigators should receive adequate training in how to conduct criminal investigations.

(5)Morale—How do investigators define morale, and what is the present state of morale among investigators? Good morale involves how individuals feel about coming to work, and accomplishing their tasks. An organization has good morale when the employees look forward to coming to work, and performing their tasks.

Generally, the tasks of investigators result in adverse consequences for the clients. Investigator tasks include: the investigation of criminal violations, locating law violators, and obtaining facts relevant to an individual's claim to certain INA benefits. Often, the investigation uncovers fraudulent attempts to gain immigration benefits. Strong support from management and the public facilitates such tasks, and public support depends on a positive image. The FBI commands a positive image mainly because of these factors. Similarly, most large organizations have a public information officer to enhance their public image. Agency spokespersons accomplish this task through press releases, or by releasing official statements to the media.

The interviewer asked investigators about their perceptions of how the agency portrayed the illegal alien problem to the public, as well as their self-perceptions about their place in the law enforcement hierarchy. In part, self-perceptions will also reflect the state of officer morale.

(6)Promotion—How are investigators rated, and promoted? How does management evaluate job performance, and what criteria do they consider important in the evaluation process? The author asked investigators to describe the promotion process, and to discuss their perceptions of it.

Ideally, merit is the sole criteria for advancement among professionals, or in a bureaucracy where candidates compete for jobs. The candidate with the best qualifications should be selected, and nepotism, or favoritism of any kind, are inappropriate practices which agents will strongly object, or disvalue.

Among legacy agents, most expressed the belief that the possibility of a promotion did not exist. The author was particularly interested in comparing the responses of GS-11, and GS-12 grade investigators. After March 1, 2003, the merger of agents from INS, and customs into ICE should eventually resolve the grade discrepancy issue. I was informed that legacy INS agents in ICE were still GS-12 journeyman officers, while the customs agents are GS-13's, but new hires are GS-13 journeyman positions.

DESCRIPTION OF SAMPLE

The average age of the interviewees was 31.5 years, and most of the sample was in the 30-32 years of age category (30 investigators). There is a mandatory retirement age in federal law enforcement. At the time of this study, the mandatory retirement age was 55 years of age with at least 20 years of federal law enforcement service. Presently, the mandatory retirement age is 57 years of age for law enforcement positions.

72% of the sample had a college degree, 4 had master's degrees, and 1 had a law degree. Ten investigators declined to provide information about their education. 72% of the sample were married, and the remaining investigators were single. The interviewees had an average of 5.5 years of service with INS. The range of service for the sample was 2 to 14 years. 12 of the respondents were GS-12, 32 were GS-11, and 6 were GS-9 grade criminal investigators.

DHS has an annual budget of approximately $60 billion with most of the expenditures devoted to ICE. The agency has more than 20,000 employees with 400 offices in the US and 46 foreign countries. ICE houses Homeland Security Investigations (HSI), and Enforcement Removal Operations (ERO). HSI investigates a wide range of domestic and international activities arising from the illegal movement of people and goods into, within and out of the US. ERO apprehends removable aliens, detains them when necessary and removes illegal aliens from the US. The Strategic Plan 2016-2020 for US ICE[11] states its mission as focused on homeland security and public safety, investigating and enforcing the nation's laws governing border control, customs, trade, and immigration. The itemized mission goals include preventing terrorism, protecting the borders (customs and immigration), strengthening employee engagement, identifying and dismantling criminal networks that traffic in weapons, narcotics, counterfeit goods and human beings, and strengthening partnerships with every level of law enforcement. The DHS Federal Employee Viewpoint Survey (FEVS) indicates that 75% of the agents worked in the field, and the rest at Headquarters. 64% of the sample were non-supervisory personnel, 64% were male, 36% female (N=40,618), 76% were White, 13% were Black/African American, 16% Hispanic; 60% had a Bachelor's degree or higher, <5% were under 29 years of age, 23% were 30-39 years of age, 32% were 40-49 years of age, 30% were 50-59 years of age, and 11% were 60 or older.[12] Official statistics from the DHS website, the FEVS, and other sources will be used to compare the DHS ICE with the legacy INS data.

The interviews with the investigators are discussed in the chapters that follow, and were also analyzed using *Atlas/ti* software. Chapter five focuses on the attitudinal perceptions of the investigators toward their assigned tasks, the mission of INS, and professional law enforcement. Thereafter, I discuss the investigator at work, and describe the internal and external relations of the investigations branch. I then turn to the continuing problems of status and morale that arise out of the investigator's perceived notions of task.

NOTES

1. C. Wright Mills, *The Sociological Imagination,* (1959), New York: Oxford University Press.

2. David S, North and Marion F. Houstoun, "The Characteristics and Role of Illegal Aliens in the US Labor Market: An Exploratory Study," (1976) Washington, DC: Linton and Company.

3. David S. North, "A Tenuous Connection: Immigration Research and Policy Making," in *The Problem of the Undocumented Worker, ed.,* by R. S. Landmann, (1979) New Mexico: Latin American Institute, p. 21.

4. Lewis A Dexter, *Elite and Specialized Interviewing,* Ohio: Northwestern University Press, (1970) 5.

5. S. M. Miller, "The Participant Observer and *Over Rapport,*" *American Sociological Review.* (1952) 17: 97-99.

6. Jim McElhatton, "Immigration Agents Accused of Database Abuse: Cartels make Corruption Easy," *The Washington Times,* July 6, 2014, http://www.washingtontimes.com/news/2014/jul/6/immigration-agents-accused-of-database-abuse-carte/

7. "Methodological concerns about research on illegal aliens parallel the methodological concerns in this study." See Wayne A. Cornelius, *Interviewing Illegal aliens: Methodological Reflections Based on Fieldwork in Mexico and the U. S., International Migration Review,* 16(2): 378-411.

8. OPM.gov, "Classification & Qualifications: General Schedule Qualification Standards," Accessed on June 27, 2016, https://www.opm.gov/policy-data-oversight/classification-qualifications/general-schedule-qualification-standards/1800/criminal-investigation-series-1811/

9. Leonel Castillo and Others, "New Immigrants," interview by Public Broadcasting System, New York: PBS, 1979.

10. David H Lambert, "Target-Adjudications Backlog," *INS Reporter,* (Spring 1978), Washington, DC: INS, 53.

11. ICE, "U.S. Immigration and Customs Enforcement Strategic Plan 2016-2020," Accessed on June 28, 2016, https://www.ice.gov/sites/default/files/documents/Document/2016/strategic-plan-2020.PDF

12. DHS, "Department of Homeland Security 2015 Federal Employee Viewpoint Survey Results," Accessed on June 28, 2016, https://www.dhs.gov/sites/default/files/publications/2015_FEVS_AES_Department_of_Homeland_Security.pdf

Chapter Five

Investigator Perceptions of Agency Policies

INTRODUCTION: INVESTIGATOR CASEWORK AND TASKS

An INS manager described the mission of the legacy INS investigator as follows:

> Investigators are the plainclothesed enforcement arm detectives if you wish, of INS. Their primary responsibility is interior enforcement, generally in the metropolitan and urban areas in more than fifty locations throughout the continental US, Hawaii, Alaska, Virgin Islands, Puerto Rico and Guam. The Investigations branch's responsibilities include area control, which is a specific search for illegal aliens primarily at their places of employment and controlled casework. Casework includes such things as character investigations, marriage and labor certification frauds, document frauds, and private bills and other miscellaneous types of investigations relating to the enforcement of the INA. [1]

Investigator tasks include assigned casework, non-file casework, and *other* tasks. In addition, interviewees perceived managers as individuals responsible for implementing policies from above. Managers included supervisors and above the Assistant District Director for Investigations (ADDI) position in the organizational hierarchy, and the terms *manager,* or *management,* are used to refer to these policy makers. Criminal investigators are agents whose main task is conducting criminal investigations. Although most of the legacy investigators conducted administrative investigations relating to low-level visa abusers, the potential to conduct criminal investigations existed. Many illegal aliens enter the US without inspection (ewi), and although this is a crime, the agency chose to handle these cases administratively. The strategy of prioritizing administrative cases and service caused conflict and morale problems, because investigators perceived their main task as criminal investigation. In addition, even the administrative enforcement of the immigration laws was secondary to the service function, and such policies caused problems for investigators as well.

The degree to which policies are aligned with operator's perceptions about mission will determine the level of morale. Legacy agents were concerned with the internal policies that made it difficult to complete their tasks, while DHS ICE agents must deal with official external policies (executive orders), as well as internal policies (Priority Enforcement Program) that, for all practical purposes, contradicted their perceptions of agency mission. The DHS mission " . . . to ensure a homeland that is safe, secure, and resilient against terrorism and other hazards" includes preventing terrorism and enhancing security, securing and managing the borders, enforcing and administering the immigration laws, safeguarding and securing cyberspace, ensuring resilience to disasters, and maturing and strengthening the Homeland Security Enterprise.[2] According to the Director, the three operational components of ICE include HSI, ERO, and CBP whose respective missions include enforcing immigration and customs laws, border security, public safety, and counterterrorism/homeland security.[3] Although the DHS mission is much broader than that of the legacy INS, the immigration enforcement responsibilities are largely the same. The creation of the ERO unit mirrors the Detention and Deportation Officer position of the legacy INS, and USCIS has a separate chain of command. Even if it is only perceived by their managers, USCIS appears to have maintained a priority status as the service arm of the agency.

POLICIES THAT CAUSE PROBLEMS FOR INVESTIGATORS

Legacy agents complained about their frustration in trying to do their job. Most of these complaints had to do with difficulties in obtaining approval for equipment, or routine investigative tasks such as search warrants, or raids. In comparing their tasks with those of other federal law enforcement agencies, investigators indicated that other agencies did not experience the same resistance from management. As one investigator stated:

> As I understand, other agencies don't have half the restrictions. We would use credit cards from cars that were down (out of service), were going to be deadlined permanently. Right? I mean too expensive to fix them. We could take these cars, use them until they need major repairs, and turn them back in, and get other cars that had been seized. . . . (unint.) from the 4th floor that got knocked out . . . I've been driving cars with 140,000 miles on it. We've gotten two new cars, one is a Chevette, and one is a Volare. They have not been assigned to any investigative section yet. The Chevette is being driven around

by an administrative officer . . . as well as the new Volare. They're really important for that use, right? They take them to go out to lunch. Meanwhile, you've got vehicles down there that are not moving, have not moved for months and months, but they need these cars . . . and then they could get it from investigations. But meanwhile, these are not being used. We've had them for 4 to 5 months. We put in for bulletproof vests. All we got is ten for Investigations. Just ten, so guys can have access to them. We don't want one per man, like every other agency has, we just want ten so if somebody needs it they can sign it out. They knocked that out, saying it's not necessary. That's criminal negligence. How can you send a criminal investigator out . . . and say he doesn't need a bulletproof vest? . . . You know, that's why they say. Don't let anybody see your holster in the office. Don't let anybody see you with your handcuffs, you know, don't let them hang on your belt, that's the whole philosophy here.

Prior to DHS, federal agents in Customs, ATF, or the FBI had government vehicles permanently assigned to them, usually each agent had their own vehicle. They had access to these vehicles whenever they needed them, unlike the INS investigators. As an investigator stated:

Well, we've got a policy on vehicles now where you have to return the vehicle to the office every day after you finish your tour of duty, whereas previously, when you're through with your work, you could take your vehicle to your home, and the next day you could go directly to the field using that vehicle. So now, that has greatly hurt the effectiveness of each investigator, because if you decide to work late at night, so that you can contact some informants, or visit some potential witnesses, you work till say 10:30 at night out in Brooklyn, and you live up in Westchester, then at 10:30 you must return to the office, and you must rely upon a transit system with a staggered schedule. So, it kind of makes your job more difficult.

Another investigator expressed a similar difficulty caused by the policy on vehicle use:

I'm down at South Jersey, which means I can't actually work down there, but I'm the only immigration officer in the county. They call me, and I have to go down to the station house where they pick up (unint) for shoplifting, they pick up a guy (unint) . . . and according to the policy . . . I can't even take him with a police officer, and drop him off in Newark. I have to pass him in, and hope he shows up. The current policies on the use of motor vehicles are absolutely absurd. If you have to pick somebody up on call from another agency, and it's late in the day, it's happened quite frequently at the passport office, you have to bring the guy back, and you may have to handle them criminally, lodge him, either in Brooklyn or (unint), you may have to drive the guy out there to Brooklyn, you have to wait, then you have to bring the car back to the office, and then you go and take the train home. Now, for me, I live in New Jersey, and I can't get a train home until late, after rush hour.

Such policies made it difficult for investigators to perform their duties, especially limiting access to vehicles. One of the main functions of the legacy INS investigator was to locate and apprehend illegal aliens, requiring the use of a vehicle to transport the apprehended alien. Even when the illegal alien is in custody, the problems only seem to begin for the investigator. Many investigators viewed the bureaucratic obstacles embedded in the processing apparatus to be problematic, as the following investigator pointed out:

> They make things difficult for you to process. You do the paperwork, and then you've got to wait for the person to sign for the bond. No one knows where he is, or else he's out to lunch and you wait. It doesn't matter your time, or how long you've been working. You wait until you get a hold of somebody. And, I think the criteria for bonds is shaky at best, in the sense that if it's a male, they'll (unint.) if it isn't a little kid or old man, fine they'll walk him up (set bond or detain). But if it's a woman, they hem and they haw if she's over 50, well then she's an old lady! If she's 21, oh well she's a little girl! (Alien will be released)

Another problem for investigators, especially those in the ACIS unit, was the policy of limiting responding to police referrals of aliens in custody. Unless the deportable alien was in police custody for a criminal offense, the investigators could not respond to the call. DHS ICE will not act on aliens in police custody unless a criminal conviction is registered, and even criminal aliens are classified according to a sliding priority scale. The main function of ACIS was to locate and apprehend illegal aliens in the community. As an ACIS member stated:

> Most of the time in area control we get calls from cops, that they're picking people up for something else, and as long as they're holding them on their own charge, that's no problem. As soon as they say that the charge is no good, it's gonna be dismissed, do you want us to hold them until you get here? He's illegal. It's no, you can't do this!

Investigators questioned agency priorities, and offered examples of programs that were more efficient in the past. At one time, the ACIS was very effective in locating large numbers of illegal aliens in the US. An investigator commented on this, and other policy matters:

> . . . it seems to me that a lot of the case work that we do is looking for illegal aliens. That seems to me as a raucous waste of time. Back in the days gone by, when Area Control used to produce much greater numbers than it does now, you would just stumble into these, to the illegals who had cases open on them by accident, "bag & baggage" cases (aliens with warrants outstanding that have already been ordered deported). It would seem to me that

just a mass low quality, but high quantity, effort in Area Control would be the most effective task. As to whether it would ever be permitted again by the courts, probably doubtful. But, Area Control in that sense I think could be of tremendous importance. They could, just by a low quality – by appearing at businesses here, there and everywhere often, they could simply every time you, you know, Immigration appears at a business, all the illegals rush out and change jobs, and it could wind up making the illegal alien look, or appear to American business as an undesirable worker, simply because he'll be there for two or three months, at which time he's going to be trained at the expense of the company, and then an Immigration officer will show up, and those who aren't arrested will just run away and not come back. So, in terms of absentee-ism, and high turnover, you could really be effective there.

Interviewer:As a deterrent effect?

Sure, as a deterrent, yeah.

Interviewer:What about the other squads in order of importance?

Well the other squads, and the other work that the rest of investigations does, is really the satisfaction of other people's priorities. Some people are –for some reason it's a kind of cross-American border EWI . . . Some manners of entry are crimes, and others are not. We make special efforts towards – we used to make a special effort with regard to crewman. We have institutional-ized, and made a special squad to take care of organized smuggling over the Mexican, and Canadian borders. And, I don't know if that's really useful as a methodology of enforcement. Whether that would make it – it enjoys a priority that I don't necessarily agree with--the Anti-Smuggling unit.

Interviewer: Why is that?

I really don't know why. I personally think that the most effective thing they could do would be go back to street hits. Taking off businesses, and neighborhoods with large operations. It would make life here in the US as difficult, and economically unprofitable for all those, you know, for illegal aliens, and those that hire them, as possible.

Although there were no official rules regarding when to arrest an illegal alien, investigators in other than the ACIS unit received informal suggestions from management that doing so was not recommended. When I began work-ing as an INS investigator, I would arrest any illegal alien that I encountered, even though I started in General Investigations, a unit devoted primarily to casework. Over time, I realized that doing so caused more problems than it solved. Many investigators alternatively issued the deportable alien notice to report to INS office the following day for processing (now referred to as a Notice to Appear). This is similar to the desk appearance ticket issued by police officers when they encounter a law violator, but choose not to arrest the person. If the alien has any documents such as a passport, or I-94 (arrival-departure record) these documents are seized. Assuming the alien would fail to appear, I would always seize such evidentiary documents, and subsequent-ly prepare a case file on the alien. If the documents established alienage and deportability, they could be used to obtain an administrative arrest warrant, and this would facilitate processing if that alien is ever encountered again. This procedure allowed for integrity while complying with the managerial preference to avoid arresting non-casework illegal aliens. In most instances the illegal alien failed to appear, but at least a record would be made including any seized identity documents that would facilitate processing the alien, if apprehended in the future. After time, the investigator learns that arresting an illegal alien not directly related to assigned cases may be counterproductive. As one investigator pointed out:

> They basically don't want you arresting anyone unless you have a warrant of arrest. I mean, if you're in the process of a frauds investigation, and you come across somebody you're supposed to bring them in, I bring them in. Some guys don't. At times, we are given a small problem, you have your own caseload (assigned cases). You're doing a case, why are you bringing bodies in? If they're illegal, they're supposed to be brought in. But, I've had supervisory personnel, not tell me directly, "don't bring bodies in!" But you know, saying why do you bring them in for? Now, you have to spend the whole day writing them up.

The President of the National Border Patrol Council (NBPC) testified before the House Subcommittee on Immigration and Border Security about DHS policies, and "catch and release":

> On February 4, 2016, Brandon Judd, President of the American Federation of Government Employees National Border Patrol Council, testified before the Immigration and Border Security Subcommittee that DHS has established a policy requiring border patrol agents to release unlawful immigrants apprehended at the border, and not place them in removal proceedings. This *de facto* policy contradicts the Obama Administration's so-called enforcement priorities issued on November 20, 2014, which state that unlawful immigrants who came to the US after January 1, 2014 and recent border crossers are priorities for removal and are to be placed in removal proceedings.
>
> Within days of Judd's testimony, the House Judiciary Committee has been informed that a manager within the border patrol submitted a complaint for alleged misconduct against him and other leaders of the National Border Patrol Council. In his letter to Secretary Johnson, Chairman Goodlatte states the timing of the complaint "raises the specter of retaliation against Mr. Judd and the other executive committee members" and calls on him to ensure that no DHS employee or contractor will be targeted for voicing legitimate concerns about compliance with unwritten departmental policies that contradict written policies.[4]

The official policy of the DHS regarding apprehension, detention and removal of illegal aliens issued through a memorandum dated November 20, 2014,[5] enumerates priorities as threats to national security, border security, and public safety, criminals (misdemeanants, and new immigration violators), and aliens issued a final order of removal on or after January 1, 2014 (the lowest priority). The problem with the last priority is that verification is difficult, especially with regard to asylum applicants.

In an unprecedented effort to counter the effects of the executive orders, immigration agents actually sued the Obama administration in an attempt to overturn the president's edicts:

> The 10 U.S. Immigration and Customs Enforcement (ICE) agents and deportation officers said Mr. Obama's policies force them to choose between enforcing the law and being reprimanded by superiors, or listening to superiors and violating their own oaths of office and a 1996 law that requires them to put those who entered the country illegally into deportation proceedings.
>
> Upping the ante, the agents are being represented by a high-profile lawyer, Kris W. Kobach, secretary of state in Kansas and the chief promoter of state immigration crackdowns such as Arizona's tough law.[6]
>
> "ICE is at a point now where agents are being told to break federal law. They're pretty much told that any illegal alien under the age of 31 is going to be let go. You can imagine, these law enforcement officers are being put in a horrible position," Mr. Kobach said.

Other problems encountered by investigators had to do with obtaining approval to do investigations, or access to equipment routinely used in conducting criminal investigations such as electronic surveillance equipment. Also, investigators in the legacy INS were allowed to carry .38 special revolvers, while most other agencies eventually made the transition to the .9mm semi-automatic, now a standard firearm carried by law enforcement officers. The perception of most of the investigators was that management did not trust them, or management did not have confidence in them. In order to successfully conduct a criminal investigation, management needs to place trust in its investigators, and this means giving them discretion to complete tasks, especially routine criminal investigative tasks. One explanation for the perception of the lack of trust might better be explained by the investigator's belief that managers lacked competence in these areas. Although there was no shortage of potential informants, if they surfaced investigators could not obtain funds to pay them. As one investigator stated:

> The investigators working the cases that require electronic surveillance will tell you that the hardest thing about doing it is getting the approval from our office to do it, and subsequently getting buyer money if we needed to buy (unint). They refuse to give us the money. The FBI has all kinds of equipment, and you never hear of them doing anything with it. They never loan them out either . . . DEA has equipment . . . postal inspectors have more equipment than we do. There is a difference in the philosophy . . . The DEA, they give more faith, or truth, or whatever you want to call it, in the particular agent they have. Here, to get anything done, you have to have it approved.

After I left INS, I transferred to the Federal Probation Service, also a dual mandate agency trying to administer a service (rehabilitation of offenders), and control (supervising offenders, and protecting the community). I quickly realized that the service mandate was a priority in this agency as well. Trying to administer a dual mandate is difficult to accomplish, and enforcement usually loses out to the service, especially when the agency is dominated with service-minded individuals. On several occasions, I attempted to utilize routine investigative techniques, such as initiating criminal investigations, or developing informants, but management discouraged such strategies. My perception is that they avoided these routine investigative techniques because they were unfamiliar with them. It was a service priority agency, and law enforcement was not considered an essential part of the mission. Whenever issues arose requiring law enforcement techniques, managers created policies that transferred the actions to other agencies. For example, although the Probation Officer prepared a warrant of arrest for a violation, and was still responsible for the case, the US Marshals Service executed the actual arrest warrant. In addition to the service mentality of the Probation Service, most of what the agency had to do was administrative in nature. Although a federal judge sentences an individual, the supervision of the offender either on probation, or parole, is administrative, not criminal. That is, all proceedings subsequent to the sentencing such as violation of probation, or parole, are administrative. Administrative proceedings require preponderance of evidence, not beyond a reasonable doubt as in criminal proceedings. One would be able to use this rule of law to facilitate the agency mission. However, agencies with this dual mandate, often apply the more stringent rule in administrative proceedings. This too reflects the overall preference to insure due process, even at the expense of public safety. Probation officers are statutorily permitted to arrest probationers in violation of their status, but managers *insisted* that such cases were to be handled by the US Marshals Service. My perception of the arrangement is that the US Marshals Service agents had little respect for Probation Officers as a result, and this was exemplified when I asked to assist them is arresting any probationers that I violated, and prepared the case for the warrant. The marshals did not want any assistance, and most likely did not consider the probation officer a "real" law enforcement officer. In my opinion, the entire Probation Service modeled a social work mission rather than law enforcement, and in this contributed to lower morale among the officers who fulfilled law enforcement related tasks. Of course, many of the probation officers were content with this policy since they were more like social workers, than law enforcement officers. Historically, probation evolved from John Augustus, a shoemaker who wanted to rehabilitate lost souls and alcoholics. The modern mission did not stray far from that model. Of course, times change and the correctional population now includes many violent offenders, and career criminals. The

Eastern District of New York (EDNY) Probation office was considered one of the more law enforcement oriented federal probation offices. However, when I transferred into the EDNY from INS I came to realize that the agency was more social work, or service oriented, compared to other federal law enforcement agencies.

At INS, the service priority seemed to blend into the enforcement mission. The border patrol was able to avoid management interference in such matters, because their mission was the accepted enforcement strategy for the agency. It was easier to support a mission that prevented aliens from illegally entering the US. However, locating and apprehending illegal aliens already entrenched in the community presented more difficult problems. The current enforcement priority program places the apprehension of low-level visa abusers as the lowest priority, which is the opposite of the legacy INS model.

Agents perceived that their agency would not support them if they were accused of any wrongdoing, and this most assuredly created a "chilling effect" on implementing tasks. In general, law enforcement work is problematic, and complaints and problems are routinely associated with investigative work. It tends to upset people, especially those committing crimes. Often, the complaints are meant to intimidate the investigator, and prevent further inquiry. Real law enforcement agencies are familiar with this tactic, and temper complaints accordingly. Organized crime members understand this process, and use it all the time. However, traditional law enforcement agencies encourage their agents to be aggressive, and support their efforts in doing so. One way to prevent investigators from taking aggressive action, or pursuing investigations with vigor, is to threaten them with litigation, and having to pay for that litigation with their own money. If they are performing their duties responsibly, police and peace officers have limited immunity from prosecution, and free legal advice. As one INS investigator stated:

> The U.S. Attorney has a policy if anyone begins to litigate against you they decline to defend you, on the grounds that should you be found culpable it may be necessary for them to prosecute you, and that would constitute a conflict of interest. So, you know right now that if someone comes out and presents you with, litigates against you, or charges you with a crime, that you're going to defend yourself at your own expense. That's the first thing you know.

The priority placed on service mandated an organizational structure set up to deal with never ending backlogs. One way to deal with these backlogs was to detail investigators to adjudication task forces. Most investigators considered these task forces as "rubber stamp" details, that ignored what they perceived to be questionable applications for further investigation. The *Cuban program* and the *Iranian problem* were two examples described by investigators as examples of this strategy. Investigators considered the Census restrictions on field investigations to be especially problematic. These programs caused investigators to solidify their opinions about the service mission, and the low priority given to investigations.

Investigators did not consider upper management to be supportive, a requirement for them to be successful in their tasks. This included internal mechanisms such as rigid adherence to the chain of command, staffing supervisory positions with personnel who did not have investigative backgrounds (border patrol, service branch personnel), and policy restrictions that curtailed their basic operations. In their everyday activities, especially processing apprehended aliens, investigators perceived the excessive bureaucracy to inhibit their mission. They referred to the processing of an illegal alien as "like pulling teeth." They regarded the paycheck distributed after payday meetings as a "piece of cheese," meant to describe the apparent relationship between the "carrot and the stick." That is, supervisors had payday meetings where they often instituted policies that were in conflict with the operators perceived notions of task. For example, if an investigator uncovered fraud, or other investigative issues not directly related to the section work, the case was transferred to the section that specialized in that matter. Some investigators believed that this was counterproductive, because the transfer would cause the case "to be buried." They believed that transferring such a case to someone who did not have a personal interest in it would cause the case to be treated as "just another case" among thousands.

Training and promotion also contributed to lowering morale, because the investigators believed they were in a dead-end job, and they could not get out. The evaluation process was standardized, and most investigators were rated the same way. The idea of the "good old boy" was a perception that many investigators held, and referred to someone who was either with the border patrol, or had border patrol experience. Being a "good old boy" was perceived to be more important than merit in getting promoted.

Legacy INS investigators stated that they were satisfied with the basic training they received at the FLETC, because it provided basic knowledge relevant to their task. However, senior officers received basic training at the border patrol academy, formerly located in Texas, and they stated that their training there concentrated on border patrol activity, such as processing illegal aliens, rather than the contemporary investigative techniques needed to complete criminal investigations. The content of basic training is indicative of an agency's goals and priorities, although investigators learn most of their skills through *on the job* training. Investigators sought training offered by other federal law enforcement agencies at FLETC, and they considered INS training irrelevant to their perceptions of task. As the following interviewee's statement affirmed:

> The best training I have received was from a fingerprint identification course
> offered by the FBI. The FBI provides police training in various fields to other

law enforcement agencies. Even though I notified our personnel and administrative offices to make contacts with the FBI police training coordinator concerning training, they have failed to do so. Furthermore, when I took the FBI
course I had to take annual leave (vacation day), since our agency would not
authorize attendance on official duty.

The training received by investigators at the district office appear to be
cloned from the border patrol Officer Training Course. According to respondents, INS revised the basic training course, but the revision basically updated the older material. It is unknown whether this was intentional, or reflected
management's belief that border patrol activity is the same as interior enforcement.

Legacy agents reported that there was virtually no incentive to pursue
training opportunities, and they believed that their agency was content with
the current quality of training, which was limited due to budget limitations.
However, the training priorities seemed to focus on administrative aspects of
the law enforcement mission. One investigator reflected:

It has been my experience that INS punishes rather than rewards an investigator who has advanced degrees. It is generally understood that having an advanced degree such as a master's or even a Ph.D., means little to management,
especially when it comes to promotion. This is probably because you are
competing with border patrol agents for some of the same jobs. Border patrol
agents usually have a high school education. Investigators have a college
degree, and some even advanced degrees. So, they give you a minimum
amount of points for your education, and a maximum number of points for
length of service, and other factors, which probably makes promotion more
equal for a border patrol agent or someone outside of investigations. It is
generally agreed that having border patrol experience is the only way to really
advance at INS, even though border patrol agents know very little about criminal investigative work in the interior US.

A trainee investigator follows a path similar to the police officer:

. . . the recruit reports to his precinct with some anxiety, but in general ready to
practice what has been preached to him at the Academy . . . he is expected to
be a good listener, quiet, unassuming, and deferential without being obsequi-
ous toward his superior officers . . . For a month or so, he receives lenience and
sympathy for routine mistakes. After that he is on trial and carefully
watched . . . His reputation is made in the next few weeks and will shadow him
for the rest of his police career . . .[7]

Most investigators are hired from a list of eligible applicants that take the
federal entrance civil service test. The agency sends the trainee investigator
to FLETC as soon as possible. The agency places an emphasis on the trainee's academic abilities during the initial period, and defines academic suc-

cess in terms of whether the trainee *knows the law,* or *can speak Spanish.* The agency threatens the trainee with dismissal if basic standards are not upheld, and instructors encourage borderline cases to *try harder* to pass the qualifying examinations.

After completing the basic training successfully, trainees return to their duty station, and are assigned to one of the sections in the investigations branch. The investigator spends most of his time in training during the first year of employment, and supervisors assign a senior investigator to accompany them in the field. The trainee is supposed to defer to the senior investigator if any *problem* surfaces on the street, where the successful trainee quickly learns the difference between the academy, and the street. The investigator learns the advantages of accepting the pragmatic (real), rather than the academic (ideal) approach. Peers judge trainees on how well they perform *on the street,* and such judgments focus on their effectiveness as enforcers. Although a relevant factor, toughness is not the sole criteria of effectiveness, and investigators define efficiency in terms of how well the trainee conforms to the image of law enforcer.

An ICE agent described some of the changes that occurred in training after the legacy INS merged with customs as follows:

> Training opportunities have improved considerably since 1980, and new classes/courses are routinely offered to agents as funding allows. INS (ICE) funds most of its own training, however a small portion is funded by other law enforcement agencies with whom the agency partners with in joint task forces such as the Organized Crime Task Force (OCDETF), High Intensity Drug Trafficking (HIDTA), or the Joint Terrorism Task Force (JTTF). For example, both the Department of Justice and the Executive Office of OCDETF have funded Financial Investigations (Money Laundering) Training Seminars for our special agents, while HIDTA and the FBI/NYPD routinely train our co-located special agents in the latest investigative methods and techniques.

In 2004, T. J. Bonner the president of the National Border Patrol Council, a union representing border patrol agents, advised that a survey of agents found that they disagreed with the fundamental enforcement strategies, that they did not have the tools, training, or support needed to combat terrorism, and that DHS could be doing more to protect against terrorism.

> . . . believes mismanagement and lack of support has caused morale to "plummet precipitously" among border agents and inspectors along America's 6,000 miles of international border.
>
> "The bureaucratic bungling that plagued and hampered the old Immigration and Naturalization Service (INS) has not only survived, it has thrived in the new Department of Homeland Security," T.J. Bonner, president of the National Border Patrol Council (NBPC), said in announcing the survey results.

"Business as usual is no longer acceptable, however, since there can be no margin of error when dealing with terrorists," said Mr. Bonner, whose council represents all 10,000 of the patrol's nonsupervisory agents. "While no system is foolproof, the current system is just plain foolish."

According to the survey, 64 percent of those questioned believe they do not have the tools, training or support they need to combat terrorism, 44 percent said the country is no safer today than it was on September 11 and 62 percent said Homeland Security could be doing more to protect the country from terrorist attacks

The survey, commissioned by the NBPC, the National Homeland Security Council and the American Federation of Government Employees, also found that 60 percent said morale within the border force is low and 45 percent said they had considered leaving the job, mainly citing poor management. [8]

To summarize, an analysis of the interviews [9] with the legacy INS agents revealed the following examples of policies that cause problems in completing their mission:

- Manager instructions to not arrest illegal aliens-especially with regard to the different units tasked to investigate cases such as fraud, special, anti-smuggling, and general investigations, that the agents focus on the assigned case and not become involved with illegal aliens they encounter that are not directly related to that case. In addition, due to the lack of resources and manpower, agents are encouraged to issue notice to appear orders to such illegal aliens even though the probability of such high-risk flight cases existed.
- Inappropriate training-agents perceived their job as criminal investigators, and that appropriate training related to criminal investigations should be available.
- Policy to not conduct random street hits (investigations, interrogations)-even if probable cause could be articulated; this operation was not recommended or utilized.
- Vehicle use restrictions-agents advised that managers made it difficult for them to get government vehicles, and that agents were required to officially request government vehicle use on a regular, often daily, basis.
- Processing apprehended aliens is an onerous procedure.
- The perception that waivers existed for all types of detained aliens.
- Placing a low priority on local police referrals of illegal aliens.
- Lack of equipment to complete tasks, especially electronic recording devices such as audio, or video equipment.
- Completing mostly administrative enforcement tasks.
- The perception that one's actions were not supported, especially if allegations were made against the agent, and that there was a high liability in whatever actions you take.

- The perception that the agency prioritized service functions over enforcement.

ASSIGNED CASEWORK

Most of the casework assigned to legacy INS investigators related to illegal aliens that were deportable. In some instances, the subject of an investigation could be a corporation, or organization such as the owner of a school requesting accreditation to offer an educational program to foreign students. Sometimes, US citizens who violate the INA are investigated, such as the owner of a travel agency trafficking in fraudulent documents, or someone smuggling aliens into the US. Deportable aliens may come to the attention of the agency through complaints from the public, referral by other agencies, or from immigration examiners that uncover fraud. An example of an internal referral occurs when an alien applies for an extension of time to remain in the US, beyond the original time granted. Although the time expired, the alien is permitted to remain in the US until the application is adjudicated. Exceptions to this provision include alien crewmen, aliens in transit (TWOV), and aliens that violate the provisions of their employment. If the application is denied, the alien must depart from the US, and if the alien fails to depart, the case was referred to the investigations branch as a *locate* investigation.

A supervisor assigns a case by opening it on Form G-600 (Case Control Form), and adds an initial call-up date. On the call-up date, the supervisor reviews the case with the investigator's findings as to whether the case should remain open, or if more time is needed to compete the case, or close the case. Regional and central office personnel regularly perform case audits in order to assure that investigators (and their supervisors) follow all rules and policies. Case assignments conform to line numbers that refer to the various units of the Investigations branch. For example, cases in General Investigations are assigned line number 100, A through D, where 100A relates to a deportable alien locate investigation, 100B to a character investigation, 100C to an applicant for admission into the US, etc. The Frauds Section assigns cases by line number 200, A through D, where 200A relates to a fraudulent document case; or 200b relates to a marriage fraud case.

Although a quota system does not officially exist, supervisors expected investigators to complete a certain number of cases every month, and included this as part of performance evaluations. In this system, ratings determine if an investigator is placed on a promotion list, and such expectations become standardized. For example, investigators assigned to General Investigations closed an average of twelve cases per month, while those in the Frauds Unit averaged three cases per month. In this study, participants stated that fraud, and criminal cases were more difficult to complete, and required more time than the standard administrative cases. Some investigators closed more than the average number of cases, but most conformed to some informal agreement to close the same, or near the same, number of cases. On rare occasions, an investigator might consistently choose to stray from this practice, and in doing so risked being ostracized by the other investigators in the unit.

Generally, the investigator assigned a *locate* investigation follows up on the available leads in the case record where there is usually minimal information. This usually involved interviewing witnesses such as the landlord, or neighbors. In addition, routine record checks as specified in the "Investigator's Handbook" were completed, usually before the investigator completed any fieldwork. If the alien is still not located after these actions, the case is placed in "pending inactive" status, and reviewed periodically to determine if further investigative action is warranted.

In conducting *character* investigations, investigators interviewed witnesses at both the applicant's residence(s) and employment(s). The purpose of these investigations was to determine whether the applicant has good moral character (based on community standards), a general criterion to be granted legal resident status, or citizenship. Typically, gamblers, habitual drunkards, criminals or adulterers, would be considered as lacking in this character. In addition, record checks on criminal, and medical history are also conducted. The investigator prepares a report, and forwards it to the appropriate section that requested the investigation. When an alien applies for suspension of deportation, or when there is a reason to believe that the applicant does not have good moral character, a character investigation is opened on the alien. For example, USCIS can request a character investigation if the applicant has a criminal record, or if some other issue regarding character surfaces.

The adjudication of permanent resident visa applications may trigger a referral to the Investigations Section, and the most common type of referral occurs in suspected marriage applications. Marriage petitions make up the most frequently occurring fraudulent relative petitions, and investigations based on marriage fraud involve the so-called "marriage of convenience," "sham marriage," or a "bona fides of marriage." In these cases, the task of the investigator is to determine whether it is as valid marriage, or whether the parties entered into the marriage simply to obtain immigration benefits.

Generally, agents disliked conducting most *character* investigations. For example, in naturalization cases, allegations of adultery often predicate a character investigation, and similar allegations surface in *bona fides* of marriage investigations. As a result, the investigative techniques involve asking awkward questions about living arrangements, and sexual behavior. One investigator commented on the latter type of investigation:

It's ridiculous. You used to knock on a door 5 o'clock in the morning, go into
an apartment and look around to see if the couple are actually sleeping together, and if the apartment has toiletries for both sexes, and the like. What it
comes down to is you go around *sniffing underwear*. Sometimes you go to an
apartment and the spouse is not there at 5 o'clock in the morning. The alleged
husband or wife then tells you that the other partner is working. You come
back different times, and he or she still is nowhere to be found. You conclude
that it is a marriage of convenience. We know there are a lot of fraudulent
marriages, but it is difficult to prove that a marriage is a fraudulent one.

It is noteworthy that the assignment of *criminal* cases differs from administrative assignments. The U. S. Attorney's Office is contacted if an investigator finds criminal activity during an investigation, and the AUSA assigned
to the case either authorizes, or declines a criminal prosecution. Generally,
projects and criminal investigations are assigned to Senior (GS-12) level
officers. A project usually involves a complex criminal investigation of numerous defendants. On the surface, it appears that the agency considers criminal cases to be more complex than administrative cases. As a result, GS-12
agents conduct criminal investigations, and GS-11 and below investigators
conduct the other work. The other work includes apprehending illegal aliens,
character investigations, and other miscellaneous tasks. If a GS-11 investigator develops a criminal case, INS management generally reassigns the case to
a GS-12 investigator. At the time, the interviewees believed that management
reassigned criminal cases to senior agents to avoid *desk audits*. A *desk audit*
is a request by an agent for reclassification to a higher grade because the
agent believes that he is performing higher-level work. In an agency where
there are few if any promotion opportunities, a desk-audit request becomes
one of the only ways to get one.

NON-FILE CASEWORK AND OTHER TASKS

The Area Control Illegal Status Unit (ACIS) attempts to locate illegal aliens
that are reported to the agency. On a daily basis, an ACIS duty officer takes
call-ins, or complaints from the public and these are logged on a complaint
form. Agents have access to these daily complaints and the criteria for selection is based on which leads will yield apprehensions. Some of the criteria
include geographical location of the target of the complaint as well as convenience of location, in order to deal with the stress of getting around in high
traffic areas. Investigators also select cases that are most likely to result in
apprehensions. Supervisors in the other units consider the number of cases
closed in determining the productivity of the investigator.

Some sources of information about illegal aliens include: complaints
made by citizens directly to INS, such as individuals who want an alien

found for personal reasons such as infidelity of a mate, or who want to *get even* for some perceived wrongdoing, other law enforcement referrals, or other government agencies. At the time, a reliable source of intelligence about criminal aliens was the local newspapers that published the names of illegal aliens apprehended by the police department the previous day. Such leads were productive in that they assisted INS agents in locating both low-level visa abusers such as day laborers, or overstay visitors, as well as illegal aliens charged with crimes.

The Coastal Control Unit, also a part of the ACIS Section, investigates crewmen that desert their ships, so called *ship-jumpers* or *stowaways*. INS creates a case file on all crew that desert a vessel and, by law, captains of vessels must report desertions to the agency. Crewman's files contain information about the desertion and any efforts to locate the individual. Coastal Control involves mostly non-casework activity. Investigators record complaints of illegal aliens on Form G-123s that serve to initiate an investigation and the investigator creates a file if the illegal alien is located, apprehended, and processed. Unlike the other units, ACIS investigators do not maintain caseloads, or a specified number of assigned files on aliens. Their work is evaluated on the number of apprehensions made.

ACIS investigators had the most discretion in the Investigations branch because they conducted patrol type operations. INS policy dictates that ACIS investigators concentrate on illegal aliens at their job sites, and this usually results in encounters with low-level visa abusers. INS recommends that investigators avoid arbitrary *street* arrests, especially at residences not specified in case files. ACIS investigators believe that such a policy is restrictive and curtails proper enforcement efforts.

Investigators are also assigned other tasks such as driving details. A driving detail amounts to chauffeuring an official around, reportedly on official business. One investigator commented on the driving detail:

> I will never forget the time I *had* to drive the DD (district director) to a luncheon. I never met the man before and he just opened the back door of the car and got in. I was his *chauffeur* and he made sure I knew it. They (upper management) always want to make sure that when an investigator uses a government auto to conduct investigations, everything is according to the book. You know, you have to sign out the car, justify in writing what you are going to do with it, have it approved by your supervisor, and God forbid if you should have an accident. They look to suspend you, or even terminate you if something goes wrong. And don't forget the gas shortage, when investigators could not use the government automobiles, or were heavily restricted in the use of automobiles. But it is strange that they always can find a car and gasoline to drive some big shot around.

Sometimes, investigators are directed to prepare special reports. Some examples of these reports include an estimate of the number of illegal aliens in the New York district, and a revision of the *Investigators Handbook*. Investigators also participate in public speaking details wherein they describe the functions of INS and their duties as investigators to interested groups. An example of this task includes the career orientation program sponsored by the Boy Scouts of America. Such details take the form of an official memorandum from the District Director seeking volunteers. Investigators believe that management often preselects the volunteers. The selections tend to be more democratic when a number of investigators are required for such projects. Some investigative details are sought after because they usually include per diem benefits and overtime pay. In addition, overnight details allow the investigator to be away from his duty station and the perceived oppression of management, or experience a sense of freedom from the drudgery of daily tasks.

Investigators are sometimes selected to perform *personnel* investigations. Such investigations are concerned with alleged corruption, or officer misconduct. The Office of Professional Responsibility (OPR) that usually conducts these investigations was originally in Washington, DC. This corruption unit reorganized and designated personnel to district offices. Prior to the reorganization, local offices could designate investigators to perform low-level corruption cases. INS utilized this practice at the NYDO.

In order to be selected for *personnel* investigations, investigators required experience in such investigations, or certification from the OPR training school. According to the investigators, an OPR investigator recommends a candidate for the OPR training classes. Selections often result from personal friendships, or favors rather than the ability of the candidate. Many investigators considered the work beneficial because experience with OPR type cases increased a candidate's promotion potential.

AGENCY MISSION AND INVESTIGATOR MISSION

It is important to discuss the dual aspects of the INS mission. In this analysis, the *professional-client* relationship depends on whether the agency is more service or control oriented. Ideally, the mission of INS is to devote an equal proportion of its resources to service, and control. If not, then INS can specify which aspect of the dual mandate should take priority over the other. A logical organizational strategy might include the establishment of goals and priorities, and how to implement them. We now turn to the perceptions of investigators about how the agency actually decides to administer the dual mandate mission. As one respondent notes:

> ... in my opinion INS is preponderantly a service agency. It provides a service
> to the public. As far as efficient, intelligent, and effective law enforcement—
> INS has not, is not now, and probably, unless things radically change, never
> will be capable of performing the enforcement part of the mission. It does not
> have the equipment, manpower, budget, congressional backing, computer sys-
> tem necessary to maintain the massive records, or, most of all, the desire to
> enforce the law.

This statement seems to contradict actual legacy INS budget and manpower allocations. Over sixty percent of the budget (1979) went to the border
patrol (42.7 %), interior enforcement (10.7 %), and detention and deportation
(9.9 %). The Fiscal Year (FY) 2015 Total Budget Authority for DHS was
$60.9 billion. 9% of the FY 2015 budget was allocated for ICE which in-
cluded HIS and ERO, while 21% of the FY 2015 budget was allocated for
CBP. The total amount allocated for border and interior enforcement of the
immigration laws was $18.1 billion, with 30% of that total for ICE and 70%
for the CBP.[10] However, a more detailed analysis of the allocation of resources enables one to appreciate the lamentation of the investigator.

Investigators consider the dual mandate to be a contradiction, and believe
the service mandate takes priority over enforcement. They also believe that
INS management ignores their perceptions of the mission of the Investigations branch.

It is important to describe how the investigator perceives his position in
the INS organizational structure. Traditionally, the title of special agent held
prestige in the law enforcement community, and was reserved for series
1811-investigators. At INS, a border patrol officer's title is Border Patrol
Agent, although their main task is to patrol the border. In the Department of
the Treasury, the border patrol agent's counterpart is the Customs Patrol
Officer. Investigators perceived that labeling the border patrol as an "agent"
gave them more status than investigators. Among federal law enforcement
agencies, INS would be unique in doing so. Border patrol officers have little
inclination to transfer to the investigations branch, and they consider their
position more prestigious. A former border patrol agent, now a criminal
investigator, stated,

> I think every investigator ought to start in the border patrol in order to develop
> a proper law enforcement attitude.

This statement reflects the perception some border patrol agents have
toward the investigations branch, and according to investigators echoes the
overall sentiment of INS management. A dominant procedure in local and
state law enforcement is for detectives to be drawn from the ranks of patrol
officers. In most federal agencies, criminal investigators are drawn from a

civil service list open to all qualified applicants. Most federal investigators begin their careers without any law enforcement experience.

One investigator that was hired *off the street*, as some border patrol agents refer to investigators without border patrol experience, discussed the issue by stating:

> I feel that the minimum education for a special agents (investigator) should be a college degree. Most border patrolmen have a high school diploma, if that, and a lot of the anti-smuggling agent positions have been filed by border patrolmen who know nothing about conducting criminal investigations, and writing complex reports. These former patrol agents still consider themselves part of the border patrol, even though their title is criminal investigator. It is absurd. INS mentality shows preference for these *"good old boys* at all levels. They are probably fine at catching wet Mexicans, but just about anybody can do that. When it comes to conducting criminal investigations, and writing complex reports, they are lost. Then a criminal investigator is expected to carry them along. I was on a detail where these *good old boys* were running the operation. All the team leaders were from the border patrol, or had been in the border patrol, even though it was an anti-smuggling detail, which dealt exclusively with criminal investigations. The border patrol people appeared to be lost and did not know what they were doing. Not only that, even though there were some investigators with higher grades than the team leaders, they were not placed in supervisory positions . . . I think the anti-smuggling program was set up so the border patrol could get higher grades.

At the 1980 INS, Congressional budget hearings, then Acting INS Commissioner David Crossland stated:

> I would like to turn now, if I may, to discussion of the major operating divisions of the Service, first focusing on the border patrol . . . I would like to comment also on my personal observation as to the professionalism of the border patrol . . . My observation is that they act in a professional manner, that they are accommodating to the alien; they recognize the reasons for which they come, and they apprehend them and process them in an efficient manner, but not in a manner which intimidates them . . . The border patrol has done a great deal with a limited budget. [11]

Mr. Crossland then went on to discuss the investigators, and stated, "Turning to the area of investigations, it should be understood that investigators are not the same as the border patrol . . . " According to Mr. Crossland, the difference is that investigators deal with casework, whereas the border patrol is almost exclusively involved in apprehending *border crossers*. Crossland did not make any similar endearing statements about the investigations branch. Even Table 33 of INS Annual Report (1977), *Principal Activities and Accomplishments of the Immigration Border Patrol,* seems to highlight the attitude of INS management towards the border patrol. Until many years later, there is no similar table in the Annual Reports to describe the principal activities and accomplishments of the investigations branch. Investigators further stated that INS rarely concerns itself with the needs of the investigations branch. This was especially evident in intraoffice publications such as the *Commissioner's Communiqué,* where the border patrol and service functions personnel often receive compliments. The fact that the border patrol commands the lion's share of INS budget mutes Crossland's claim that the border patrol does a great deal with a *limited amount of money.* In addition, investigations activity is subsumed within the category *Interior Enforcement.* This category includes a border patrol program *Other Than Border.*

The Border patrol made up 44% of the legacy INS, and Investigations (interior enforcement) made up only 7%. Patrolling the borders of the US was clearly an INS priority. However, the illegal alien problem is just as serious, if not more serious, *inside* the US. This matter is compounded further by the popular notion that interior enforcement strategies are *drastic measures,* although the facts contradict this image:

> About 300 investigators are assigned to area control operations—INS' principal program for locating deportable aliens in the interior of the country. In fiscal year 1979, the program accounted for about 150,000, 15 percent of the total number of deportable aliens located.[12]

INS devoted more than twice its personnel and resources to *Service to the Public,* than to *Investigations Activity.* This further indicates INS priority regarding interior enforcement. It is somewhat humorous to note that there were more program directors than investigators in INS, even though a common complaint among investigators was that INS had *no* direction. Compared to other activities, *Service to the Public,* showed a significant increase in personnel for 1981.

Although INS funnels the largest part of its budget to the border patrol, it is important to note that most of border patrol activity involves arresting Mexican border crossers. The agency returns most of these aliens to Mexico, which seems to substantiate a *release valve* theory of enforcement. The same aliens that are *turned around* at the border, make repeated attempts to enter the US. This is so because once they succeed in their attempts, it is unlikely that they will be apprehended inside the US. Due to this *arrangement,* border enforcement is not as effective deterrent as it should be. As such, interior enforcement complements the border patrol by locating and apprehending illegal aliens that escape border patrol detection. This is a different strategy than the investigator's presumed main task of criminal investigation—enforcing the criminal violations of the INA. As a result, the deterrent effect of the INA is diminished, and serves as an incentive for the intending illegal immigrant to *try harder.* One investigator commented:

> . . . if we were allowed to pursue some of the cases, God knows where it would lead us, probably to drug trafficking, crime, possibly the mob. We do not have the capability to investigate along these lines. We have the capability to pick up *wet* Mexicans, not investigate criminal activity.

The organizational structure of INS placed the Investigations branch under District Directors that also directed the service aspects of INS. Therefore, District Directors were burdened with a contradictory dual mission of service, and enforcement. It is not surprising that such a system did not facilitate effective law enforcement. As Senior Executives, District Directors must answer to higher (political) authorities and quickly realize that there is much less liability in catering to the service aspect of INS mission. Doing so garners positive responses from those *served.* Enforcement operations generally involve involuntary and asymmetrical professional-client relationships, producing negative responses from those caught up in the processing system. Similarly, groups sympathetic to the illegal alien quickly criticize enforcement measures. The legacy border patrol did not suffer from similar pressures, because it was detached from the service sections as an enforcement agency. For this reason, the border patrol was able to maintain an appropriate enforcement identity. During budget hearings this became a critical factor in explaining the operational needs of field personnel. INS often described the investigations branch as a minor, and often inconvenient extension of the dual mandate. DHS also has a separate chain of command for CBP and ICE, or border enforcement and interior enforcement. This changed under DHS, especially after President Obama issued his executive orders on DACA, and DAPA. The border patrol had to process these applicants that were released into the community, and essentially the process is a service function.

CRIMINAL PROSECUTIONS AND ADMINISTRATIVE ENFORCEMENT

While the stated policy was to prioritize criminal prosecutions, most investigators did not pursue criminal investigations. Investigators also believed that managers were incompetent, or unwilling to pursue criminal investigations.

Except for the ASU, most of the cases worked by investigators were administrative in nature. Furthermore, the way INS managers handled locate case closings is further indicative of an overall agency attitude about the illegal alien problem. Managers made no distinction between cases that were closed by an apprehension, or simply exhausted all leads in attempting to do so. Other than self-satisfaction, there is no real incentive to exert one's self to apprehend an illegal alien. The investigator might just as well close a case by exhausting available leads, and avoid problems associated with an apprehension. The sheer volume of the illegal alien population contributed to the routinization of work associated with these investigations.

An interesting pattern surfaced concerning an investigator assigned to a unit other than ACIS. As indicated earlier, if an investigator encountered an illegal alien while conducting routine investigations, managers discouraged arresting the alien unless the alien was the subject of the case file. The investigator either *ignores* the alien by not pursuing the matter, or could ask the alien to voluntarily surrender to INS for processing at a later date. Investigators from other sections could instruct the alien to report to ACIS for processing. Rarely does the alien show up for processing when *passed in* by an investigator. If the alien does appear, the ACIS officer of the day will process the alien, and get credit for the arrest. Furthermore, the routine apprehension of an illegal alien is an administrative matter. However, most investigators perceived illegal aliens in the US were a problem that should be addressed. As one respondent points out,

> . . . the law enforcement part of INS is completely different from the non-enforcement part. For example, dealing with people becoming citizens, or changing their immigration status from illegal to legal. Our role as investigators is supposedly to apprehend illegal aliens, conduct criminal investigations in areas where people try to circumvent the INA through using fraudulent documents, anti-smuggling activities, and various other administrative investigations. Which, although not criminal, could lead to criminal prosecution. But again, what it amounts to is paper shuffling. There is no firm direction. We are expected to go out on the street and close a certain number of cases every month. There is no preference to bring in a body, or do *all* that you can do to close a case. It is a numbers game. It is my impression that it is preferable not to bring in the body. They just want to show that an effort was made, and you did everything you could do, or shuffled one more case through the system . . . In my opinion, the lowest priority is on locate type investigations, the highest is on investigations where another branch of INS is involved. For example, if a person applies for citizenship, this person does not fall within the criteria of the law in which he must establish five years' residency with good moral character. There might be some question concerning the person's character. An investigation may be requested by the citizenship section, and this investigation (a dual action case) will be given a higher priority than a locate investigation.

ASU investigators were members of an elite unit in the investigations branch, and derived this status because their cases were solely criminal investigations. ASU members routinely developed cases leading to criminal prosecutions, and these tasks were preferred over administrative arrests. However, the ASU investigators also criticized INS policy regarding anti-smuggling operations. As one ASU investigator pointed out:

. . . there are other sections in INS that work criminal cases. Our unit (ASU) does 100% criminal prosecution work. As time passed, I have seen ASU go from a completely independent unit being brought more and more back into the mainstream, or become more administrative . . . We have just been told that we are spending too many hours closing our criminal cases, they want more *closings*. So, what we do, we have our category smugglers, Category IV smugglers, who are just a waste of time, mother, father deals, father smuggles his son, etc.; to appease the directives that come down we will sit down and write up these bullshit cases. This gives us time to work on our more important category smugglers without hearing from above.

ASU investigators considered the lack of funds available to pay informants a major impediment to their perceived notions of task. Informants obtain otherwise unobtainable evidence necessary for successful criminal prosecutions. Investigators believed that they could develop major cases similar to the DEA or the FBI if they had the resources available to develop informants. Agents in those other agencies had relative ease of access to funds for informants if the case merited investigation. Obviously, the availability of funds implied a willingness on the part of managers to pursue the development of informants.

More than $135 million was budgeted for DEA in 1975-1976. In 1976 DEA had a budget for buying information and drugs of $9.9 million while in 1974-1975 it was over $10 million. This latter figure, only about 5% of which was recovered (for example, through buy-busts where the money and the drugs are confiscated) provides each agent with a working capital of about $4,300 a year. [13]

Illegal aliens acting as informants often receive *extensions of time* to stay in the US in exchange for the information they provide. Paid informants received relatively small amounts of money. Obtaining funds for informants or to make *street buys* often required complex and time consuming bureaucratic *red tape*. An example of an INS *street buy* occurs when an undercover agent, or confidential informant, poses as a buyer of fraudulent INS documents from a vendor. If INS managers approve a *street buy* operation, agents usually have to guarantee that the money will be recovered immediately. For example, if an exchange requires $1,000 to buy false documents, the arrest of the vendor is immediate so that the money is recovered at that time. Obviously, this limits the scope of an investigation. Higher-level vendors, or criminals in a large organization of vendors become insulated, and lower-level criminals in the organization are the ones that usually face prosecution.

In order to avoid complications, INS investigators preferred offering time to illegal aliens, rather than money in exchange for information. Most of the investigators expressed views similar to those expressed in the following statement:

It is very difficult to get money. You have to go all the way to Washington, and do everything, to kiss people's asses, and not the asses of the people you would expect to have to kiss. Instead of dealing with the Associate Commissioner for Enforcement, you have to beg someone in Finance . . . the people who really have no idea of the importance of an investigation, or the activity in question.

The FBI has paid informants with annual salaries of $15,000, or more. (1982 estimate) I'm not saying that INS does not have anything like that, it is possible but I've never heard of it, although there are provisions where we could have it as well. For example, we tried to make a criminal case a few months ago where we needed $4,000 quickly to buy some documents, or to give the impression that we were going to buy them. It simply was not available; we could not get the money for the buy. INS came up with one reason or another and the case was almost jeopardized. Luckily, we had another avenue to pursue and we did not need the money; but, not having access to fairly large sums of money could seriously jeopardize such cases.

INS investigators also believed that managers knew very little about how to conduct criminal investigations. Investigators further believed that Headquarters and Regional Offices did not care about the investigations branch, or mission. They believed that INS wants to *give the store away.* By this, investigators mean that INS places a low priority on interior enforcement of the INA, and has a liberal policy on illegal aliens. Investigators believe that managers actually attempt to obstruct their mission. They further believe that INS goes out of the way to make illegal aliens permanent residents, or citizens, instead of enforcing the INA.

Investigators suggest that Congress and the public would be more sympathetic to the interior enforcement of the INA if they were fully informed about the scope of the illegal alien problem. As one interviewee points out:

I had to testify before a Congressional committee about immigration problems . . . and present information on criminal activity in one ethnic group. When the committee wanted to ask questions, the Acting Commissioner spoke, and we were *gagged.* I brought a recently smuggled . . . alien with me and the panel was visibly impressed with my presentation, but when they asked questions about what INS was doing I was not allowed to answer . . . The Acting Commissioner answered all the questions. I do not think he had any conception of our problem. I do not think the panel was given an accurate picture of what the problems were. When the panel asked if INS needed more money, more investigators, a reorganization, or whatever, the answers (given by the Acting Commissioner) were not responsive. They were general, vague answers. He was more interested in dealing with the telephone system than with criminal activity. Questions were directed at me, but the Acting Commissioner grabbed the microphone and answered for me.

After processing illegal aliens, investigators present the cases to their immediate supervisor for review and approval. Supervisors rarely change the recommendations made. This is so because most cases are basically the same. Routinization of work is typical in such organizations, and investigators are encouraged to seek out cases that *fit* the processing routine. It appears that the Area Control Illegal Status (ACIS) Section follows these patterns in the organization. The primary function of ACIS investigators is to locate and apprehend illegals. Investigators rely on complaints from the public as the primary source of information about the whereabouts of illegals. This information initiates strategies to conduct *hits*, or investigations. A duty officer stationed at the District Office radio room also fields complaints phoned in from the public. The complaints are recorded on a form and referred to the ACIS supervisor for assignment. Obviously, an experienced duty officer will select complaints for his next field day. Although the complaints are supposed to be filtered through the supervisor, the duty officer screens the complaints informally for good leads to follow. Regarding processing illegal aliens, pretyped forms were used in most cases. As such, investigators encounter routinization of work at all levels.

When investigators seek approval in unusual cases, supervisors are forced to make unprecedented decisions. When this occurs, the supervisor rarely makes the decision until consulting a second line supervisor. Managers do not encourage investigators to vary their procedures, or rely on imagination in fulfilling their tasks. Such instances can cause the organization to grind to a halt. This is especially so if a second line supervisor is hesitant to call upon upper mangers to approve investigative activities.

Investigators that process illegal aliens with pending applications for adjustment of their status, had to refer the case to the service branch of INS. The application takes a priority over the arrest process and disposition. Investigators believed that many marriage applications are fraudulent, and that other applications are equally questionable. As such, investigators believed that such practices undermined the enforcement of the INA.

Investigators followed operating procedures that were based on the established practices of the border patrol. The routine procedures of the border patrol were deeply entrenched in the agency's concept of law enforcement. The border patrol is more suited to the administrative apprehension and processing of illegal aliens, and this may account for the preponderance of the administrative enforcement efforts that filtered down to the investigations branch. The investigators voiced disenchantment with their tasks, and the direction of INS. They believed that the agency confused criminal investigations with border patrol activity. One interviewee states:

> . . . it seems that they are trying to do away with the investigator's mission . . .
> to give asylum to all the illegals here, and just let anyone who wants to come

into the US, come in. Carter and his humanitarians, and that whole idea of the *melting pot* is where it comes from . . . which might have worked when this country was beginning. We have too many people here today . . . we cannot handle them . . . look at the unemployment rate . . . all we are doing is adding more people to the unemployment rate. I do not care what they say about these illegal aliens being hard working, there just are not enough jobs available for them, unless you want slave labor, which is exactly what a lot of the factories have: illegal aliens in sweat shops working for below the minimum wage.

GOALS & POLICY DIRECTIVES

The investigators believed that INS did not have clear goals regarding the interior enforcement of the INA. The agency offered a general definition of mission by stating that it enforced the INA. Some of the policies that impacted on the way investigators implemented their tasks included:

(1)INS restricted the use of government automobiles partially as a response to a gas shortage and the Census of 1980. The use of a government vehicle is often required because investigators complete most of their work in high crime areas and outside normal business hours. Most field stops are not readily accessible to public transportation and the possibility of taking someone into custody usually exists. To accommodate these problems, Investigators take automobiles home overnight in order to conduct early morning *hits*, to work late in the evening, and to arrest illegal aliens. Investigators stated that having to return the government vehicle to the district office after work is counterproductive to these work activities. In many instances, taking the vehicle home saves the government man-hours of work as well as resources (gasoline). INS policy governing the use of government vehicles varied over time. Management insisted that investigators abide by the *outstanding regulations* governing such use. Such regulations are *always* in effect in order to deter the misuse of government vehicles that includes personal use. Investigators believe that taking government vehicles home overnight is essential in the New York City area for the proper and efficient implementation of their tasks. Investigators stated that the policy restrictions on the use of government vehicles essentially brought the Investigation Branch to a standstill.

(2)From April 1980 through mid-January 1981, the Attorney General of the US mandated that INS officers obtain search warrants before seeking out illegal aliens at businesses, farms, ranches, or residences. The Attorney General implemented this policy based on allegations that INS used Census information, or could use Census information in investigating illegal aliens. Although without merit the restrictions impacted severely on the interior enforcement of the INA and the Investigator mission.

(3)At the time, INS policy regarding identifying personnel in the investigations branch further demoralized the Investigators. Managers advised officers to refer to themselves as *investigators* only, and to delete reference to the title criminal in Criminal Investigator. INS managers also decided to refer to illegal aliens as *undocumented persons.*

(4)Investigators should not display their weapons, handcuffs, or other police equipment unnecessarily, either in the office or in public. Upon entering
the office, the investigator must store his weapon in a locked gun cabinet.
Investigators believe that mangers are concerned about public perceptions of
agents as law enforcement officers doing *police* work. Managers readily satisfy the service part of INS mission by minimizing the law enforcement image
of the investigations branch. Although the government vehicle assigned to an
investigator is a police type vehicle, at the time policy proscribed the use, or
installation of, emergency lights and sirens.

One investigator comments:

> They do not want you to take cars home. That is a big waste of time. I find it
> more effective to do my work early in the morning. I find this to be very
> productive. You can go out to the sight of an investigation early and get your
> people. This is your job. That is what you are supposed to do. In my situation,
> there are not any trains running that early in the morning, to come into the
> office, and then return to the area where I am working, which is near my
> residence many times. Much of the information I work is near where I live or it
> is between my house and the office. To come into the office, go back out there
> to get the people, and return to the office, is idiotic. It is pointless.

Overall, investigators believe that such policies prevented them from doing their jobs effectively. Subsequently, INS rescinded the automobile use
and census restrictions, but investigators believed that the immigration policies of the Carter Administration stifled interior INS efforts. These beliefs
seemed to be substantiated since the policies were removed after President
Carter left office. Investigators believed that INS used the 1980 fuel crisis as
an excuse to obstruct their tasks even further, even though agencies had to
curtail gasoline consumption. Many investigators believed that managers *had
it in for investigators* who were perceived as taking great pleasure in implementing the restrictive policies. Investigators displayed an enormous lack of
faith in the ability of INS managers to conduct enforcement operations, especially criminal investigations. This lack of trust in the competence of management is one of the main contributors to low officer morale, especially in
police agencies.[14]

Dual mandate agencies such as INS often attempt to minimize the association with law enforcement. One way to do this is by using special terms to
identify officers. In dealing with the public, INS managers ordered investigators to delete "Criminal" from their official title--Criminal Investigator. Administrators commonly employ such techniques to display a certain image to
the public. Another example of such a tactic occurs when University administrators decide to label the campus security force as the *Department of
Public Safety.* Actually, such public safety officers perform primarily security (police) functions. This is an appropriate form of deception for a college

campus. The public views colleges as scholarly preserves. Why would there be a need for a police garrison to protect such a community? Another example of a change in job tile includes custodial engineer for janitor. Such a change is meant to enhance employee morale. Investigators should be exclusively concerned with the enforcement of the INA. There should be no confusion about the nature of their tasks. When INS directs its officers to distance themselves from their main task of criminal investigation by renaming them, one can logically conclude the reason behind such a maneuver. Such organizational decisions highlighted the service priority or had a deeper meaning. Most of the investigators interviewed in this study shared the feelings expressed in the following interviewees statement:

> The law enforcement aspect of INS has been shot down so badly . . . we are so limited in what we can do because of the policies which come from Washington, the Region, and our own office. But the basic policy is to do nothing so you cannot be blamed for doing anything. There was an injunction placed on us for stopping people on the street even though the INA authorizes us to question anyone we believe to be an alien and their right to be in the US. Policy has evolved . . . that we do not create too many problems in enforcing the INA. For example, we use certain criteria to make arrests that local police cannot use; the police can use other criteria to make arrests and turn people over to us if they are illegal aliens. But the way INS operates now we are prohibited from working *joint operations* (with other law enforcement agencies) because INS might be subject to civil suits. If we cannot cooperate with other law enforcement agencies how do we expect to get cooperation from them?

Investigators also commented on the overall attitude of INS towards the enforcement mission. Investigators believed that INS policy at the time of the study was to maintain a low a profile in the law enforcement community. Managers adhere to the policy even if doing so endangers the safety of investigators. ASU investigators reported a continuing problem they had with management involving restrictions on using emergency lights and sirens in government vehicles. The ASU investigates alien smugglers and routinely encounters situations wherein smugglers are transporting their cargo in automobiles. Attempting to stop such vehicles is extremely hazardous without proper police equipment and poses a risk to the public as well as the investigators. Investigators stated that high speed chases without proper emergency equipment (flashing red lights and sirens) leaves the investigator and the government liable for law suits in the event of an automobile accident. Furthermore, investigators stated that suspects arrested after fleeing a pursuit can claim that the pursuers were not agents because they did not have the flashing red lights and sirens. More importantly, agents stated that suspects assaulting arresting officers can likewise allege that the arresting officer was not a law enforcement officer. Assaulting a federal officer is a serious federal offense. A legal defense of such an assault might include failure to know the person assaulted is a federal officer. Although ASU investigators officially stated their concerns, INS continued to deny them permission to equip their vehicles with the police equipment.

Regardless of the unit, a criminal investigator can encounter situations requiring emergency police equipment in government vehicles. The nature of police work presumes the possibility of physical injury. Investigators stated that serious physical injury and assaults do occur. Such a reality further highlights the task of criminal investigations as law enforcement activity. Investigators believe that INS management defined their mission more as a service function, and implemented this policy with severe organizational restrictions. They further believed that this showed a lack of concern for the safety of investigators.

Investigators voiced strong resentment toward INS management because of the restrictions imposed on the investigations branch due to the 1980 Census. INS investigators pointed out that other federal law enforcement agencies did not experience these restrictions: "Drug smugglers did not receive a moratorium. Rapists, murderers, and other felons did not receive a time out to file a Census return." Investigators believed that such a policy blatantly imposed a priority on *counting illegal aliens* that were illegally in the US. In addition, INS managers continued to impose the restrictions on the investigations branch, even after the effectiveness of the restriction lapsed.

NOTES

1. Glenn A. Bertness, *Acting Associate Commissioner, INS, Remarks Concerning Department of Justice Authorization—INS,* before Committee on the Judiciary, Subcommittee on Immigration, Refugees, and International Law, US Senate, April 1, 1981, pp. 1-2.

2. DHS, "Our Mission," Accessed on June 30, 2016, https://www.dhs.gov/our-mission

3. DHS, "Written Testimony of ICE Director Sarah Saldana," Accessed on June 30, 2016, https://www.dhs.gov/news/2016/03/15/written-testimony-ice-director-senate-committee-homeland-security-and-governmental

4. Brandon Darby, *Breitbart,* "Retribution: Border patrol Agent Suffers After Blowing Whistle To Congress," (April 18, 2016) Accessed on July 5, 2016, http://www.breitbart.com/texas/2016/04/18/retribution-border-patrol-agent-suffers-blowing-whistle-congress/

5. *DHS,* "Policies for the Apprehension, Detention and Removal of Undocumented Immigrants," (November 20, 2014) Accessed on July 5, 2016, https://www.dhs.gov/sites/default/files/publications/14_1120_memo_prosecutorial_discretion.pdf

6. Stephen Dinan, *The Washington Times,* "Immigration agents sue to stop Obama's non-deportation policy," (August 23, 2012), Accessed on July 5, 2016, http://www.washingtontimes.com/news/2012/aug/23/immigration-agents-sue-stop-obamas-non-deportation/#pagebreak

7. Arthur Niederhoffer. *Behind the Shield: The Police in Urban Society,* New York: Doubleday, 1967, p. 52.

8. Jerry Seper n.d., "Border Patrol Union Survey finds Job Discontent," *Washington Times,* The (DC), *Regional Business News,* EBSCO host (accessed June 29, 2016).

9. The author used Atlas/ti software to analyze the perceptions of the interviewees formulating a network view of policies that caused problems for the agents in completing their tasks.

10. DHS, "Budget-in-Brief: Fiscal Year 2015," Accessed on July 7, 2016, https://www.dhs.gov/sites/default/files/publications/FY15BIB.pdf

11. US Congress, Department of State, Justice, and Commerce, The Judiciary, and Related Agencies Appropriations For 1981. Hearings Before a Subcommittee of the Committee on Appropriations House of Representatives, 96th Congress, 2nd Session, 1980, Washington, DC: U. S. Government Printing Office, pp. 587-590.

12. Comptroller General, Report to the Congress of the US, Prospects Dim for Effectively Enforcing Immigration Laws, Washington, DC: U. S. Government Printing Office, 1980, p 24.

13. Peter K. Manning, *The Narc's Game: Organizational and Informational Limits on Drug Law Enforcement,* (Massachusetts: MIT Press, 1980) 12.

14. R. Wayne Boss, "It Doesn't Matter If You Win or Lose, Unless You're Losing: Organizational Change in A Law Enforcement Agency," *Journal of Applied Behavioral Science,* (1979) 15(2): 198-220.

Chapter Six

The Investigator at Work

UNIT STATUS

Investigators commented on the status associated with placement in various units, and perceived General Investigations as having the lowest status. The interviewees were 1811 criminal investigators, as distinguished from 1810 general investigators who usually do not carry firearms, or make arrests. For this reason, 1810 investigators may be perceived to have lower status than criminal investigators. Except for the ASU, most casework involved locating a deportable alien for processing. Investigators considered criminal cases to have more status than non-criminal cases, and preferred them to administrative casework. This was especially true in the ASU, where agents attempted to disassociate themselves from noncriminal cases, and the investigations branch in general. Since the ASU investigated smuggling cases, this limited their work to criminal prosecution cases, and members were able to more easily identify with the traditional criminal investigator perception.

Investigators assigned to the Special Investigations Unit investigated illegal aliens with criminal, or subversive backgrounds. The Fraud Unit primarily investigated cases relating to bona fides of marriage, or fraudulent document vendors. The investigators assigned to the General Investigations Unit spent most of their time looking for low-level visa abusers, such as overstay visitors that had no known criminal background. If they uncovered any criminality, the case would be transferred to the appropriate unit for investigation. Most of the respondents shared the feelings expressed in the following statement:

> the way it is set up now we have two types of investigators: the elite ASU investigators, who are given a higher grade which creates a lot of jealousy and animosity; and the rest of the investigators. Another example is APG (Alien

Processing Group). INS considers it part of training, and assigns the investigator there for three months when he comes on the job. Since there is a hiring freeze they have to recycle investigators through that unit again. Of course, if you got your GS-12 you do not have to go into APG. APG exists to expedite cases for immigration lawyers. They can bring their clients into the office after they attain some equity, and have their applications processed because the alien is technically illegal. All it amounts to is speeding up the application process so the alien can get his residence visa, or permission to work which is normally granted if an alien has a pending application. Otherwise the illegal alien would have to wait, like many others, and risk detection and arrest. APG is a valuable waste of man-hours I think investigators should be strictly involved in investigating criminal violations: rings set up to bring in illegal aliens prosecuting unscrupulous lawyers, travel agencies who violate the INA, and smugglers. This work could keep us occupied for years. The rest of the investigations could be eliminated, or completed by an administrative workforce.

In ACIS, the primary task was to locate and apprehend illegal aliens, especially at their places of employment, which offered the advantage of locating other illegal aliens who often worked as similar employments. This policy was based on the belief that removing such deportable aliens would make more jobs available for legal workers. This unit also worked leads based on complaints, but did not carry formal case files on aliens. Leads came from other units in the agency, other government agencies, the public, and supervisors did not assign regular caseloads to ACIS investigators. Complaints received by the agency about illegal aliens are recorded on Form G-123, and if one does not already exist an official case file is opened when the alien is apprehended and processed. This less formal process enables more officer discretion in completing tasks especially with regard to selecting the most promising of the available leads. For this reason, ACIS investigators had more *control* than investigators in other sections over their environment[1]. In addition, ACIS investigators also seemed to have more camaraderie than investigators assigned to General Investigations. ACIS investigators routinely responded to complaints from police, and this increased their relative status because it involved dealing with police type work, or their perceptions of the law enforcer image.

As previously stated, the ASU had the highest status and its members stressed that they only worked criminal cases. However, agents within that unit also complained about the lack of agency support, the main determinant of their lower morale as well. As a veteran ASU agent indicated:

As time goes on, I've seen the Anti-Smuggling unit go from a completely independent and unique operation here within the New York district to a unit that is gradually becoming more and more brought into the mainstream of what's happening administratively in the NYDO. And thus, more and more of our time is being spent doing administrative garbage here in this office.

Most of the investigators stated that they would prefer to work in the ASU primarily because it involved a promotion, and would allow them to work exclusively on criminal cases. The investigators advised that they could avoid dealing with many of the administrative restrictions imposed by the agency if they were assigned a criminal case. Certain tasks are mandated when working criminal cases, such as having the use of a government vehicle to conduct investigations. The AUSA, who also supervises the case agent in a criminal case, is often less concerned about administrative policies. The AUSA wants to obtain a successful prosecution, and the requirements to do so are often hampered by administrative policies such as automobile use, or lack of resources. As one investigator recalled an incident that reflects these issues:

> I had a criminal case where I had to serve subpoenas early in the morning. The supervisors at INS would not authorize me to take a car home overnight to serve these subpoenas. When the (Assistant) U. S. Attorney found out about this he contacted INS at the regional level and was advised by them that it was a district matter. The (Assistant) U. S. Attorney said that he felt that INS management was actually trying to impede the investigation.

Investigators advised that criminal investigations are more complex than other cases, and the Frauds Unit routinely dealt with such cases. Investigators assigned to the Special Investigations Unit tend to equate task with the title of the unit rather than the actual work performed, and perceived such work as important because it dealt with criminals. The Criminal, Immoral and Narcotic Unit (CIN) dealt with criminal aliens administratively, in that most of the cases involved aliens that were deportable because of a criminal conviction. The criminal conviction made the alien deportable, and the ensuing investigation involved administrative proceedings. The investigator was assigned the case to locate and process the alien for deportation proceedings. Law enforcement agencies usually notified the agency when they arrested an alien on criminal charges, and then the INS investigator would lodge a detainer on the alien if still in custody, or place the alien under deportation proceedings if released by the police. The CIN Unit concentrated on these administrative deportation cases, but generally did not develop criminal investigations. Managers did not encourage their agents to go beyond locating, apprehending, lodging detainers, or placing the alien under proceedings. In this regard, the CIN Unit is very much like the General Investigations Unit, except that the clients have criminal backgrounds.

However, most of the investigators in the CIN Unit agreed with the following statement:

> I'm in the criminal section. I know there are other sections which deal with
> aliens who are not criminals, they have merely broken an administrative law.
> That is not my case. I often try to describe my job by telling people that I deal
> with hookers, drug pushers, drug users, importers,those are the people that I
> see

At INS, investigators were assigned to units on a relatively permanent basis, and the only way to obtain a transfer was to request one through official channels. Most investigators perceived that such transfers were based on personal, rather than objective reasons. The following statement reflects this belief:

> I have been assigned to General Investigations for over seven years and I hate
> the work in that unit. I have requested transfers to Special Investigations
> several times because I feel that I could be more productive in that unit. They
> don't even acknowledge my requests, not that they have to. During my time,
> here at INS I have seen people transferred to Special Investigations from other
> units overnight because they were friends with the ADDI (Assistant District
> Director Investigations) or knew one of the section chiefs, who put a good
> word in for him. In order to get into Special Investigations, you have to be an
> ex-border patrolman; when they come to New York they usually go right into
> that unit. Or if you were an ex-cop, or you know someone, you can get into
> Special. Just like everything else in this agency, it is who you know, not what
> you know.

The transition from INS to DHS ICE involved the blending of two agencies, US Customs and INS. US Customs had higher journeyman grade levels, and more status in the law enforcement hierarchy. This resulted in an initial conflict between the legacy investigators, in which customs related investigations became more important than immigration related cases. The conflict had less to do with the actual investigative relevance than with the ability to again detach from the immigration mandates. Customs agents could avoid working the immigration cases since they already were trained to work other than immigration cases. INS agents would be relegated to the obvious resolution of immigration related matters. Over time, both legacy investigators would be cross-trained to accomplish the respective tasks, and new agents would be hired without any conflicts inherited. As previously indicated, few would argue the relevance of the investigative importance that most other federal criminal investigators completed such as narcotics, criminal organizations, firearms, and terrorism. However, immigration law enforcement had clear disadvantages for the criminal investigator about policy restrictions, and general political ideologies that were pro-immigrant.

INVESTIGATIVE WORK AND THE ELEMENT OF DANGER

An example of what might happen during a routine investigation illustrates the element of danger as perceived by investigators. An investigator assigned to the General Investigations Unit attempts to interview a witness for a routine character investigation. In such cases, the investigator sets out to determine the character of an applicant for residency, or citizenship in the US. The investigator might find the witness in an apartment building located in a high-crime area in the Bronx, New York and attempts to interview the witness there. The witness admits the investigator into the apartment, and the investigator observes narcotics' paraphernalia in plain-sight, as well as two illegal aliens hiding under a bed. The investigator decides to arrest the individuals, and a subsequent search finds an illegal handgun. As an illustration of what could happen, this routine investigation turns out to be anything but routine, and such scenarios can unfold at any time when conducting field work. Investigative fieldwork creates stress for the investigator, which in turn causes the officer to become suspicious of those being investigated.

> Accordingly, the element of danger isolates the police officer socially from that segment of the citizenry that he regards as symbolically dangerous and from the conventional citizenry with whom he identifies.[2]

INS investigators arrested thousands of illegal aliens annually, and although the arrestee usually offered little resistance, the unpredictability of such encounters makes them like maintenance of order tasks performed by police officers. Agents had little to do with maintenance of order activity where unpredictable outcomes tend to occur.[3] However, the routine arrests they made contributed to their working personality, which mirrored police officers involved in maintenance of order work. The agent might presume a worse-case scenario, and could never be sure about the outcome of official fieldwork encounters, some of which could be dangerous. Agencies that stress courteous and humane treatment of foreigners in all situations exacerbate this process. Most likely, it would be less stressful if the investigator perceived his role and status the same way the agency did. However, agents perceived their agency as service oriented, and they had little faith in the ability of managers to deal with the problems associated with law enforcement. These issues contributed to the working personality of the INS investigator. The following statement expressed the feelings of most of the legacy INS investigators:

> I consider it a dangerous job anytime you go out on the street. Most of our work is in high crime areas, and the residents see you as "the man." They don't know that it is *only* immigration. Furthermore, you never know how someone is going to react when you arrest them. A lot of *wets* will run if they have the

chance, and chasing them can be dangerous. Several investigators have been injured chasing *wets*.

Another investigator states:

> People are culled into thinking that the job is a safe one, when, in fact, it is not. Investigators are not prepared for the worst. It is potentially dangerous work. I do not think it compares with drug enforcement, or serious firearms enforcement, but it is potentially dangerous.

The working personality of agents also impact on the people they officially encounter. Investigators routinely ask questions about a person's immigration status when they conduct investigations, and individuals other than the target of an investigation turn out to be illegal aliens.

> to the person stopped, the patrolman seems hostile or edgy, and if, as is often the case, the citizen has no intention of attacking the officer, he sees the patrolman as *unjustifiably* suspicious, hostile, or edgy. If the citizen then shows his resentment, the officer is likely to interpret it as animosity and thus to be even more on his guard. Both sides may be caught in an ascending spiral of antagonisms. [4]

In routine locate investigations, the investigator may become suspicious of those encountered, and needs to be prepared to deal with a hostile witness, or a potential threat. A significant difference exists between an INS agent and a police officer, and this also applies to other federal agents such as the FBI, or DEA, that more closely fit the police image. The participants shared the perception that most illegal aliens were not serious criminals, but they did encounter serious criminal law violators during their duties, and such encounters became part of their working personality. Routine investigations do not guarantee routine encounters, and experience might dull the working personality. In some instances, the potential stress involved in the agent's working personality may surpass that of the police officer. Although INS arrests are routine, most arrestees perceive the encounter as a traumatic experience. In such encounters, INS investigators advised aliens that they were in the US in violation of the law, and that they were being taken to the immigration office where they would be placed under proceedings. To diminish the probability of a negative reaction, they avoided using the term "arrest," and diffuse the encounter by offering additional options available to the alien. For example, advising the alien of the right to be released after posting a bond could soften resistance to the arrest process. Part of the processing of an apprehended alien includes checking whether the alien has any applications pending, or is eligible for relief based on a relationship to a lawful immediate relative. If an application is pending, the alien might be eligible for temporary legal status with employment authorization, and in such instances the alien benefits from the encounter.

Since aliens migrate from every country in the world, it is difficult to predict how they might react to an encounter with an agent. An alien from a country with a military dictatorship has a different concept of the *federales* than one from a democratic country, where the former might imagine anything from torture and a lengthy incarceration, to death. In describing their treatment of illegal aliens, legacy agents expressed their perceptions of fairness, and compassion. Most individuals caught up in this process soon understand how it works. Illegal aliens often attempt to run away from immigration officers, and may remain free indefinitely if they can elude a future apprehension. The sheer volume of illegal aliens in the US creates a haven for them, and therefore they have everything to gain, and nothing to lose by running away. Even if the illegal alien is apprehended, the possibility of release by posting an affordable bond is possible. After that, they can simply abscond, and never encounter an agent again.

The ramifications of current enforcement policies impact on these interactions immensely. If the illegal alien believes that an encounter with an immigration agent is unlikely, or that any encounter will not result in detention, the interaction process changes accordingly. Sanctuary cities, catch and release, executive waivers, and enforcement priorities, contribute to the interaction processes involving both the investigator, and the illegal alien. The investigator is severely restricted in such encounters, and the illegal alien benefits from the ensuing confusion. These interaction processes may seem less constraining for the border patrol agent, but they too become involved when they attempt to apprehend illegal aliens who fall within the exceptions resulting from executive policies, such as *catch and release*. US Customs and Border Patrol stationed at ports of entry, such as international airports, may have less confusion about their role. Usually, such encounters are meant to interdict illegal contraband such as narcotics, or visa fraud, which are criminal investigations, not administrative. Such cases are less constrained, or not constrained at all, by internal agency policies, or executive orders.

MANAGERS AND SUPERVISORS

Investigators perceived that the primary concern of their supervisors was implementing the policies from the *top down*. Supervisors rarely went into the field, and confined their activities to office work such as assigning cases, reviewing investigative reports, and preparing monthly work reports. Investigators indicated that supervisors assigned cases as they were received, and rarely initiated an investigation, or project on their own. Investigators did not consider supervisory critiques very constructive, nor did they seek advice.

They perceived the supervisor's role as ensuring that policies were followed and that cases were assigned equitably. However, even random allocation of cases would make little difference since most cases were similar. Investigators stated that supervisors based annual ratings primarily on the number of case closings. An investigator stated:

> I can't do anything to change policies that come from above. I keep hoping that things will change, but even if they don't there are good aspects to this job. Supervision is minimal, which I like. I can conduct my investigations any way I like with minimal interference. There are not many agencies where you can say that happens. That is probably the best aspect of our job.

Although ICE agents had far less discretion than legacy agents, they could rationalize their conflicts with the higher-grade levels that occurred after the transition, and the increase in status that accompanied the creation of an agency meant to insure the national security. Immigration matters could become less important in their self-perceptions, or they could accept the policy changes that muted immigration enforcement as standard operating procedures beyond their control. They had all *the bells and whistles* associated with the special agent, including a government vehicle, salary, and benefits, and could repress the negatives associated with the politics of immigration enforcement. They were ICE agents, not INS agents.

Supervisors had control over investigators because they completed their annual performance rating, and promotions were based on these ratings. A supervisor could also rely on other methods to control investigators, such as requesting that an investigator complete a daily activity log if a sufficient number of cases are not completed. This would strictly restrict the investigator's duty time, and is meant to bring the investigator "into line."

Most of the investigators believed that if they completed an acceptable number of cases, they would receive a highly recommended rating at the end of the year, and the supervisor would yield discretion as to how they handle their time in the field. Not all investigators shared this understanding. As one pointed out:

> There are annual ratings, and your supervisor fills these rating forms out. There are official guidelines as to how a person should be rated, in terms of production (quantity) and quality of work. These guidelines are not uniformly followed. Some supervisors have a policy of rating all the investigators in their squad highly recommended even if they were just promoted a week before the rating, and even if they did not deserve a highly recommended rating. Other supervisors will give an investigator a recommended, or not recommended if the investigator was recently promoted; or sometimes, although rarely, a supervisor may not like an investigator, or a personality problem erupts. Many investigators are penalized unfairly by this arbitrary system. Ratings have little to do with quality of work performed.

Sometimes supervisors recommend investigators for cash awards if the investigator performed above the norm. Managers determine the criteria for defining above the norm. Investigators consider exemplary investigative work or extraordinary law enforcement efforts to be better qualifiers for awards. Investigators stated that entire squads routinely received cash awards at one time. The criterion used for such rewards was the number of case completions by the squad. Ratings and awards sometimes caused strain as the following statement reflects:

> Because of certain events which occurred in the past year, I was detailed away from the office to work on special projects. Because of this, my closings were down over the year, as can be expected. But, when I returned I found out that my supervisor recommended several investigators for awards. He did not take into account the other factors or the quality and kinds of work I performed. I think he was unfair and I know he gave an award to one of his gofers who took care of the monthly statistics for him. I really felt cheated, but I know also that it was a personality thing too. I have experienced discrimination, and I have seen my supervisor play favorites several times.

Although supervisors had this control, rating an agent as other than highly recommended was the exception rather than the rule, since doing so drastically reduced the chance for a promotion. Both supervisors and investigators viewed immediate supervisors as individuals that did not want to "rock the boat." Supervisors and investigators wanted control with the least amount of coercion. The problem of low morale coupled with the promotion freeze also suggested that supervisors would be reluctant to impose low ratings on investigators.

Investigators perceived that supervisors were mostly concerned with official policy, and less concerned with their needs, even regarding the mission of the investigations branch. Several respondents indicated that their supervisors rewarded investigators that "followed orders," or those that assisted the supervisor in completing mundane tasks. For example, the investigator that volunteered to calculate the monthly statistics for the supervisor received an award for this service. Investigators perceived that the agency did not support them, especially about completing their mission. The perception of the distrust that agents had of upper management is described in this comment:

> The majority of the time, the supervisor would not back the investigator. I was sued myself by the American Civil Liberties Union for $100,000, and the DD at the time . . . had a meeting with all the investigators, and read aloud all the allegations. I was new at the job at the time. I was only on about nine months, read allegations that two investigators were kidnapped, assaulted, spit on, beat, stepped on, and at the end of the speech I thought he would say you see what you are up against. However, he did not state that. He stated, "is this the way

that investigators should operate?" At this point I knew what the immigration service was all about.

It would seem obvious that managers reward those following their mandates and priorities, but the agency priority was service related. For example, the agency considered completing a naturalization case more of a success than conducting surveillance, or developing a good criminal case. This is because criminal cases are often time consuming, and do not always lead to a successful prosecution. An investigator that completes a naturalization case, in which the applicant becomes a voting citizen, seems more appealing to headquarters than a criminal prosecution.

Investigators interact with their first line supervisor daily, but rarely with upper-level managers. Several investigators pointed out that one ADDI had an open-door policy, and they preferred that to the standard "through official channels." If an investigator had a problem with a case, he could walk into the ADDI's office and get it resolved more rapidly. However, an open-door policy requires a charismatic leader who can effectively control allegiance through personal power, rather than relying on bureaucratic traditions. The charismatic leader receives personal requests for favors as well, but can usually limit such problems and still get the job done. Investigators seemed to prefer open channels of communication, since such a system facilitates law enforcement.

In this study, the perceptions of investigators determined the attitudes of supervisors and their conceptions of task. Since many of the supervisors were former investigators they most likely identified with the agents they supervised, even though they could do little to accommodate their perceived complaints, or concerns. Upper-management could easily avoid dealing with the everyday problems of investigators, and agents perceived that they ignored them entirely.

To get approval for field operations, investigators had to submit requests *through official channels*, and this process usually causes delays. Supervisors interpret the requests from below in terms of how they think their supervisors will respond to the initial request. As the request moves up the chain, it often is revised to conform to perceived top-down views, and the first line supervisor will rarely approve a sensitive request for fear of it being rejected at the upper level. The final disposition of the initial request reflects perceived notions about probable outcomes based on misguided suggestions, and the process triggers routine requests that assume expected outcomes. As such, the investigator hesitates to submit even routine requests, unless necessary. Unfortunately, some of these routine requests could be important in implementing the enforcement mission. Similarly, Gresham's law points out that such actions involve "ritualistic routine minimizing the likelihood of energetic search for more satisfactory solutions."[5] Perceptions about the "good old boy," and those that meekly follow the whims of upper-management was a perception that investigators held.

> I think what we have left as managers, and even as investigators and the old investigators are the "good old boys," the former border patrol, and the company men. You know, you didn't need a college education to get this job before, and even in some cases you don't need it now. But, you get the people who would say yes to any ridiculous order that you're given. They didn't make waves. They do exactly what the managers want and these are the people who are now in the manager spots. And to me they are incompetent, because their concern is answering to their next higher superior who is also, in turn, concerned with answering to his boss, and on, and on, and on, until the buck stops wherever. These managers don't want to take a stand. Here in the Cuban detail, I don't know if they don't care, or if they just don't know what the hell to do.

Because of President Obama's executive orders, and the Priorities Enforcement Program that resulted from them, DHS agents were confronted with a plethora of waivers and inconsistencies that made enforcement a frustrating task. Congressional testimony notwithstanding, the laxity of enforcement operations, and the *de facto* amnesty for millions of illegal aliens most certainly exacerbated the confused perceptions of the deviant population, stigma, and deterrence. The most likely perception in the environment was that even if the illegal alien is encountered, there will not be any sanctions imposed.

Sheriff Paul Babeu of Pinal County, Arizona which is located in the CBP Tucson sector, was interviewed on The Green Line Podcast, a NBPC podcast, and reflected on the apparent disconnect between the Obama administration's policies and the rule of law.[6] Sheriff Babeu's comments suggest that a rift exists between the managers of DHS and the field agents, and that agents were threatened with prosecution if they failed to comply with the policies relating to the DACA program, and enforcing the INA in general. During the podcast, the interviewer stated that the current budget allows for 21,370 CBP agents and that the agency is 1500 agents under that mandated level. In addition, the interviewer asserted that the Obama administration called for a further reduction of 300 CBP agents. Sheriff Babeu, who was strongly supportive of the CBP stated that, "There is a neon sign that says if you make it to the border you are home free." Babeu believes that the government should be hiring more agents to patrol the border, not reducing the number. Such comments suggest that the lack of support for enforcement continues at DHS.

PAPERWORK

Conducting criminal investigations, and apprehending and processing illegal aliens generates a good deal of paperwork. Most bureaucracies keep records, especially about accountability, and liability issues. Arresting someone carries with it the potential liability both for the arresting officer, and the agency, but agents considered the paperwork related to such tasks as onerous, and restrictive. Here, an investigator described the ways paperwork impedes the investigative process:

> Today, I was informed that you do not work with any other agency, especially the local. You have to have it approved by management, by the regional commissioner or something. And if you do go on ahead, it has to be an open case, whereas before, you know, you develop informers in order to really succeed in your work. You cannot use the informers any more. You must have an open case with a G-600 on it, it has to be reviewed by two supervisors, then they tell you, "oh yea, you can go on this," where you know you have the criminal address here, because your informant, and your expertise, and you, your knowing undercover work, tell you that the guy is in there. You cannot get the guy. But yes, they make you work arrest reports, which are about 5 or 6 months old, that the address does not exist, or the name that the person uses is a fictitious name, so they love to see pieces of paper, paperwork, (rather) than actual bodies.

As with most police agencies, investigators believed that the real work to be accomplished was "on the street". Office work is considered dirty work, and agents prefer to work "in the field." As one investigator pointed out, INS seemed to create an avalanche of paperwork that prevented investigators from working in the field. Other policies, such as making it difficult for investigators to take vehicles home overnight, restricting field investigations due to the census, assigning officers to service related task forces, and enforcing a strict "chain of command" also contributed to this perception.

> It seems that all these decisions; the policies are keyed toward the field person, keeping him in the office. Keeping him stamping, just looking through paperwork. Making a lot of decisions, and completing cases through examination of files without actually having to go out and contact people, or just to slow it down so that there's not that high profile, like the 190 arrests in Washington, or something like that.

Every two weeks Investigators had to attend "payday meetings" where updates and instructions regarding operations were presented. The payday meetings often focused on how to fill out paperwork. As one investigator pointed out:

Interviewer: When they have a payday meeting every payday, what do they talk about at the payday meeting? Don't they brief you on what to do?
Investigator: Make sure you fill out the gas slips. Yeah, right! The 22-12's. (Monthly Statistics Report) It's superfluous bullshit. Gibberish. Gibberish that my six-year-old, my eight-year-old nephew . . .

According to one legacy investigator, the border patrol agent does not have to complete the same amount of paperwork as an investigator. Since they apprehended over one million aliens annually, the agency attempted to facilitate the processing apparatus. However, if the agency wanted to discourage interior enforcement, it could create a complex web of forms and procedures that would discourage those involved in their attempts to implement it. As one investigator stated:

They (the border patrol) do it completely different. We have in-depth paperwork that we have to fill out here. Sheets, and sheets of stuff, 217's, 213's, 215's, 214's. Border people fill out the top part of a 213 (I-213 Record of Deportable Alien), five or six lines, and people ignore it. I think we waste a lot of time on this administrative nonsense. We find one of these people, the file that gets sent up from El Paso, or Laredo, or anywhere down in the southern border or the northern border, completely different paperwork.

Because of President Obama's executive orders for DACA and DAPA, a surge of illegal entries occurred along the southwest border. Most of the illegal entrants were from Central America, and this necessitated a reassignment of a significant number of border patrol agents to complete the paperwork, or processing of these illegal entrants. Comparing the perceptions of the legacy investigator about the border patrol, it appears that DHS has extended the paperwork problem to the border patrol as well. This is another example of how the agency staffs administrative task forces with enforcement personnel, which adversely impacts on the enforcement mission.

. . . a Democratic congressman, decrying what he terms a "critical situation" in Texas' Rio Grande Valley.
"[I]f you're just looking at the lower Rio Grande Valley, we're getting about 1,200 people a day. Over 70 percent of them are not from Mexico but from other places, and 300 to 400 of them are young people coming in without parents," says Rep. Henry Cuellar, a Texas Democrat, reports.
As this human tide pours into the U.S., Cuellar says "almost 40 percent of the Border patrol agents are not at the border. They're actually filling out paperwork, transporting, feeding, moving these folks around."[7]
Cuellar says illegals from Central America seem motivated by a belief that if they arrive in the U.S. with small children, they will not be sent back.

In comparing earlier times, investigators reported that arresting an illegal alien is a time-consuming task, and it is not encouraged by unit supervisors outside of ACIS. The arrest process requires completing a good deal of paperwork, as well as waiting for supervisors and upper management to approve all the paperwork associated with the task. The investigator advises the alien about their due process rights, conducts an interview, and completes the arrest report. If the alien does not have proper travel documents, a sworn statement is obtained from the alien, and the case file is forwarded to the supervisor for approval. If the supervisor approves the recommendation made by the agent, the file is then sent to the ADDI for approval, and then the file is sent to the Deputy District Director for final approval. Such a process was contingent on the availability of all the participants. In ACIS, the typical workday begins early in the morning, and often involves a foot chase with illegal aliens who ordinarily flee when encountered. As such, the workday is both stressful and exhausting. However, agents indicated that morale was higher when ACIS was making a lot of arrests, such as in the 1970s. As one investigator points out:

> The office now goes crazy if you bring in 10 (aliens) to process, and I remember when you used to bring in 20 to 30 a day, and just a small group to process. They make things difficult for you to process, you do the paperwork, and then you've got to wait for the person to sign for the bond . . .

Even where paperwork is expected, the investigators pointed out that quantity over quality was preferred by management. This is especially true due to the numerous backlogs that existed. Many investigators believed that there was a great deal of fraud involved in applicant petitions, especially the "sham marriages". One relatively easy way to obtain legal permanent residence is for the applicant to submit an immediate relative petition on behalf of the illegal alien. The beneficiary is not subject to visa limitations in such petitions. However, investigators pointed out that the agency did not scrutinize these applications carefully, even though apparently, agents were not coerced to push applications through.

> " . . . there was no pressure to *rubber stamp* the petitions . . . we were trying to move paper, they wanted to know how many petitions were completed each, to rubber stamp everything, but there was no pressure to *rubber stamp* the applications . . ."

Even though there was "no pressure to rubber stamp" it is obvious that the way the project was set up, rubber-stamping was admittedly facilitated by managers, and in this sense rubber-stamping was not hindered. This may be more a determination by the interviewee that pressure must be overt, or obvious for it to be real. Sometimes subtle mechanisms influence the direction of action. If it is easier to do it without finding problems, or fraud, then the investigator might fall prey to the subtlety. Another investigator commenting on the adjudications task force stated:

> . . . if you had a thousand investigators working full time on these old backlogged petitions for adjudication you would never successfully adjudicate one without all questions being answered. There would always be doubts about certain applications. Just because you go out in the field, by speaking to people, you can't prove beyond a reasonable doubt that these people are living in a fraudulent state. By that, I mean that the marriage is fraudulent and the application is viable only for inequity. Because you can't prove that the marriage is not viable, because you can't prove that the marriage is a fraud, and by prove, I mean, conclusively, 100%, actually get a petitioner or beneficiary or both to give you a statement form, the fact that "Yes I did marry so and so for money, yes I did marry so and so for a favor." In my mind, even though these things are being rushed through, adjudicated, quote unquote adjudicated, set down, these people are getting their residency, their green card, in my own mind, I am not satisfied with any of them that I close out . . . all they're trying to do is get rid of numbers, they're trying to . . . it's statistical and that's all it is. Look, it goes to Congress a year later, and says hey look we closed 85,000 cases and we adjudicated 85,000 petitions because of this new program I put through. Ain't we doing good? We need more money. We need a bigger budget next year, ok? It's bullshit! 85,000 may have been adjudicated, 85,000 people may have gotten green cards or residence, or half may have gotten green cards and residence and the other half may have been proven fraud. But that doesn't mean that you've done a good job. All of these Goddamned things have been rushed right through. They've been stamped, or proved, or not proved, document seen. They were approving applications at one time in this operation just based upon whether or not the petitioner and the beneficiary submitted the proper documentation. Neither alien was seen. Neither the petitioner . . . nor the beneficiary was interviewed, or even seen. If the accompanying documents were attached to the I-130 (Immediate Relative) petition without doing an outside investigation, or without even having seen the petitioner or beneficiary. The documents were there. By documents I mean the birth certificate proving a relationship, a marriage certificate, proof that the petitioner was a US citizen, types of documents like passport. If all the documents were intact by the time the I-130 was submitted, it was stamped, approved, instant approval desk. What a load of shit that was! And in 101% of every one of those documents submitted there was fraud. And if you couldn't find it on the surface, if you dove into file someplace you would find it. I hope I answered your question about Castillo's program.

The overall effects of never ending amounts of paperwork coupled with the service priority hardly encourage investigators to pursue illegal aliens inside the US. Internal policies and mandates seemed to reinforce the belief held by most investigators, that INS did not want them to fulfill their mission, at least aggressively. As this investigator summarized:

. . . paperwork "so damn many forms one of the many things that turn off investigators" investigators learn how to complete these forms expeditiously but they still create a tendency to avoid having to do it. " . . . part of the never-ending paperwork." The outcome of creating forms and paperwork causes the investigator to avoid having to do it and so may diminish motivation to appre-hend illegal aliens in the first place, or actively enforce the immigration laws.

FACTORS THAT AFFECT MORALE

Law enforcement officers share similar assumptions about mobility and pro-motion in their profession. In most instances, federal agents have higher pay and prestige than their counterparts at the state and local level. However, most law enforcement officers do not seek careers in law enforcement to make a lot of money. The recruit has alternative compensation in the form of a secure job, employee benefits, and the belief that one is serving the com-munity, and we may assume that agents share goals based on their similar backgrounds and qualifications. The legacy INS agents expected the same career opportunities as other federal criminal investigators, and assumed that opportunity for advancement existed beyond the journeyman level. As an organization, INS had to contend with efforts to enhance job satisfaction, and morale for all its employees. This is especially important when the agent reached journeyman level status, such as the GS-11 grade for legacy INS investigators. Investigators are mobility-oriented people and will be dissatis-fied with the idea of a dead-end job. If such a condition persists, members of the organization may lose motivation, become alienated, and most likely attempt to transfer to another agency that offers more advancement.

If these role behaviors fall below an adequate minimum, then the effective operation of the organization and, perhaps even its very survival, are in jeopar-dy.[8]

At the time, the government-wide hiring and promotions freeze essential-ly locked agents into their positions. As a result, their expectations of attain-ing a promotion was very low, even though getting the GS-12 is a standard expectation among most federal criminal investigators. This promotion in-cludes working more complex and interesting cases, which can lead to both recognition, and more promotions. The policies of the legacy INS followed a border patrol strategy in enforcing the immigration laws, and this made it more difficult to achieve success. Border patrol agents had lower journeyman grade levels than the investigators, and this factor justified keeping the inves-tigator journeyman level lower as well.

Most of the legacy INS investigators shared the feelings about promotion, incentive, and morale expressed in the following statements:

Investigators are nothing in this Service. The real positions are in personnel. They create the jobs. Many of the promotions work like this: they have someone they want, so they write the requirements of the job around that person's qualifications. That is how it really works. I've seen promotion folders with check marks next to some names. What do those marks mean? There are all sorts of techniques to work around the system which is supposed to be based on merit. Merit has very little to do with the selection process.

Until recently, my belief was that INS was not in opposition to its investigators, and had their interests at heart, and would not interfere with our operations. However, now we are under full assault by the Administration (1980), especially Investigations. We are facing dismantling, if they can get away with it, and they have pretty much gotten away with it through their policies on vehicle use and enforcement. I would strongly advise, at this date, to any investigator who could financially do it, to leave INS if he could find an opening in another agency. I never would have given that advice to anyone before. Of course, anyone who is in my position is sunk (GS-11) since no other agency wants you.

I think good morale is the situation where guys look forward to the casework assigned, to doing their work, volunteering. A sort of unselfish attitude. I feel morale is the worst since I've been on the job. I've seen it slowly deteriorate due to the restrictions placed on the job morale is past the point of being bad. Guys have given up, they don't give a shit, don't care, and just come in to pick up their paychecks. I know allot of guys who are trying to get out. I think the car situation instigated it, and the lack of GS-12's solidified it.

Another investigator comments on the promotion process:

It seems to be a mystery board in Washington, D. C. As far as rating investigators, when I came to INS it was understood that if you were border patrol, a *"good old boy"*, you were pretty much in good running for a promotion if you got to investigations. I think allot of it is subjective. I've seen dummies get *highly recommended* (annual evaluation rating) by their supervisors, and I've seen great investigators get *recommended.* As far as promotions in the future, it looks pretty bleak. There have been two GS-12's posted in the last year and a half. There are about 130 investigators in New York competing for these positions, not including people who can lateral over from outside of investigations, or from another agency. I would say that promotions, unless they go to an automatic field 12, are almost non-existent, and as that problem worsens, you will have more and more investigators seeking other jobs, or other career options.

Investigations is managed by incompetents. The basic problem I think is that they have hired a group of educated guys who can think. We sit down and ask ourselves why certain things should or should not be. The basic attitude of INS management is to be punitive. They feel that punishing you will increase productivity. What they fail to realize, in the case of New York, is that New York City is a unique city with a unique set of problems. They can't understand why the New York office does not run smoothly or conform, and compare our problems with some one-horse town out in Kansas, or El Paso, Texas.

The problems are multiplied in New York, but INS management does not seek to identify or address these problems. They just say that New York will fall into step with the rest of the country, or else. You take for example an investigator stationed in Hartford, Connecticut, compared with an investigator in New York City. An investigator in New York City has to commute to the office by public transportation, it takes him two hours to get into the office and two hours to get home, if he lives anywhere in the suburbs. Even if he lives in the surrounding city it still takes an hour or more to get into the office. Furthermore, it costs him $150 a month to commute. The same investigator in Hartford can drive into the office with his personal car in fifteen minutes and have a parking space waiting for him when he gets in. In this case, having a government car assigned to you not only enables you to do a better job and be more productive in New York City, it also becomes a matter of survival. But management does not even address that problem. They simply go by the book and say that government cars are not for commuting. The rules are meant to avoid misuse and abuse and I agree but let's face it, without a government car you can't really do an effective job. The rules work great in small towns, but when you try to apply them to New York City they do not work as well. I'm looking to get out. I can't afford to stay here. I'm going to school now and I intend to go into another career as soon as I can. There is no incentive left here at INS, no promotion potential, and no job satisfaction. I don't know any investigator here who likes what he is doing, or what is going on. My advice is to get out if you can.

GS-12 investigators made the following statements:

I wouldn't consider myself as being more successful, or a better investigator. My GS-12 came from being at the right place, at the right time. If I had come to INS late, I would still be a GS-11.

I'm not happy here. I've got a total of twelve years to go with INS, and then I can retire. I intend to stick it out for the pension, but I wish I would have started at something else. I cannot afford to leave now, because I have too much federal time. I have no intention to apply for a supervisor job. I'm tapped out, and I've got twelve years to go.

I was told that it is not what you guys can do, not how many criminal cases you can prosecute, it is how long you have been here. No cases, no problems. Small cases, small problems. Big cases, big problems. If you want to get ahead, you become a *"good old boy,"* a throwback to the border patrol days. They are dedicated men and women and all that, but the basic mentality, the way they perceive things, is considerably different from what we have to deal with.

There are enough criminal aliens, and subversives for every investigator to work for twenty years, with no problem. Why they spend time concentrating on the dishwasher, when you could be out there looking for real criminals, I don't understand it. In Subversives (unit), it is the same thing as in any other section. They immediately try to play down an investigation, if they think it could become notorious. In other words, if you have a terrorist, they say let the FBI do it. They try to play it down. I'm not talking about my immediate supervisor, but the general policy, let the FBI handle it, don't get involved. I'm talking about matters clearly within out jurisdiction. In fact, I know where there is a guy, there is an allegation that he is a Polish communist, and I can't get a car to investigate it. I mean it is ridiculous. So, I don't give a shit, if they don't. I mean they won't give you a car to go and get that guy. Another thing that is very bad for morale is this no promotion thing. No matter how hard you work, you are not going to get promoted. This is unheard of in any other industry, or job. What kind of shit is that?

Most of the investigators believed that upper management would not support them if problems arose during an investigation. They further perceived that their actions would be subject to criticism, even if they did nothing wrong. The respondents believed that if they investigated cases aggressively, the likelihood of encountering problems increased. Criminals that believe they are targets of an investigation sometimes attempt to divert attention away from their activities by making allegations against the investigator. Most of the investigators believed that INS managers would entertain even the wildest of allegations against them, and this can easily cause an investigator to avoid "getting involved." Such factors as these contribute to lowering morale. As one investigator stated:

We were involved in a case with about fifteen different subjects, involving cocaine, guns, and the rest of it. The cases were tried, and the people were found guilty, or plead guilty. Later, through channels, by one of the defendant's attorneys, an allegation was made that I lied under oath, that I did not act in the proper manner as an immigration officer, and that I fraudulently submitted evidence. I was called in on my day off by the ADDI, to come in and defend myself on the charges. I called the US Attorney, and she gave me a *good guy* letter which indicated that I acted properly. Later, I submitted that letter, and you know what I got? Not even a thank you, or I'm sorry. But they were *hot to trot* to call me in on a bullshit letter from an attorney.

Agents also perceived that officer morale was low because policies placed a low priority on interior enforcement. They also believed that the policy makers did not have an accurate appraisal of the seriousness of the illegal alien problem.

DEA can always go after illegal drugs, ATF (Alcohol, Tobacco and Firearms) can always go after the illegal guns, the FBI will always be able to go after bank robbers and white collar criminals, the IRS can always go after tax frauds. Nobody is ever going to come out and oppose these kinds of enforcement efforts. You will never hear an Administration come out and say, *for the next four years, dope is okay.* That is exactly what this Administration (1980) did with INS.

Supervisors assign cases to investigators based on their grade level, and they are careful to avoid assigning complex cases because they fear that the investigator will request a "desk audit," or reclassification to a higher grade. If a GS-11 investigator develops a complex criminal case, management will reassign it to a GS-12 investigator. Sometimes, lower grade investigators do develop complex cases, and this offers them an opportunity to bargain for a promotion, or become a top candidate when a promotion becomes available. Due to the promotion freeze, the desk audit became one of the only ways to get promoted. A GS-12 agent is supposed to develop criminal cases, and this also enables further advancement in the agency. This may also cause some conflict with first line supervisors, and make them less reluctant to reassign complex cases developed by lower grade agents. Obviously, this strategy does not enhance motivation, and lowers morale as well.

Sometime in 1982, I was assigned a high-profile case. At the time, I was a GS-11 investigator, and management assigned me what I considered a highly sensitive case. It was a challenge, and I put everything I had into the case. Among other factors, the case involved dealing with foreign dignitaries and consulates, as well as complex and sensitive contact with other federal, and local law enforcement agencies. The scope of the investigation was immense. The target was an internationally known, powerful, and wealthy individual. And I was a lone investigator that had to beg for a government car to make an arrest, or conduct surveillance. I tried to deal with all the policy restrictions, but I believe INS did not want me to do what was necessary to prosecute the target, or his organization, and I became fed up with the way the case was going. Since I was doing what I considered GS-14 level work, I put in for a desk audit for reclassification to a GS-12. I really believed that I had a chance, because I knew that the work I was doing fit the description of the higher grade. The desk audit denied the promotion, and I did not get the GS-12. As a reward, INS took me off the case, and reassigned the investigation to a GS-12 investigator. Eventually I was promoted to a GS-12, but the experience left me disillusioned. I had mixed emotions about what happened. On the one hand, it was a major case, and could have resulted in my successfully completing a difficult investigation. On the other hand, it was obvious that INS did not want to pursue the case vigorously. It was another example of how INS failed to take advantage of an opportunity, probably because it feared political, or media repercussions.

Most of the investigators are college educated, and attitudes linking education and promotion have an impact on officer morale. My experience may illustrate this issue.

> During my initial interview, the interviewer stated concerns about my educational level and job aspirations. Why would someone with a Master of Arts Degree want to be a criminal investigator with INS? The interviewer told me

that I possessed the qualifications for the job, but perhaps I was overqualified. The interviewer's main concern was that I would seek other employment later.

Law enforcement agencies equate professionalism with education, and there is a tendency to recruit more educated personnel to make the job more professional.[9] Unfortunately, there is a perception that too much education can be counterproductive to the law enforcement mission. This is especially so in police work, where mundane and routine tasks predominate everyday activities. Most of the investigators share the sentiments in the following statement:

When I told my supervisor that I was completing my master's degree he frowned and said, "you'll be sorry you got your masters. After *they* find out, it will hurt instead of help your career. *They* don't want educated people in the Service. They ask too many questions, and cause too many problems."

An example of issues that are associated with morale included the Cuban program, where investigators were detailed to assist in the processing of immigrant applications. The numerous loopholes in a complex immigration law cause backlogs to flourish. Service personnel control these programs, and when investigators are detailed to work there, they are under the authority of the service personnel. The following extract from an interview with an investigator who served on the Cuban detail reflects the conflicts between service and enforcement. It also shows the service priority, over interior enforcement operations.

. . . when we got down to Arkansas, there was a change in . . . and there were people there who were going to be first, second, third line supervisors. There was to be an interview procedure . . . investigators would handle cases that were problems, where first line inspectors said this guy should be excluded. After we were on duty for about 24 hours, management came down and said, "It looks to us like investigations isn't working hard enough, you're going to perform both the first line section function, the primary section function, and the secondary function." We said ok, fine, they're afraid of us sitting on our asses. It perhaps reflects a problem with their mentality, as much as their desire for greater efficiency. We noted shortly after we arrived . . . that there were tremendous problems in regards to security, the alien state of mind, the safety of service employees, . . . as well as other personnel problems. The government did not want employees to be taking a day off. They wanted employees to work 12 hours a day, 7 days a week, for the duration of the project. After a list of grievances was presented to the manager, the manager agreed the employees could have a day off. Nothing was done about security. It had become public knowledge that Cuban aliens were breaking into employee's cars. It was also known that local hire employees were bringing weapons onto the base, leaving them in their cars, and at least two weapons were stolen from employees. We were having small skirmishes several times a week, with

Cubans who would rush the barricades, and were surrounding the refugee compound, knock down the saw horses that were used there to keep them in their compound, and would take the ropes that were hung between the saw horses, would break up the saw horses and use the wood to throw at the MPs, and the buildings, and stones at the buildings as well. On several occasions, different people who were working there went to management, and said, "hey, listen you've got to do something about this situation. You're going to have riots here. Cubans don't know how long they're going to be here. They don't' like the food. They don't like the fact that it's hot, nothing's being done to . . . you must do something or you must really secure this place, or you're gonna have riots!" On three different occasions, the two processing buildings that were being used by the service had to be evacuated. Cubans began throwing stones at the buildings . . . and we had to evacuate those buildings. When the buildings were evacuated, the service employees were not evacuated to another building several hundred yards away, they were evacuated in the three cases that I had seen, to large open fields behind the officer's club . . . In other words, they were taken from inside four walls and a floor, and put into a wide-open area where they were immediately accessible to the Cubans. If the Cubans just decided we're gonna run . . . On one occasion when one of these little skirmishes broke out, we took some investigators from our old unit, down to the other building where the skirmish was going on, to help break it up . . . Management officials said this is not your function . . . you have no right to do that, we're providing security, and I said to the management official, in fact, you're not providing security . . . I said let's go outside, show me where there are MPs. And the management official said, "So they're not here right now," and I asked why aren't they here right now, and the GS-13 supervisor says, "Well they're somewhere else, they're down the street, we just sent them to service," and I said, "And so the point you're making then is that if there is a disturbance down the street, there's no protection for the people up here in this building!" And the buildings we were using were 1000 yards apart. There's no protection for service employees, or government employees, local hires or permanent employees, whatever. At Building A if there is a disturbance at Building B, and vice versa. So, in effect, you are saying that the government can't provide security at all times under all circumstances. And of course, we had to agree to disagree because the service officials there wouldn't make waves, wouldn't say to the emergency federal management agency, or to the army, or to the present staff, that we will not process people unless you provide our employees with a secure environment in which to work. Their main concern was processing through as many Cubans as physically possible in a 24-hour period, no matter what the cost for the health and safety of the employees. As a result of that philosophy, and the failure of management officials to do anything about the lack of security, or to do anything in terms of securing the compound where the Cubans were supposed to remain, the status quo continued for another week or two, until there came a point where we actually had so severe a riot that a 1000 aliens left the base, three buildings were burnt down, and unknown number of Cubans were injured, an unknown number of MPs were injured, their weapons, and their sticks taken from them, and a few service employees were also hurt. Now, what we had was a situation that was totally avoidable, if the service reacted rapidly and said you must secure that

compound with barbed wire, you must put up enough security, enough barricades, restrain the aliens, they could have avoided the injuries to the Cubans,
the unknown injuries towards the MPs, the unknown injuries towards to a few
service employees, they could have avoided the destruction of several buildings there on the base. Who knows what they cost the government. The bill
was 25 years ago, but we do know that it's gonna cost them a hell of a lot more
to replace those buildings now. All of that happened because the people in
management in INS were afraid to put their foot down. And that's the whole
service in a capsule. People in management here are so afraid of making waves
and saying "Damnit! I want to do my job right, and I want to serve my
employees at the same time," that your job and your neck are put on the line
every day. We are a tool of the State Department. We are a tool of Customs,
when something looks bad. And anything good that comes out, another agency
takes credit for.

Morale is clearly an important variable to consider in analyzing the issues
discussed in this study. It was the key determinant for legacy INS investigators in defining their perceptions of mission and task. Since the original
study, following up on perceptions about morale after 911 was simply a
matter of asking agents to compare current perceptions of morale with perceptions they had prior to the shift to DHS. The agents that provided information about this shift in perceptions seemed to agree that morale was still a
problem at INS right up until its merger into DHS. At the time, most agents
indicated that it was still too early to determine whether morale would improve or not. An ICE agent stated:

Morale has never really been good. There has always been friction between
management and the troops. I think management is just trying to manage its
people but going about it the wrong way. The rank and file just see it as
someone just trying to bust chops. It may be more an issue of personalities. As
other agencies have journeyman GS-13 there may be a feeling of being sec-
ond-class in the federal arena. The fact that INS agents are Journeyman GS-12
and Senior Field GS-13 positions are rare, there is not much room for advancement.

Another ICE agent commented about morale as follows:

Currently, it is confused due to the transfer to DHS. Morale has never been
high. HQ (Headquarters) leadership is dismal.

The transition from the 1980s through the merger in 2003 and thereafter
can best be summarized in the following statement by a former ICE agent:

Still an accurate job description for most CIs (criminal investigators), but there
are now substantially more criminal prosecutions of INS violators than in the
past. When interviewed in 1980, I stated that " . . . we don't get very many

criminal prosecution cases because it's too lengthy and time-consuming to make one case." Since then, however, criminal prosecution of INS violators has become a standard element in every CIs Performance Work Plan, and in my case, I've worked nothing but criminal cases since I was assigned to OCDETF (Organized Crime Drug Enforcement Task Force) . . . Since last interviewed in 1980, INS has become an integral part of several multi-agency task forces including the OCDETF, High Intensity Drug Trafficking Area Task Force (HIDTA), and the Joint Terrorism Task Force (JTTF) and, while there will always be non-criminal (administrative) cases to work, it's encouraging to see that INS (now ICE) is finally taking a proactive stance in aggressively arresting, and prosecuting criminal aliens, and major INS violators (aggravated felons, alien smugglers, drug dealers, suspected terrorists and their associates, etc.). Re: the two-fold mission of INS: With the abolition of INS in March 2003, this is no longer a problem. The former INS Investigations Division has merged with the former USCS Investigations Division and is now called Immigration & Customs Enforcement (ICE). A pure enforcement agency, similar in structure to the FBI and DEA, each ICE District is headed by a Special Agents in Charge (SAC) who has a single, focused law enforcement mission, and the means to support it (unlike our former INS structure where a District Director was in charge of both the enforcement, and service components, and could whimsically allocate/re-allocate human, financial and material resources as he saw fit.) While the merger with USCIS is a great step forward for INS, growing pains are inevitable and I'm sure more unique problems will develop as the new agency continues to reshape itself. Right now, though, it's far too early to tell what those problems might be.

Other issues associated with morale include task and mission. Since ICE is not in the same chain of command as immigration service functions, one might assume that agents would no longer have to defer to service in completing their tasks. ICE is supposed to focus on criminal investigations, primarily on criminal aliens, or the other initiatives in ICE. Legacy INS agents continued to perform INS functions after the transition to DHS, but reportedly cross-training, and new hires were to alleviate the conflicts between the immigration and customs special agents. Eventually both legacy customs, and immigration agents should be the same. With the passage of time, and the hiring of new agents perhaps the old allegiances will begin to blur, and one unified identity should surface. Yet, as previously indicated the San Bernardino incident suggests that service and enforcement still have a problem regarding immigration law enforcement.

CODES ON FACTORS AFFECTING MORALE [10]

Buck upper-management

Investigators perceived their managers as unwilling to aggressively fight for them. This was most obvious when investigators submitted routine requests for resources, warrants, or other matters needed to complete their perceived mission.

Commissioner of Immigration

Investigators considered most of the Commissioners weak on interior enforcement and the Investigations program. The only Commissioner that seemed to encourage the Investigator mission was Leonard Chapman during the mid-1970s. Investigators experienced higher morale and apprehensions during this period.

Executive courage

Executive courage was a phrase used by a Section Chief (manager) during a payday meeting. Overall, investigators were instructed to follow case management procedures ritually approved by supervisors with the sole purpose of avoiding problems.

It's like pulling teeth

Investigators viewed the mountain of paperwork and restrictions as impediments to their perceived mission.

It will be buried

Investigators were not encouraged to develop related cases or pursue unrelated (but criminal or mission related) tasks and to focus only on assigned cases, completions and high number of closings. If leads were developed that were not directly related to the case, the investigator was supposed to transfer the case to the section that worked such cases.

All they can get you for is disagreeing with you

This comment was also made during a payday meeting wherein the Section Chief was encouraging investigators to follow the safe path of least resistance in case management. In this regard, mundane and relatively useless leads should be covered and cases closed expeditiously if they were not deemed productive. Many criminal investigations are time consuming and require time to complete. Supervisors did not encourage the criminal investigative strategy and preferred quantity over quality. The main concern was to cover yourself and the rationale was "all they can get you for is disagreeing with you . . ."

Always been in enforcement except for a brief stint with inspections

During a payday meeting, the Assistant District Director for Investigations (ADDI, head of the Investigations branch) attempted to identify with Investigators by stating that he was in enforcement throughout his career with INS "except for a time when he was with Inspections." This bias showed the Border patrol mentality that permeated the legacy INS since Inspections is an enforcement branch of INS. The ADDI was a former border patrol agent and shared the perspective that only the border patrol was worthy of law enforcement status.

Piece of cheese

Salary checks are distributed during the payday meetings where policy instructions are also discussed. Investigators compared this process to the "the piece of cheese" given to a rat in an experimental maze to encourage acceptable behavior.

Managers/Supervisors

Investigators viewed managers and supervisors as impediments to their task.

Paperwork/Part of the never-ending paperwork/So damn many forms one of the many things that turn off investigators

Investigators viewed paperwork as another restriction and impediment to their perceptions of task and mission.

Promotion

Promotion to a GS-13 was rare in the legacy INS although most criminal investigators in other federal agencies become journeyman GS-13 level investigators. The disparity and lack of available higher-grade positions contributed to lower morale and high attrition rates at the legacy INS.

Recognition

Investigators believed that workers should be recognized for doing a good job. They also believed that investigators did not receive any recognition, or that the agency promoted its own recognition for the work completed overall carefully excluding the investigations branch in the description.

Whatever good you do you get shot down for

The investigator considered enforcement, especially criminal investigation, as the main task that investigators should be completing. Investigators believed management discouraged their efforts to complete such tasks in an agency that preferred completion of low-level administrative functions and service related duties. Many of the problems experienced by investigators had to do with the issues listed above. The conflict between service and enforcement and the service priority contributed to these problems.

Verbal Cue: Morale

Morale is perceived as a combination of mission, supervision, training, policy directives and promotion. Overall, morale was low in the legacy INS and continued through the transition to DHS.

I'm just biding my time

Most investigators indicated a willingness to transfer to other agencies if the opportunity surfaced. They would continue to mull through the daily routines in order to survive but always were on the lookout for opportunities to transfer to another law enforcement agency. In such an environment, motivation to do a good job is effectively stifled by the practices of management and the policies that came from headquarters.

LANGUAGE: INVESTIGATIVE JARGON AND POLICING

The legacy INS investigators used special jargon to describe their perceptions about task. Investigators tended to play down their educational achievements, and they preferred to mirror the traditional perception of the law enforcement officer held by the "old timers," who usually had less education. Old timers considered above average education a hindrance to doing good law enforcement. They perceived the intellectual as incapable of understanding the law of the street. Media stereotypes of academics and intellectuals contribute to such perceptions, and these stereotypes include the absent-minded professor, or the liberal social worker.

Although investigators did not use the term "rabbi"[11] extensively, they did make references to individuals that received a promotion because they had one. Investigators made comments such as, "How was he connected?" Or, "Who did he know?" when referring to individuals that received promotions, but did not appear to merit them.

Investigators used the terms "hairbag" and "dirtbag" quite often. The context determines the meanings of such terms, and imbues the individual so characterized. A hairbag is incompetent, or ineffective in conducting investigations. Hairbags are lazy, goof-offs that do not have an interest in law enforcement activities. They might also be sympathetic to the illegal alien, or not consider their main task to be criminal investigations. Dirtbags are individuals with low moral character. Investigators rarely refer to other officers as dirtbags, except jokingly. Some of the individuals that investigators considered to be dirtbags included: coworkers that are "company men" that are not trustworthy, corrupt individuals without principles or integrity, and employees that did not share a sense of fraternity with the officer corps, or the investigator mission. Investigators also considered serious law violators such as murderers, rapists, drug dealers, and pedophiles dirtbags.

Investigators frequently use the term "asshole."

> The asshole—creep, bigmouth, bastard, animal, mope, rough, jerk off, clown, scumbag, wiseguy, phony, idiot, shithead, bum, fool, or any of a number of anatomical, oral, or incestuous terms—is part of every policeman's worldpolice tend to view their occupational world as comprised exhaustively of three types of categories(1) *suspicious persons*—those whom the police have reason to believe may have committed a serious offense; (2) *assholes*—those who do not accept the police definition of the situation; and *(3) know nothings*—those who are not either of the first two categories but are not police and therefore, according to the police, cannot know what the police are about. [12]

Investigative work is similar to police patrol activities, and both identify with the law enforcement ethic that focuses on apprehending criminals. However, only a small percentage of the time spent is spent doing real police work. [13] Police Officers perform mostly maintenance of order activity, and agents perform mostly tasks involving the apprehension of illegal aliens. Using the term asshole allows the officer an opportunity to voice frustrations in a hostile environment.

> Since real police work is seldom available, marginally legitimate arrests of assholes provide a patrolman excitement and the opportunity to engage one's valued skills. [14]

In their daily work activities, agents confronted at least three different categories of people on the street: (1) citizens—individuals that are born in the US, or become citizens through judicial naturalization; (2) legal permanent resident aliens—individuals authorized to reside in the US. For purposes of this discussion, this category also includes temporary visitor aliens, or nonimmigrant aliens in status; and (3) illegal aliens—individuals that are in the US in violation of the INA. One can view the categories along a continuum, wherein investigators have more discretion (power) in their dealings with illegals, less with legal aliens, and the least with citizens of the US.

By law, all aliens must carry alien registration, and if they fail to do so they are subject to arrest and prosecution. As a policy, INS did not consider such violations serious enough to warrant prosecution. Although a misdemeanor, the failure to carry alien registration was an offense the agency had the discretion to automatically decline prosecution without contacting the US Attorney's office. Nevertheless, this offense gave the agent an opportunity to deal with assholes on the street, or aliens who intentionally failed to carry registration, or who were uncooperative. An investigator encounters such individuals all the time, and during questioning usually asks about the interviewee about their immigration status, even though the witness might not be the target of the investigation. Most people want to avoid involvement, and often refuse identifying themselves to the investigator, but immigration agents have the authority to question any person in the US about their immigration status. If the alien refuses to produce evidence of lawful status, the investigator might consider that person to be an asshole, especially if the alien is in status. Most aliens know they must carry and produce alien registration when requested by an immigration officer.

As previously indicated, anyone that fails to recognize lawful authority can be a suspicious person, asshole, or a know-nothing. Because of the complexity of law, police officers might confront all three kinds of people. On the other hand, an agent confronts many citizens that might be "know-nothings," not subject to their jurisdiction, and aliens that are here legally, or illegally. Rarely are illegal aliens ignorant of their immigration status, and failure to carry alien registration places the violator in the suspicious person category. The investigator will most likely treat the permanent resident alien who refuses to produce alien registration as an asshole, because there is difficulty in placing the person in the know-nothing category. Without doubt, investigators consider an illegal alien that questions their authority deserving of the asshole characterization.

Another common phrase used in law enforcement is "cover your ass." The phrase implies that the control agent must deal with the possibility of adverse actions resulting from official duties. To some extent, it represents a life style for some law enforcement personnel, but is also generally applied to most operators in many industries. Discretion and manager-operator relations dictate the degree to which the cover your ass syndrome operates. Anyone can be subject to sanctions if they make a mistake, intentionally violate rules, and more importantly if they are accused of wrongdoing, whether the allegations are true, or not.

The investigator does not always base discretion on rules, procedures, and policies. As previously stated, one is more likely to find procedures on what not to do, rather than on what to do. This is characteristic of police organizations where control agents are expected to produce, regardless of the consequences that might occur. The nature of investigative work precipitates hostile client responses, and the agency wants the operator to work within guidelines to minimize mistakes and their consequences. Investigators believe that managers blame mistakes on failure to follow organizational policy and rules. However, when they make mistakes, the operator must "manufacture *post facto* a legally defensible account of his action in order to, in the vernacular of the day, *cover his ass*."[15]

One might argue that if operators do what they should, then the need to *cover your ass* disappears, or at least diminishes significantly. However, the control agent deals with unpredictable variables, and a *cover your ass* philosophy develops. Furthermore, the degree to which operators adhere to this philosophy depends greatly on how the managers want tasks completed. An organization that demands strict adherence to official rules inevitably creates routine mechanisms that push control agents toward accepting a *cover your ass* philosophy. Such organizations are inherently punitive, and routinely proclaim edicts on what *not to do*. As one investigator so aptly described this philosophy,

> I will say one additional thing. There is a philosophy throughout the management of the service of making no waves whatsoever, either to save more money to do our job, effectively whether it's the job of cranking out petition approvals, or closing out insignificant rather than significant smuggling cases. And there is just a philosophy, don't make any waves, don't attract any unnecessary publicity, don't do anything that will cause the government, or the present administration of the government to be subjected to unfavorable attention, or criticism from ethnic or political organizations, that might cater to illegal aliens in the society, or not necessarily illegal aliens, but groups of immigrants in the society. They fear any attention from the public at all, whether it's good or bad, but especially bad publicity. So, we're shackled, we're shut down, the Census shut us down for business. Without even attempting to justify the law enforcement functions of this service, or to say our men will not use Census information . . . this information will not be available to immigration. It's just to say that we were sold out before we get a chance to do anything.

Managers can easily "cover their own asses" by mandating that all personnel "go by the book." Obviously, if a control agent "screws up," the supervisor can easily escape reprisals from superiors, and put the blame on the investigator. This is accomplished by pointing out that the investigator did not follow the rules. Such top-down mandates are often forced on personnel. Broad mandates cover everything, but they do not take the practical aspects of task into account. Individuals understand that restraining law enforcement is important in a civil society, and control agents understand this fact as well. To complete law enforcement tasks in a civil society, managers and operators must cope with the adverse effects of their actions. The federal assault on the Branch Davidian[16] compound in Waco, Texas is an extreme example of what could occur when the situation becomes insurmountable, and normal strategies fail to resolve a conflict between law-breakers and the police.

If an investigative team arrests a female, headquarters is contacted immediately and advised that a female is in custody. The location, time, and odometer reading at time of custody is reported, and the estimated time of arrival is given. Investigators do this to control for possible allegations of mistreatment, or sexual assault by the female in custody. Hopefully, the information provided will document a direct and timely route back to the office. It further serves as evidence to refute any allegations of misconduct.

The investigator cites any physical force used to detain a suspect. Investigators record such information to alert detention personnel that the detainee is a risk of flight. It also *covers the ass* of the arresting officer. The recorded data describes how the investigator used necessary force, and serves as a defense against allegations of mistreatment, or unnecessary force if the alien decides to sue INS or the investigator, for excessive use of force.

Investigators also cover their ass by using careful terminology in their reports of investigations. An investigator can state that he made several attempts to interview a witness who refused to speak with the investigator. With some perseverance, an investigator can usually obtain the interview with most witnesses. The investigator has discretion in determining the amount of persistence required. Usually, the practicality of closing cases, minimizing hostile encounters, and avoiding possible repercussions, tempers such persistence. If a witness states, "I'd rather not talk about it," the investigator just leaves it at that. In the report, the investigator indicates that the witness refused to discuss the matter under investigation. Since most of the investigative work involves administrative law enforcement and character investigations, the *criminal* investigator usually opts for routine encounters and dispositions.

I was fortunate to obtain an interview with Martin Ficke, the Special agents in Charge of the New York Office, Department of Homeland Security, ICE. In this interview, SAC Ficke describes the then status of ICE, and covers some of the aforementioned issues.

INTERVIEW WITH SAC MARTIN FICKE, DHS-ICE[17]

The following interview was conducted in 2004 during the George Bush administration. SAC Ficke was kind enough to offer an interview with the author, and the interview provided up to date insights about how the agency planned to implement its mission. It should be noted that SAC Ficke, and the author worked together at the legacy INS, and there was excellent rapport between the interviewer and the interviewee. In retrospect, the information that SAC Ficke provided involved an accurate portrayal of the initial plans of the agency, but obviously through the perceptions of a manager, not a field agent. This would imply a top-down view of operations.

Interviewer: What about the new programs such as Detention Officer and criminal aliens? Are you doing that at all?

SAC Ficke: Clearly we are doing it. The goal is to get out of that. The direction from headquarters is to get out of that and we're working very closely with Detention and Removal to transition that over to them. And, there is on the books, we are attempting at the point to slowly withdraw ourselves from that and allow Detention and Removal to take over that function. The problem is we just can't leave now until they have an opportunity to fill various vacancies that have been unfilled for many years. And a lot of those are INS agents which I think are 1801's (General Investigators), which are people who have been hired to basically work in jails. On March 1, 2003, we left Treasury and they left Justice and went to DHS. On June 8, we consolidated the offices of investigations at INS and Customs and broke away Customs and Border Protection (CBP) which is uniformed inspectors which is Customs INS and one Border patrol and of course Citizenship and Immigration Services which would be Naturalization.

Interviewer: What about the legacy INS, and Customs credentials?

SAC Ficke: Everybody's got the same credentials (they had before the merger). We have not switched over yet. Nobody has. There's some talk as to whether we will be called Immigration Customs Enforcement or whether we're going to be Investigations Criminal Enforcement. Before they start to issue new credentials, badges, we're trying to make sure we get that correct. Now they are trying to get it changed to Investigations Criminal Enforcement. There are about 5500 special agents in ICE, 3,500 from customs and 2,000 from INS.

Interviewer: When the agents go out on a case how do they identify themselves?

SAC Ficke: When they go out on a case they identify themselves as ICE agents even though we carry customs or immigration credentials. We still refer to each other inside the building as the legacy INS and legacy customs. The point of perspective you need to understand sometimes but even that every day that goes by we are getting less and less of that.

Interviewer: What types of cases are you working on?

SAC Ficke: Our number one priority is terrorism. We have made a much more significant contribution to the Joint Terrorist Task Force (JTTF). Clearly made a much more significant contribution to the FBI. As far as personnel who work in the JTTF on a daily basis, NYPD has as many as the FBI, we are the third largest agency outside of the FBI and we are moving to increase that slowly but surely we will have an ASAC (Assistant Special Agents in Charge) there.

Interviewer: One of the key points in my first book was about morale. What struck me was that the legacy INS journeymen were grade 12 and the customs journeyman were grade 13. Since the merger to DHS was there an equalization? Are INS agents now GS 13 grade?

SAC Ficke: Yes, they are. I have not personally noticed, but talking with (other managers) the legacy INS agents experienced a drastic change. We are going through the paperwork making sure we have not missed anybody. This occurred in the last pay period.

Interviewer: How does that affect the legacy customs agents? How do they feel?

SAC Ficke: What do they care? It doesn't affect them at all.

Interviewer: There was an article I read, and rumors that customs agents look down on INS agents.

SAC Ficke: I think there's some of that. Let's face it we have some . . . in the world, but every day it's getting closer so that it is indistinguishable who we are.

Interviewer: You feel that things are good, and getting better?

SAC Ficke: Absolutely. I am very positive about it. To be honest with you I think that the greatest jolt, and I can tell you this that happened this year. The biggest effect I've seen in the operation of customs, pretty much the customs operation maintained doing what we are doing. INS side has money for informants, and they are obtaining an education on how to go about requesting resources. INS side is learning how to do the paperwork.

Interviewer: What about your relationship with the US Attorney's office?

SAC Ficke: The agent, or the supervisor calls the AUSA. We went out to the US Attorney's office and sat down with the SDNY, EDNY and told them that this is DHS, this is how we do things. They were very receptive. I can't recall one case on INS side that I got a call over there where I can't understand why you guys won't prosecute from simple reentry after deportation to a document case. There is a significant number of immigration related cases. Document, criminal entry after deportation, we have a gang initiative, some narcotics work as it relates to alien smuggling. Those are big issues now.

Interviewer: What about the so-called "sanctuary laws" where police don't cooperate with the federal authorities on immigration?

SAC Ficke: We get calls all the time from police, NYPD. They don't call us, they call the Law Enforcement Support Center and they filter it down to us and we get calls, and we respond to them.

Interviewer: But, what if someone calls about an illegal alien that is not criminal?

SAC Ficke: If it is within, we have our specific concentration now on alien's form specially designated countries, countries associated with terrorism, we respond zero tolerance policy on that. Now, if you call us on a Mexican dishwasher that is not our priority. If it is connected to a criminal investigation we run out and deal with it, but if we encounter an illegal alien we bring him in, or we pass them in if we think they are going to come in, like we used to. If we bring them in, we process them, but they are going to walk (be released). It happens, but it is more of an aggravation, because you put the guy right back on the street. Customs guys here thinking all I have to do is call INS guys, and they walk away from it. Some of that is going on, because they haven't been trained yet. Which is the way they process aliens, now it's all electronic. We don't have the capability of doing that yet in this building; as soon as we get it, that is over and done with. The processing is all done in the computers electronically down at 26 Federal Plaza. We haven't trained the legacy customs people to do it yet. We're going to train our people on it moving all our agents to this building within the next six months. Altogether, in New York we have about 400 agents, of which 150 is legacy INS, give or take a few.

Interviewer: What about the ACAP (Alien Criminal Apprehension Program)?

SAC Ficke: ACAP is operational. Agents respond to police referrals if it is within specially designated countries (terrorist related). All aggravated felons, and absconders as in the IRP (criminal aliens in institutions). We have agents in the prisons, but I got to tell you we're trying to get them out of there. We don't consider that (type of work) to be 1811 (criminal investigation). We're desperately trying to get them out of there.

Interviewer: What percentage of your agents is working in prisons?

SAC Ficke: About 40 agents. We're staying with it until we can transition to D & R (Detention and Removal). Headquarters is involved. I am the only SAC that worked on both sides (INS and Customs). I had ten years with INS and over twenty years with Customs and I am very optimistic. Just like everything else in life, we don't have everyone on the same page, but every day we're getting there, moving more and more there. I could leave this job tomorrow, but there are more days I want to stay in the agency, because I like where we're going.

Interviewer: The most important criticism about Washington, is that policy makers have abandoned the interior enforcement of immigration laws. What can we do about it?

SAC Ficke: You've got to have more resources to do that, more responsibility, more areas they're getting more people. That is why we concentrate on criminal aliens.

Interviewer: That is a neat resolution. It pretty much avoids the problem.

SAC Ficke: We are not looking for work. We have more good INS customs cases that we can work. This summer we have other things on our plate—the Republican National Convention, the economic summit in Georgia. We even have people in Iraq doing money laundering, and art cases.

Interviewer: What is your opinion about amnesty for illegal aliens?

SAC Ficke: The way I see it, if there is a documented need for a job, fill it! Why not? I think there has to be some degree where the employer has to document it that an lpr (legal permanent resident alien), or US citizen can't fill it. I have no problem with that.

We are actually sitting down with New York State tomorrow, and we are going to propose that they cross-designate Department of Corrections to do the jail work, not for us, but with us, until we can fill our vacancies.

NOTES

1. Roger Schaefer, "Law Enforcer, Peace Keeper, Servicer: Role Alternatives for Policemen," *Journal of Police Science and Administration,* 1978. 6:324-335.

2. Jerome H., Skolnick, *Justice Without Trial: Law Enforcement in Democratic Society,* (New York: John Wiley and Sons, 1966), p. 44.

3. James Q. Wilson, *Varieties of Police Behavior: The Management of Law and Order in Eight Communities,* (Massachusetts: Harvard University Press, 1968).

4. Wilson, 1968, p. 20.

5. Murray Edelman, "Power and Symbol in Administrative Regulation," in *Social Problems and Public Policy: Inequality and Justice, ed.,* by Lee Rainwater, Chicago: Aldine Publishing Company, 1974, p. 20.

6. The Green Line Podcast, Episode 68: Blue Plate Special, starts at 34:00 minutes, (March 11, 2016) Accessed on July 5, 2016, http://www.bpunion.org/index.php/newsroom/the-green-line-podcast

7. Joe Schaeffer, "Paperwork Hampers Border Patrol as Illegals Flood Into US," *Newsmax,* (June 9, 2014), Accessed on July 6, 2016, http://www.newsmax.com/Newsfront/Henry-Cuellar-Texas-border-paperwork/2014/06/09/id/576016/

8. Edward W. Lehman, "Opportunity, Mobility and Satisfaction Within an Industrial Organization," *Social Forces,* 1968. 46: 492.

9. Arthur Niederhoffer. *A Study of Police Cynicism,* New York: New York University, Ph. D. Dissertation, 1963.

10. Codes were created using Atlas/ti software.

11. Niederhoffer, 1963.

12. John Van Maanen, "The Asshole," in Peter K. Manning and J. Van Maanen, *Policing: A View from the Street,* California: Goodyear Publishing Company, 1978, pp. 221-223.

13. Van Maanen, 1978.

14. Van Maanen, 1978, p. 235.

15. Van Maanen, 1978, p. 232.

16. Frontline, "Waco: The Inside Story," Accessed on July 28, 2016, http://www.pbs.org/wgbh/pages/frontline/waco/timeline.html

17. Martin Ficke, Interview by George Weissinger, New York, NY, April 29, 2004.

Chapter Seven

Internal and External Relations

THE COMMISSIONERS: SERVICE VS. ENFORCEMENT

The Commissioners and Secretaries of the agency are appointed by the President of the US, and their backgrounds, for the most part, coincide with the ideological and political views of the President. In May 1977, President Jimmy Carter appointed Leonel J. Castillo as Commissioner of INS, and from that time through the last Commissioner, James Ziglar, who was appointed by President George Bush, and Jeh Johnson[1] who was appointed Secretary of the DHS by President Obama on December 23, 2013, the service priority dominated immigration law enforcement. Although the statutes and laws relating to immigration enforcement inside the US clearly state that illegal aliens are subject to apprehension and removal, and that immigration officers can remove them, the entire apparatus of the agency seemed to freeze in place.

The large number of apprehensions of illegal aliens is a deceptive statistic. Over 90% of these apprehensions are on the Mexico-US border by the border patrol. As indicated later on in this study, most of these arrests end in a voluntary departure (returns) of the alien, who can simply turn around and make another attempt the very same day. Similarly, even though DHS has ICE to enforce the interior immigration laws, it appears that ICE is ignoring the illegal alien inside the US except for criminal aliens, and terrorists. To understand the historical development of this enforcement policy I looked at the available statements made by several of the Commissioners, and analyzed them in terms of the investigator's perceptions of the mission of INS.

From 1992 through 2003, the investigations program continued to increase its apprehensions of deportable aliens, but it is still less than half of what it used to be during the Nixon-Chapman era.[2] After that, the investiga-

Table 7.1. INS Commissioners by Years of Service and Deportable Aliens Located.

Commissioner	Years of Service	US President	Aliens Located	Removals during Presidency	Returns during Presidency
Leonard F. Chapman	11/73-5/77	Richard M. Nixon	2,868,390	1969-1977 194,601	5,130,255
Leonel J. Castillo	5/77-10/79	Jimmy Carter	2,392,721	1977-1980 105,378	3,527,878
Alan C. Nelson	2/82-6/89	Ronald Reagan	9,095,546	1981-1988 168,364	8,108,489
Gene McNary	10/89-1/93	GHW Bush	3,895,304	1989-1992 141,326	4,020,157
Doris Meissner	10/93-11/2000	William J. Clinton	11,176,663	1993-2000 869,646	11,421,259
James Ziglar Michael Chertoff Tom Ridge	8/01-11/02 2005-2009 2003-2005	GW Bush	1,551,712	2001-2008 2,012,539	8,316,311
Jeh Johnson Janet Napolitano	12/13- 2009-2013	BH Obama	4,378,202 (2009-2014)	2009-2014 2,427,070	1,950,820

tions program made significantly fewer alien locates that ultimately reduced the numbers dramatically. From 2000 through 2009, investigations located 138,291 to 21,877 deportable aliens respectively. In 1977, the investigations program contributed 19.6% of the total apprehensions of INS. During this period the ACIS program was in effect, and investigators actively located and apprehended illegal aliens inside the US. In 2003, the investigations program contributed only 10.7% of total apprehensions (112,007 deportable aliens). The average total investigations contribution to deportable aliens located from 1992 to the present is 7.26%. Most the apprehensions are low-level border crossers completed by the border patrol. The investigations program was an effective tool in locating and apprehending illegal aliens, but the agency did not seem to encourage its use. IRCA was supposed to deal with employers who hired illegal aliens, but failed to stop the flow of illegal aliens across the border. Since a foolproof identity card does not exist, it was difficult to prosecute the employers who could claim ignorance of any document validity. In addition to not having enough investigators to do the job, it would be difficult to prove intentional violation of the law in such cases. The agency policies supported border enforcement, but avoided interior enforcement. It appears that it was acceptable to apprehend law violators attempting to enter the US, but once they entered, their status changed. Border patrol agents apprehend illegal entrants after they enter the US. INS inspectors at ports of entry can exclude aliens from entering the US, but the border patrol, and the investigations program primarily deal with aliens who are in the US. For this reason, there should be little difference in which program inside the agency apprehends the alien. However, there is a significant difference in policy, and resources allocated for each program. For most of its history, and at least through the 1996 Act, the legacy INS was a border patrol agency. The border patrol received the lion's share of operating budget, and agent perceptions regarding their lower priority in the agency persisted. Most likely, the main reason for this imbalance was the politics surrounding immigration enforcement. Whatever the reason, the fact remains that interior enforcement could be extremely effective in locating and removing illegal aliens, if policy makers so desired. Apparently, they do not.

Commissioner Leonard F. Chapman, who served under the Nixon administration stated:

> The problem of illegal immigration to the US has grown to the point where it is out of control, and our nation faces the dim prospect of even greater numbers of aliens pouring into the country unless steps are taken soon to halt the movement . . . between 5 and 10% of the six million foreign visitors annually do not depart, but remain in this country to find employment . . . .it is painfully evident to our officers that they are capable of handling only a small percentage of the violations because of the limited funds and personnel.[3]

As an investigator in the NYDO, I personally witnessed the rapid decline in morale after General Chapman retired, and Commissioner Castillo took over. Castillo immediately began implementing his personal agenda by focusing on the humanitarian aspects, and civil rights issues so strongly held by pro-immigrant activists in the field. During his tenure, some of the edicts that came out of Castillo's office included policy memorandums instructing investigators not to use the word "criminal" in their official title, and to refer to illegal aliens as undocumented workers. In addition, managers and supervisors enforced a strict dress code, and warned investigators not to display any law enforcement equipment such as holsters, speed-loaders (devices used to load bullets into the cylinder of a revolver), or handcuffs. Since the Commissioner viewed the illegal alien as more of a contributor than a drainer on society, these policies were meant to portray interior enforcement through a service image.

In March 1980, investigators from the Central Office conducted a routine audit of INS NYDO, and an inspection team conducted so-called *gripe sessions* wherein they asked investigators to voice any complaints they had about how INS operates. All the investigators stated that morale was low because they believed INS considered Investigation Activity a low priority. In addition, investigators stated that INS seemed to place a higher priority on service related functions. Investigators complained that this arrangement impacted adversely on officer safety due to the lack of needed equipment, appropriate office space, and clerical support. Investigators considered these deficiencies relative to other INS activities. In response to the complaints, the inspection team stated that INS Commissioners favored service over enforcement activity.

In an effort to clear the enormous backlog of applications for permanent residence, former Commissioner Castillo instituted an *Adjudication Task Force*. This task force processed the applications with a view towards eliminating any backlogs as quickly as possible. Investigators considered the task of adjudication as a service function. Although processing units attempt to carefully review the applications, and documents submitted in support of them, such efforts usually uncover only the most flagrant examples of fraud. Even with minimal effort, INS routinely uncovered substantial fraud in applications. INS decided to use investigators to assist in this task force, and used enforcement personnel to give the appearance of proper vetting. Unfortunately, investigators viewed the *detail* as a misuse of investigators, and their mission. Management described the task force as an opportunity for investigators to gain expertise in areas that could be useful in conducting investigations. Most of the investigators shared the sentiments expressed in the following statements:

> I think the task force was an example of how a politician works at his best . . . it was a disgrace for INS, or worse, to the American people. Not only were I-130 petitions (relative visa applications) accepted without a single shred of proof to back up the validity of the marriage but I actually had one case where I arrested the beneficiary three months earlier and saw his name on another I-130. I pointed this out to the officer in charge of the project and he rubber stamped it over my direct refusal to sign (approve) the petition. It was an example of how INS moves paper without regard to the INA. As far as increasing expertise, all it did was dishearten and demoralize investigators even further. If an investigation were ever launched into it, it would probably uncover massive malfeasance.
>
> I know that during the task force investigators were directed not to review the files and petitions and just check for documentary sufficiency, not to look for age discrepancies or anything that could be an indicator of fraud in the petition. It was not an investigative task at all, merely an examinations (service) task.

In 1997, former INS Commissioner Doris Meissner made the following statement that seems to support public perceptions about the nature of INS inside the US, as compassionate in tone, but essentially service oriented.

> Well, INS will not be engaging in any mass deportations of any kind. We will not be taking—we will not be doing sweeps. We will not be doing round-ups, and we certainly will not be targeting specific nationalities. We will continue to deport people in accordance with what our priorities have been, which is to focus first on criminal aliens, focus on people who are employed illegally. People who are here illegally are always subject to deportation and they will continue to be, but the cases that you just cited where people are trying—are

claiming hardship, people that have been here for long periods of time, the rules have changed for those people, and judges will be operating according to different standards.[4]

The continued decline in morale among legacy INS investigators was reinforced by the mission statements of the Commissioners. One can only imagine the impact that the last Commissioner of INS, James Ziglar, had on the investigators as he implemented another restriction on investigators trying to do their job. It supports the sanctuary city position held by open borders, pro-immigrant groups. It clearly expresses the inherent bias of someone who is supposed to both enforce the law, as well as administer a service to the public.

> All of us in INS family have been deeply shocked and saddened by the terrible loss of life and destruction in New York. We are committed to supporting the rescue and recovery efforts taking place at the World Trade Center. We have heard disturbing reports that some people whose loved ones are missing have not come forward because of immigration issues. We cannot let that happen. It is crucial that local authorities get the help they need in identifying victims and the missing. I want to personally urge the immigrant community to come forward, and assure everyone that INS will not seek immigration status information provided to local authorities in the rescue and recovery efforts.

Such a statement is made to a nation in shock, but the underlying message is similar to the one proclaimed in an effort to implement the Census mandate, and the underlying purpose is to restrict interior enforcement of the immigration law. In order to count illegal aliens in the US, INS shut down investigations to assist in the enumeration of the population. Investigators made parallels to other law enforcement agencies such as the FBI or DEA, and logically pointed out that such agencies did not stop doing their jobs because of the Census, and suggested that enforcement increase as a result of the terrorist attacks, not decrease. On the contrary, acknowledging that illegal aliens were involved in the World Trade Center attack should have caused the Commissioner to implement even more aggressive interior enforcement. It is no surprise that six months after the World Trade Center attack, the agency under Commissioner Ziglar issued approval for change of status applications previously submitted by two of the hijackers, who were not only ineligible, but also deceased.[5] Such actions are representative of the history of the service priority, so dominant in the agency.

The philosophy and statements of Commissioner Ziglar are indicative of how the perception about the lack of support by management was created in the minds of investigators. If most of the illegal aliens in the US are not terrorists, the Commissioner essentially negated the entire interior enforcement mission in the following statement:

No one likes the idea that people came into the country illegally, but it's not practical or reasonable to think that you're going to be able to round them all up and send them home. We need to set up a regime where we don't have to spend so much of our time and effort in enforcement activities dealing with people who are not terrorists, who are not threats to our national security, who are economic refugees. [6]

As indicated elsewhere, labels such as economic refugee, and undocumented worker are carefully peppered in the illegal alien debate to characterize the deviant as something different from what they are. In so doing, it creates an image that the rule-breaker is not a rule-breaker at all, or is not a deviant. This relabeling is quite effective in redefining the behavior. However, illegal aliens are not undocumented workers; they are persons in the US who are in violation of the INA.

Employees should expect to complete tasks within the parameters of their official job description, defined by the employer (Office of Personnel Management). Most of the investigators agree with the sentiments voiced in the following statement:

In the past, I have seen one branch of INS play against the other. If the need for adjudicators or examiners arises, investigators are pulled from their duties to adjudicate petitions . . . I know of instances where deportation branch personnel, who are supposed to receive a certain amount of hazardous duty pay, have refused to back the investigative branch in time of need. Investigators are pawns in INS game, to be used by anybody who needs us. Investigators have been directed to do inspections, adjudicate petitions, and detention work, whereas no other branch of INS has been manipulated like this, and only investigators do investigative work. Take for example the bond detail which investigators are forced to do. They will make a team of investigators stand by all day so that they can escort some clerks to the post office with cash, and the daily receipts from application fees. You are acting as an armed bodyguard for money. Why can't they hire people to do that work, instead of wasting an investigator's time to take care of non-investigative work? Only investigators are forced to do this escort, which I consider really demeaning. Even though deportation officers and inspectors are authorized to carry firearms, they don't have to do this escort. It is really unfair. Every time some administrator has a *shit* job to do, an investigator usually ends up doing it. Investigators are even asked to move office furniture. Another time there was a riot in the detention facility, and they had all the investigators go there to straighten up the mess. Why didn't deportation officers, or detention personnel do it? Because every time there is some dirty job to do, they call on investigators to do it.

If an investigator determines that an illegal alien has equities the case is referred to a service branch of INS for adjudication. One of the most common forms of equity involves marriage applications. In such cases, the alien derives a benefit by marrying a US citizen, or legal resident alien and also bypasses any visa quota restrictions. Even if the Investigation Branch has a *wanted* file on an illegal alien, the Travel Control Section (service) takes precedence in processing the marriage application. As such, the investigative function is secondary to the service function. However, criminal cases take priority over administrative policy and that is why investigators preferred to work them. If given the opportunity, investigators disassociated themselves entirely from the administrative enforcement process. Investigators also sought positions that insulated them from the administrative hierarchy. Officers assigned to such units as the Organized Crime Drug Task Force experienced a relief from the formal chain of command. It also meant that the investigators in these elite units did not have to participate in administrative task forces as described above. An investigator assigned to the ASU states:

> I don't have anything to do with the administrative enforcement part of INS. I couldn't care less about it. My function is to work criminal prosecutions against smugglers. That other work (administrative enforcement) is just a waste of time.

The ASU investigator classified administrative duties as service work. This is similar to police officers that view *community relations* as necessary, but not *real* law enforcement work.[7] ASU investigators further considered criminal casework the only real work for an investigator. For the most part, investigators in the other sections agree with this perception but must perform the administrative work assigned to them. Most of the investigators shared the following sentiments:

> I was working a case, and this has happened to me before. And it turns out that one of the subjects I ran a check on was wanted by INS (an illegal alien). This could have been useful to me, because I intended to use this guy as an informant and obtain important information. Well, it turns out that the alien got married to a citizen who submitted a visa application for him, which I'm sure was a phony marriage too. I finally found his file which was in Travel Control (unit that adjudicates petitions), and I knew I lost control of the case. The people in Travel Control feel that their function is more important, and so does INS. I told them about the case, they listened and shrugged their shoulders, but there was nothing they could do. They are not enforcement minded, so they can't understand our problems. It all comes down to this service and enforcement division, and investigators usually lose out to INS service priority. If you really analyze it carefully, you can say without any question that the service part of INS is more important than enforcement. It is a policy that any alien who has a pending application, and can adjust his status in the US, is permitted to stay in the US until his application is adjudicated. In reality, this means that most illegal aliens can delay leaving the US, until they exhaust all the various schemes available to them. It is very convenient for immigration attorneys, who charge large fees for their services. The system really is beneficial to

anyone who can afford a lawyer, because their departure can usually be delayed. The poor alien will leave the US shortly after he is apprehended.

Immigration law is similar to tax laws in complexity, and many individuals need the services of professionals to assist them through the INS maze. This creates an environment that attracts disreputable persons involved in immigration scams, and in some ways, the legal system contributes to this environment. Parallels to Prohibition, and other black market ventures are obvious. The millions of people that want something they cannot obtain through legal channels will turn to criminals instead. Investigators believe that certain factors aggravate the illegal alien problem as the following statement indicated:

> INS creates the atmosphere for illegal aliens to do what they do, and here is an example: we know that aliens go to a top attorney for I-130 forms (relative visa applications), and pay up to $1,500 for the attorney to fill them out. Why don't we publicize in the Spanish community that there are certain associations that can tell aliens what is affordable to them under the INA, or make an I-130 in the Spanish language? What is your name? Where do you live? People are going and paying $1,500 to have an attorney fill out the forms . . . I have been working on . . . that are really ripping off the people, and the reason that . . . are making millions of dollars is that we create the atmosphere for them. The illegal alien does not want to pay an attorney $1,500 to fill out an application. Instead, they go to a travel agency and pay $400 to fill out that sixteen question form, and that is where they get into buying counterfeit job letters, the whole bit . . .

Throughout my tenure with INS, upper management often referred to INS as the "service with a heart". This meant that although the task of enforcement meant locating and arresting illegal aliens, the investigator should keep in mind that INS is a very compassionate agency with an underlying sentiment of service. Immigration legislation is traditionally molded to keep families together, and this accounts for the numerous immediate relative petitions submitted and generally approved by INS. This statement by an investigator reflects the inherent contradiction between service and control. The investigator is not without passion, but perceives a different underlying reason for the service priority.

> If one more time I'm told that we're the service with a heart, I'm almost going to vomit. Um, it's thrown in our faces that we're here to serve people, which on one hand is true. There are aspects of our branch which are made to help people legitimately, and legally enter the US. But, at the same time I feel that we're being used to a certain degree by um, it's my personal opinion, by groups of attorneys who practice immigration law to pad their pockets, and disapprove our own law.

ILLEGAL ALIENS: DRAINERS OR CONTRIBUTORS

An Atlas/ti network view of the illegal alien as drainer, or contributor to society includes the following:

As Contributor

* Illegal aliens are a source of cheap labor
* Illegal aliens take jobs nobody else wants
* Illegal aliens contribute to cultural diversity
* Illegal aliens sustain certain interest groups

As Drainer

* Illegal aliens take jobs away from legal workers
* Illegal aliens are law breakers
* Illegal aliens obtain benefits and services they are not entitled to
* Illegal aliens send money out of the country
* Illegal aliens do not pay their share of taxes
* Illegal aliens commit crimes
* Illegal aliens use fraudulent documents to obtain benefits
* Illegal aliens cause overpopulation, and overwhelm services to the community

Some of the investigators believed that illegal aliens were drainers on society, because they took jobs away from the general population. As one investigator pointed out:

> They are drainers because they take many jobs where general population— kitchen workers, cooks, sewing machine operators . . . can't get these jobs, because they are taken by illegal aliens.

Other investigators were more concerned with those illegal aliens that were involved in fraud, especially welfare fraud, and would prefer focusing on the apprehension of these law violators as the following interviewee stated:

> The people who stay home and milk the government, the people who are working. So, what? I'd rather be getting the ones that are hurting us. The Dominicans who get green cards, and next day are on welfare. Jordanians who bring in families, go on welfare, buy up property, keep bringing in more people, those are the people I'd like to apprehend.

Another investigator stated:

. . . with or without documents, I might add, being picked up at welfare.
Coming in as illegal aliens to begin with is bad enough, but as soon as they get
into the country they don't take jobs. They go out and buy counterfeit, or
forged documents, indicating that they're Puerto Ricans, or US citizens, or
some such national, and go right down to welfare. Get themselves on a welfare
roll, and then bring in Jose and Davilla, and 12 thousand kids from Santo
Domingo the same way, fraudulently, and get them all on welfare.

With regard to aliens as net contributors to society, one investigator working in the ACIS unit stated were those with:

. . . fewer incidences of welfare, work at jobs, pay taxes, contribute social
security using fraudulent social security cards so they don't get the benefits,
but the money goes to the social security administration, have babies on Med-
icaid, but should be entitled to it.

Another investigator indicated that some illegal aliens are in fact contributors, but like the previous quote was far from the norm among the interviewees. This statement is in complete contrast with Commissioner Castillo's statement that aliens are more contributors than drainers on society. It
represents the majority perception of most of the investigators.

I would say illegal aliens, in the predicament and the situation they are in, as
being illegal aliens, are mainly drainers. On the majority, taking money from
our economy, and placing it back into a foreign government. There are numerous undocumented aliens that are on welfare. That has not reached the public
ear due to various squelchers in the government. I mean, there are some good
people, but I can't actually see it now. They are draining our hospitals, our
welfare systems, our schools. I mean it would again be like inviting a foreign
government to place its army into the US, and let us support it. I've interviewed various people. I've picked up a few illegal aliens that were actually
doctors. And, under labor certifications they were actually doctors, and I
would say they are contributors. But, the average illegal aliens are not contributors.

THE US ATTORNEY: CRIMINAL VS. ADMINISTRATIVE CASES

The US Attorney's office reviews all requests for criminal prosecution, and
decides whether or not to accept them. At INS, a designated *liaison officer*
presented cases on behalf of the agent to the AUSA. The intent of this
arrangement was to create an efficient line of communication between the
agency, and the US Attorney's office. In many instances, INS can automatically decline to pursue a criminal prosecution based on a "blanket waiver"
for certain cases granted by the US Attorney. Generally, these include aliens
that enter the US without inspection (ewi), reentry of aliens previously de-

ported, and crewmen that desert their vessel. The agency tracked all declined cases, and provided the US Attorney's office with summary statistics regarding them. The US Attorney's Office is primarily interested in prosecuting cases that have a significant impact on the administration of justice, and most INA violations generally do not reach this standard.

> ... The U. S. Attorney acts as the attorney for the government in all proceedings in which the federal government is a party . . . His decision whether to prosecute is not subject to review by any court . . . The discretionary power to decide whether to prosecute is awesome . . . Although the Attorney General can overrule a U. S. Attorney . . . this type of action runs risks in the arena of public opinion.[8]

In order to pursue a criminal prosecution, an agent needs the AUSA to approve it, and AUSAs often need criminal investigators to obtain the evidence necessary to complete a successful prosecution. It is a symbiotic relationship. Since the INS investigator had to go through a designated liaison officer, the AUSA received second hand information about the case. Sometimes, it is necessary to sell your case to the prosecutor, or else it might be viewed as lacking merit, or not important enough to pursue. The liaison officer was not directly involved with the case, and might not know all the facts, or the significance of it.

Most INS agents worked administrative cases, rather than criminal prosecutions. ASU agents quickly characterized themselves as "working criminal cases all the time," perhaps in an effort to distance themselves from the routine, non-criminal work. ASU officers advised that they had a more direct relationship with the US Attorney in presenting cases, and often bypassed the designated liaison officer. The following statement from an ASU agent reflects these differences:

> We spend a lot of time working with the US attorneys. Most of the time we will speak to our liaison officer here rather than, and usually they will say to us, alright you make the call yourself . . . too detailed, or they'll recognize that they're not competent to pass on the evidence in any way, and we will call the deputy chief in the eastern or southern district, give the essentials of our case ourselves, and they'll tell us who we should go speak to. We have a pretty high degree of success with the US Attorney (office), and with the criminal courts, in the smuggling unit. Pretty much, whenever we call they know us, and they've known us as a result of cases that we've presented, and they'll go along with us, even with some cases that might seem unimportant, or perhaps a little doubtful. Whereas I think their general policy is, I think, to downplay immigration . . .

The key to success in criminal investigations is to make cases that result in a successful criminal prosecution. Regarding prosecutions, the agents perceived conflict between them and the agency, over the enforcement mission. Agents would like to prosecute criminal aliens, and remove them from the US. On the other hand, INS encouraged apprehending mostly low-level visa abusers such as dishwashers, landscapers, day laborers, and service workers. Essentially, the conflict revolves around having to implement policies that make it difficult to work on criminal prosecutions. The agency measured success by counting the number of apprehensions, not criminal prosecutions. What occurred during the Vietnam conflict is similar to this process with the use of the phrase "bring in bodies," which translates into apprehending as many illegal aliens as possible. Success in criminal prosecutions is measured differently than arrest rates.

Most of the agents work on administrative cases, and processing criminal aliens for deportation proceedings is an administrative function. Deportation is an administrative function without punishment involved, in which the alien is simply removed from the US. In a criminal prosecution case, the intent is to prosecute a defendant, which may result in punishment including incarceration, fines, probation, and in some instances death.

AUSAs considered INS cases fairly simple to prosecute with high success rates, but otherwise low priority in the criminal justice system hierarchy. They accepted certain cases such as passport fraud for these reasons, but declined the routine, or blanket waiver cases. These perceptions are expressed in the following investigator comments:

> I don't really know . . . they didn't voice any opinions . . . something fairly simple for them (AUSA), they are not interested in them, but a high success rate, not much contact with US Attorney's office, you fill out an affidavit, go to the arraignment. In one case, had to go to Grand Jury, took about an hour.

> I'd say maybe about ten cases were presented by me. About two were accepted. I think the policy at the U.S. Attorney's office is such that they don't consider immigration violations serious violations, although they are rethinking certain areas of immigration violations like passport fraud. They're pretty simple cases usually. We had high quality evidence. They recognized the fact that they can easily get a successful prosecution by following up on them. So, recently they had been accepting that type of immigration case.

> The US attorneys have been given directives that they are to increase the number of complaints they are to accept to get a higher prosecution rating, and higher convictions. . . . (Liaison officer) said that this would mean that they were going to go for faster, easy types of cases.

Most of the investigators believed that it was more effective to deal directly with an AUSA, rather than attempt to present a case through a district liaison officer.

> Trying to explain your case to a liaison officer really hampers law enforcement. A lot is lost in the process. When you make an application to an AUSA

you are acting as a salesman, you are trying to sell your case . . . And the AUSA is looking for a case that will result in a conviction. He is in tune with the media, he is not interested in a simple B-2 overstay (alien that overstays the time allowed to remain in the US), or the guy with no prior criminal activity. And, once you have established credibility by presenting good cases, you can attain an open-door policy, even to the extent of calling AUSA's at their homes, about cases.

Agents believed that other agencies, government officials, and the public identify INS enforcement exclusively with the border patrol. They perceived that the portrayal of the investigator is rarely accurate, if portrayed at all. Considering the following statement, it appears that the US Attorney's office did not view the INS as a professional law enforcement agency. The statement seems to be directed more at the agency, than the agents.

"The border patrol is 50% mediocrity, 40% stupidity and 10% corruption," said Stephen G. Nelson, a U. S. District Attorney in San Diego. "It is absolutely the worst federal law enforcement agency. No service does more to stifle bright young guys than INS . . . " In trying to enforce a seemingly unenforceable law, the U. S. Border Patrol, "is just effective enough to create the need for smugglers," said Peter K. Nunez, a U. S. District Attorney in San Diego.[9]

A network view[10] of the relationship between the legacy INS and the US Attorney's comparing apprehensions and prosecutions, or administrative as opposed criminal casework includes the views that:

- INS cases are low priority cases filtered through a liaison officer.
- Direct contact is better than presenting cases through a liaison officer.
- INS cases are fairly simple, and the AUSA accepts such cases.
- INS is used by other agencies to prosecute offenders.
- The ASU had a relatively high success rate, and often dealt with AUSAs directly

LIAISON WITH OTHER AGENCIES

INS agents perceived that other federal law enforcement agencies such as the FBI, DEA, Customs, Secret Service, and ATF, considered INS to be low in the law enforcement hierarchy. However, this perception varied when there were more personal contacts between these agents.

I view INS investigator positions in relation to other federal criminal investigators as lower echelon simply because we are a lower journeyman grade level. Investigators from most of the other important agencies have journeyman GS-12's, and their priority is criminal investigation. We all enjoy the same title of criminal investigator, but they do criminal work primarily, we do not. I have contacts with agents in almost every other agency, and most of them look down on us. Other than federal, say local police departments might show us a little more respect, simply because our talents are a little more specialized, and require a little more expertise. For example, many agents are impressed with our ability to speak Spanish.

This "looking down on" INS appears to lessen as personal contacts between the agents increase. The following statement summarizes most of the investigators' sentiments regarding these relationships.

> I know agents from the FBI, DEA, Customs . . . they like us as men doing what they do, as professionals. They know our agency has been strapped for a long time, and they know that the INA, and the US Code have to be revised. All of their laws relating to the crimes they investigate are very clear . . . The FBI and DEA have everything written down to the letter. They prove a case before they go out and arrest someone. They know that our law is very cloudy. For instance, we don't even have a statute for possession of a counterfeit alien registration card (*green card*), that it is a felony, or misdemeanor. Investigators in other agencies know what we are up against, that we don't have the tools to do the job. We have a fairly good reputation as professionals, but unable to do as good a job as the other agencies because of the way the law is written.

Sometimes, the U. S. Attorney's office uses the INS in the prosecution of other criminal cases involving aliens. In the past, prosecutors used deportation to remove undesirable aliens from the US. In the absence of the INA, these undesirables could continue to reside in the US, and continue to commit their criminal acts. This is especially useful in dealing with members of traditional organized crime, or the Mafia. As previously stated, prosecutors also consider deportation more efficient than criminal prosecution, and AUSAs do concern themselves with the fact that deportation proceedings can go on indefinitely due to appeals, or that the alien may have an equity, such as a marriage to a US citizen. Other agencies also turn to INS to dispose of cases, through deportation when prosecution is not feasible, and one might conclude that INS plays an important role in the criminal justice system. Yet, INS investigators still perceived that they occupied a low position in the 1811 hierarchy. The following statements focus on relations with the FBI, but INS agents perceived they generally applied to the law enforcement community. According to ICE, the perception regarding the place of ICE agents in the criminal investigator hierarchy has improved compared with the legacy INS model. Due to the new legislation that expedites deportation and removal proceedings of criminal aliens, other agencies want task forces to include ICE agents.

> The FBI is a loner in criminal investigations. It simply will not work in close cooperation with any other investigative office. The reasons are largely

narcissistic, although the Bureau attempts to rationalize it on the basis of security and integrity. As a result, FBI agents frequently hold back information that can be valuable to other federal, or state agencies. Because of the FBI's secretiveness, these other agencies are reluctant to turn over their information to the Bureau.[11]

We were at a training session with agents from the various law enforcement agencies, and one of the FBI agents was telling a story about his encounter with some illegal aliens. The FBI agent said that it was embarrassing to him, because the alien thought he was with Immigration. The FBI agent seemed amazed when I told him that I feel the same way when people confuse me with the FBI. He thought I should feel proud if someone thought I was an FBI agent.

We had this assignment where the subject was under investigation by the FBI for ten years. They were trying to get this guy for ten years. Well, we got the information and in one day we arrested the subject. The next day he was deported. This is an example of the importance of INS agents in the total enforcement effort, but when they have a task force to combat organized crime, like the DEA and the FBI, and Customs, they never include INS agents. Very often, they come to us and we provide valuable information on illegal, or legal aliens who are involved in the criminal activity they are investigating. But, it seems that we rarely are treated as equals. Maybe it is our own agency that does not want us to get involved, but INS agents should take a more active part in task forces on criminal investigations.

I was assigned a case where I had to locate an illegal alien who was also a parole breaker (fugitive). He was convicted for smuggling narcotics. The subject was being sought by the FBI for jumping parole, and by INS for being convicted of the drug charge (a deportable offense). The FBI agent who had the case came down to talk to me about subject. His attitude was that the FBI considered such cases *low priority*, and implied that this was an opportunity for an INS agent to get something that could be interesting. Basically, he was talking down to me, but the lowest point was when he tried to give me some tips on how I might catch the guy, not information, but investigative techniques. What they don't realize is that most INS investigators arrest more people in one year than an FBI agent does in his career. One thing we know how to do is locate, and arrest people.

We went out on a case once with the FBI, and they insisted on taking control of the situation. We let them. They wanted to arrest this guy and went to his residence and knocked on his door. The first thing this guy does is escape through the back door of the house. Any INS investigator knows that you have to cover the back exits if you want to avoid losing the subject. Anyway, we went back to the subject's residence at a later date and (INS investigators) apprehended him.

Investigators also had perceptions about the way other agencies viewed their place in the overall criminal justice system. One investigator voiced his perception about this, especially with regard to the FBI:

I don't know anybody in the Bureau, but I think it's apparent from the way the relative positions, and the hierarchy within the Justice Department, that each organization is regarded as a whole, how INS stands up. And, when the Bureau moved here there was no question we had the inferior parking spaces. We were shifted all around with the physical facilities for the cars. When it was time for civilians to leave the country, it was the FBI that stayed outside the consulate. They wouldn't use Immigration people. It seems to me, it's almost a foregone conclusion that whenever something of national importance takes place that has to do with aliens or illegal aliens, there are no investigators in on the job. It's always FBI.

Members of the ASU filed a union grievance, and requested that INS provide technical equipment and training, so that they could safely complete their tasks. The investigators requested bulletproof vests, emergency lights, sirens installed in government owned vehicles, and shotgun training. INS denied the request, stating that such equipment, and training was unnecessary.[12] During the litigation that followed, investigators and their supervisors described their tasks in relation to dealing with other law enforcement agencies. The following statement made by the ASU supervisor highlights inter-agency problems that developed in the investigation branch.

Well, we work very frequently with the Secret Service on different cases. The Agent in Charge of training . . . from the Secret Service, told me that the Secret Service has a policy of wanting any agency that cooperates with them out in the field to have that individual capable of operating the weapons that they use, and that he thought it was a safety factor. Not only for ourselves, but for the Secret Service agents we come in contact with to have us be familiar with their weapons.[13]

THE MEDIA

Investigators perceived that the media distorts descriptions of the illegal alien problem, and promotes a pro-immigrant characterization of the illegal alien. The activities of the investigation branch are vulnerable to media criticism, and agents indicated that their agency does not actively attempt to defend the distorted image created by the media. Most of the investigators perceived that a positive image would assist them in completing their tasks. The following statements summarize most of the perceptions expressed by investigators regarding the media:

INS is a politically disadvantageous agency to be associated with, and INS enforcement in particular is politically disadvantageous . . . The only way that it is advantageous is when INS processes immediate relative applications, or goes out of its way to give the impression that it is helping settle refugees, or letting thousands of Cubans, or Haitians, enter the US . . . to make it look like we are helping the poor people out . . . That is the way the administration decides to portray this agency, because it is politically advantageous to do so.

Most of what I've heard or seen in the media shows INS investigators as "the bad guys." We are coming down on the poor aliens who can't get a job, who come here to work and earn a living. We walk around with clubs in our hands, and try to get them out of the US. We are routinely referred to as the "Gestapo." Investigators are very humane, and not out to hurt anyone . . . it is just too bad that the people we are apprehending are the ones who are working, not the ones slumming off the government, the people who stay home and soak off the taxpayer, like the welfare frauds, and the criminal aliens . . . I would rather get the illegal aliens who are hurting us in these ways. The ones who get their green card, and the next day are at the welfare office. Some groups bring their whole families in, they go on welfare, buy up property, the owner petitions others who then go on welfare, and he collects the rents from them, and it goes on and on . . . these are the people that are really hurting society.

The image of the illegal alien as a "victim" causes concern for most of the investigators.

I have a very bad taste in my mouth about the way the media depicts the illegal alien. It is true that most of them enter the US to feed their families, but the US is not in a position to feed the rest of the world. Immigration laws are fair, and attempt to rationally regulate those who want to come to the US. Those who decide to violate the laws must suffer the consequences. Unfortunately, we do not adequately enforce the law. But, the idea that the public gets from the media is that the big bad Government is out there in the form of INS, especially the alien population picks up on this image. Or, items such as INS agents making big sweeps and dragging out poor aliens, that INS is the Gestapo, and so on. Once, we executed a search warrant on a firm that had illegal aliens working in it, and also had a defense contract with the government. We took a number of illegal aliens out on the search warrant. Later, the owner of the firm sent a complaint letter to Washington. He said we came into his place like Nazi storm troopers, like the Gestapo. This is the kind of thing we have to deal with. And the sad part of it is that there really isn't anybody here, the higher-ups, to rebut these fabrications. And that is very bad. On different occasions, we have gone out with the press. And later, you see what they report on television. Not that they ever gave you the impression that they were going to accurately report what they saw. The sentiment of most of the media reports tends to favor the illegal alien. He comes here, gets a job in some sweatshop; is underpaid. INS arrests him, or her, and puts him in a jail, which isn't fit for animals, and so on. It is a slanted view of reality. You never hear about how INS doesn't even detain some of these people, or how an investigator has to catch them four or five times before they leave the US. You rarely hear about investigators being assaulted, or injured. Or, how we arrest illegals with guns and narcotics. I don't think the media is giving a fair accounting of what we do.

Investigators believed that their agency should counter the bad publicity about INS with accurate press releases that concentrate on the contributions made by the investigations program. They also perceived that upper management did not support interior enforcement. Investigators advised that the NYDO did not have a press officer, and having one would probably provide a more positive image about the agency. Investigators advised that when INS did make press releases, it often was service oriented, or used for political reasons to enhance the image of politicians. Investigators further believed that the agency feared bad press from the media. In avoiding press attention and failing to correct distorted press, INS created a vacuum in which the public was not accurately informed about the illegal alien problem. Investigators believed they would have received positive support if the facts were presented, and they perceived that the public rarely heard about how the agents attempted to assist aliens who were entitled to assistance.

Investigators believed that the agency should concentrate on criminal cases, instead of focusing on the apprehension of aliens in the work place. Media coverage could enhance the investigator's mission, if the public were informed about the widespread involvement of illegal aliens in criminal activity.

> It is always the sad story of the illegal alien who comes here, who is hard working, who came here to work and support his family. I can understand, and appreciate that image of the illegal alien. We see it every day. On the other hand, we also see the illegal aliens who are involved in criminal activity, who are involved in all kinds of illegal schemes against the government. This is the segment of the illegal alien population the media has not concentrated enough on. It is also the part of the illegal alien population that INS should be concentrating on. If only five percent of the illegal alien population is criminal, and it is probably much more than that, that segment could keep investigators busy all the time. If INS devoted more time investigating the criminal element of the illegal alien population, we would get the press coverage we deserve.

DHS is an agency with a specific mission, and clear objectives. The media are kept informed, and initiatives are described in press releases meant to enhance the law enforcement image of that agency. However, a statement by a former ICE agent indicates that little has changed with regard to the interior enforcement of the immigration laws.

> Media? Nothing's changed since 1980. Eternally poor press for an eternally mismanaged agency. When the public discovered that INS went ahead and posthumously approved the change of status NIVs (non-immigrant visas) for two of the WTC terrorists, that was the proverbial straw that broke the camel's back. For a multitude of bad INS press since 1980 . . .

NOTES

1. DHS, "Jeh Johnson," Accessed on July 9, 2016, https://www.dhs.gov/person/jeh-johnson

2. INS Statistical Yearbook, 2009

3. Leonard F. Chapman, Jr., "A Look at Illegal Immigration: Causes and Impact on the US," *San Diego Law Review*, Volume 13: 34, 1975.

4. Elizabeth Farnsworth, (April 1, 1997) Real Audio Interview, Newsmaker, Interview with INS Commissioner Doris Meissner.

5. Timothy Noah, (March 14, 2002). "INS Approves Student Visas for 911 terrorists six months after they toppled the World Trade Center." Retrieved from http://slate.msn.com/id/2063213/#ContinueArticle

6. Retrieved from http://www.vdare.com/mann/what_do.htm

7. Roger Schaefer, "Law Enforcer, Peace Keeper, Servicer: Role Alternatives for Policemen," *Journal of Police Science and Administration*, 6: 324-335, 1978.

8. Whitney North Seymour, *US Attorney: An Inside View of Justice in America Under the Nixon Administration*, (New York: William Morrow and Company, Inc., 1975), pp. 47-48.

9. James Neff, (June 17, 1981). "1500 Aliens Arrested Every Day in 12 Mile Border Stretch," *Staten Island Advance*, p. 1.

10. Network views were created with Atlast/ti software and derived from interviews with participants in the study.

11. Seymour, (1975). p. 109.

12. *Matter of USINS and AFGE Local 1917*, New York: General Services Administration, Docket Number FMCS 81K-01805, 1981.

13. Matter of USINS and AFGE Local 1917, 1981, p. 98.

Chapter Eight

Interpretation

Problems of Status and Morale

PROBLEMS OF MORALE IN A DUAL-STRUCTURE ORGANIZATION

This study supplements existing research by focusing on the ways a dual mandate agency impacts on operator's tasks.[1] It is not unusual for investigators to perceive managers as impediments to their perceived definition of mission. However, concerns of typical federal agents about management involve differences of opinion about how to fulfill the mission, rather than with the mission itself. Immigration agents shared the philosophy of their peers in federal law enforcement, and experienced difficulties in coping with the service priority part of the INS dual mandate. In addition, they sensed their agency catered to the border patrol, and this further demoralized their perceptions that interior enforcement was equally important.

> Even when policy is set, articulated, and flows down the line to agents, it rarely actually constrains them, and they continue to act in line with their own perceptions of the practical problems of drug enforcement.[2]

Due to these perceived inconsistencies, INS investigators found it difficult " . . . to act in line with their own perceptions of the practical problems . . . " Although investigators perceived their task as law enforcement, and preferred to focus on criminal investigations, they had to deal with an agency that discouraged their perceived notions about how to operate. It follows that the expectations of the operator will conflict with the goals of the managers. Whenever paired with a service function, it is inevitable that the investigator will analyze the components of that function as if it were an enforcement strategy. Regarding the overall perception about task forces and service operations, an agent stated in response to former Commissioner Castillo's adjudication task force:

> But, that doesn't mean that you've done a good job. All of these God damn things have been rushed right through, they've been stamped, or approved, or not approved, document seen. They were approving applications at one time in this operation just based upon whether or not the petitioner, and the beneficiary submitted the proper documentation. Neither alien was seen; neither petitioner was interviewed; nor, the beneficiary was interviewed. Or, even seen if the accompanying documents were attached to the I-130 petition, without doing an outside investigation, or without even having seen the petitioner, or beneficiary. The documents were there. By documents, I mean the birth certificate proving a relationship, a marriage certificate; proof that the petitioner was a US citizen, types of documents, like passport. If all the documents were intact by the time the I-130 was submitted, it was stamped, approved, instant approval desk. What a load of shit that was. And in 101% of every one of those documents submitted, there was fraud. And, if you couldn't find it on the surface, if you dove into the file someplace, you would find it. I hope I answered your question about Castillo's program.

The findings illustrate how loosely coupled organizations with dual mandates operate. The legacy INS had a service and enforcement branch, but investigators viewed their status as secondary to the service mission. As such, investigators operated in an environment with adverse working conditions, and the service priority continuously lowered their morale. On the surface, the DHS appears to be tightly coupled, with a clear demarcation between enforcement and service, with priorities clearly stated. It was hoped that agents would not be involved in service related tasks. However, the service function again surfaced and priorities shifted toward that end.

The *Final Report of the Select Committee on Immigration and Refugee Policy* stressed a need for a separation between service and enforcement functions at INS. The Select Committee believed that INS could perform both functions, and were opposed to a reorganization that would separate the dual mandate. The Select Committee based their recommendation on the fact that many illegal aliens are also eligible for benefits, and keeping both mandates connected seemed to be logical. However, the findings indicated that such an arrangement hampered enforcement because the service part of the mandate often overshadowed the enforcement part. In most instances, an illegal alien can delay his departure from the US indefinitely by exhausting the available administrative options. The findings further reflected that INS sought to expedite the service mandate, since the focus on administrative enforcement complements the service mission. This is especially evident in the investigation of so-called "dual-action cases" that combine enforcement related actions with a pending application for immigration benefits. The distinction between service and control is blurred when enforcement must take special care to facilitate the service mission. Investigations are hampered when they must defer to the service mandate and its apparatus. Criminal cases are less ambiguous, since they supersede administrative cases, and the system prioritizes criminal investigations. Investigators perceived that their agency does not encourage them to develop criminal cases just for this reason. The agency avoided the criminal control mission by failing to provide investigators with special training, equipment, and funds for paying informants.

This study focused on rules-in-use, with a view from the bottom-up, and the findings provide a more accurate assessment of how control agents operate. Investigators believed that INS was a service-oriented agency, even though the agency invested most of its resources in the border patrol, which over the years apprehends millions of illegal border crosses. Border apprehensions are deceptive in the sense that many of the aliens are granted voluntary departure, not deported. In addition, deportation and removal are administrative, not criminal cases. The dual mandate structure of the legacy INS has implications for control agents working in similar organizations.

> When the tasks people perform are well understood, predictable, routine, and repetitive, a bureaucratic structure is the most efficient . . . Where tasks are not well understood, generally because the *raw material* that each person works on is poorly understood and possibly reactive, recalcitrant, or self-activating, the tasks are nonroutine. [3]

Service related tasks tend to be repetitive and routine, and therefore more easily bureaucratized. On the other hand, the agency preference for investigators' strict adherence to rules and procedures does not complement the nonroutine nature of investigative tasks. The findings indicate that the service priority invariably pushes enforcement functions in line with the service approach. For example, control agents seem to prefer more open lines of communication with managers. Regarding agent requests for approval, the formal organizational structure was perceived to be less efficient than an informal chain of command. The preference for informal decision-making does not mean that investigators do not adhere to basic rules governing their tasks. On the contrary, agents considered themselves competent decision makers regarding enforcement operations, and considered the chain of command rule ineffective in a service-oriented agency. Although chain of command decisions should enhance effectiveness, investigators stated that supervisors tended to defer decision making to the next higher level, in order to avoid making the wrong decision. Such an arrangement caused supervisors to go to the next higher level of command, even when it was not necessary. A top-down agency operates on expectations, and operators might accept such a decision-making process if both parts of the dual mandate were implemented equally.

Directors of federal law enforcement agencies request funding annually at budget hearings in congress. The factors that justify the amount of the budget depends on whether the agency is effectively meeting it mission objectives. Investigators questioned how a service-oriented agency such as INS could represent the needs of the Investigation Branch at such hearings. Even if requests come from the bottom-up, they are diverted through official channels with a top-down perspective. It is not surprising that requests for routine law enforcement resources such as "buy money" and money for informants, or special equipment become special items instead of routine needs. In other law enforcement agencies, such items are routinely included in budget requests.

The decisions of Section Chiefs, and other managers at INS were often politically motivated, and the Central Office did not encourage district level administrators to make important decisions without consulting them. Regarding critical enforcement operations, the control agent must obtain permission through official channels from these politically aligned administrators, and the investigator depends on such individuals to obtain resources required in conducting criminal investigations.

Some of the factors preventing investigators from focusing on criminal investigations include:

1. The agency priority on low level arrests of illegal aliens employed in industry.
2. Severe manpower shortages in the investigations branch, and the failure of the agency to request adequate funding for interior enforcement.
3. The policy of the agency to pander to interest groups by ordering investigators to delete reference to the term criminal in their official title, or to relabel illegal aliens as undocumented persons.
4. The agency's failure to provide investigators with emergency equipment, and necessary law enforcement training.
5. The policy of the agency for investigators to use a liaison officer instead of direct access to an AUSA.
6. The policy of the agency to place a priority on service related functions.

Investigators viewed interior enforcement of the INA as an extension of the border patrol function, and they believed that the agency was unprepared, and unwilling to conduct criminal investigations. Thus, investigators believed that INS ignored their mission.

These issues reflect organizational strain between mangers and control agents in the agency. As professionals, investigators took offense at directives that limited their ability to make decisions, or question their responsibility and integrity. The agency seemed to prefer to view them as white-collar employees, rather than as professionals.

The media portrayal of the illegal alien problem matches the top-down view of INS because most of the media content comes from official statements. Furthermore, media coverage depends on "newsworthiness." The investigator perceived that news accounts were inaccurate, and that the media contributed to perceptions of low status and morale.

INTER-ORGANIZATIONAL AND INTRA-ORGANIZATIONAL RELATIONS

The findings showed an antagonistic relationship between INS upper management (policy makers, managers and supervisors), and the field agents. The agents perceived management as either incapable, or unwilling to actively implement their tasks. Agents also believed that managers did not have the experience, or knowledge about how to perform investigative tasks. This may not be unique since control agents generally view managers, and their environment as antagonistic to their tasks.[4] INS investigators also had to contend with conflicting impressions about the illegal alien problem. In addition, most of the investigators believed that other federal law enforcement agencies gave agents more responsibility. Managers tend to be older, and more detached from street work at INS, and agents considered managers' tasks mundane, as well as service oriented. As a result, there was little incentive to seek such positions.

Agents advised that the last four ADDI's at the NYDO were near retirement, and were former border patrol agents. In government agencies, there is preference to maintain established policies by placing individuals who pose little threat to change in positions of power. A GS-12 investigator expressed this point in the following way:

> At one time, the border patrol was the reserve officer pool for INS. Investigations originally was made up of border patrolmen who disliked working in urban areas and entered Investigations for the experience and promotion potential. These border patrolmen were assigned to areas such as New York City and their assignments were a hardship. Because of these hardship assignments, they were promised reassignment to a city of their choice after a short tour of duty in these cities. Because of manpower shortages and the inability to replace the positions, these border patrol officers had their tours of duty extended. Many of them found it difficult to adjust to urban areas, and eventually the situation developed into a feud between the border patrol and Investigations, which lingers to the present day.

Investigators believed that some of these former border patrol agents became managers, and that since they deal with more varied forms of urban enforcement, and complex investigations, special agents posed a threat to the higher status of the border patrol. In some instances, the border patrol is either unwilling, or incapable of dealing with such cases. All of this centers on their perception that the agency preferred to concentrate on border enforcement, and considered interior enforcement a low priority activity.

The control function of the agency is concerned with doing *dirty work*, or " . . . something considered beneath one's dignity, or as potentially disgusting."[5] As such, upper managers have little inclination to become directly involved with these activities. They insulate themselves by mandating that agents go "through official channels, " with strict adherence to the "chain of command." The loosely coupled nature of the legacy INS perpetuated the established service priority, and continued to add to morale problems among the investigators.

After March 1, 2003, DHS merged the legacy INS and US Customs agents into ICE, which included a management directorate to assess the human resource needs of the agency. One issue that surfaced in the merger of INS and Customs agents was the difference in their respective grade levels where INS agents were one grade lower than customs. DHS addressed that problem through cross training of agents, and hopefully the discrepancy will eventually be resolved. An ICE agent who was also a legacy INS investigator summarized the problem as follows:

> For years, the former INS was plagued by an incredibly high attrition rate. Funds that might have been put to far better use were squandered on a veritable revolving door in which the agency continually recruited and trained qualified young men and women who came to INS, highly motivated to serve their country, but who quickly became disillusioned by the inept leadership of the agency, and resigned so that they could pursue satisfying careers at other agencies. No one at INS seemed to care that so many talented, and motivated employees were fleeing to other agencies. If we are to run a more cost effective agency, management at ICE, USCIS and CBP must be made accountable for the attrition rate of the respective offices to which they are assigned. This would save significant money, and result in a more effective and motivated workforce.[6]

PROFESSIONALIZATION

Agent's notions about professionalization, and expectations of how to define and implement tasks impact on their morale. Agents perceived that agency policies, and control of resources impacted on the amount of discretion they had. Ordinarily, they did not perform maintenance of order work, and job satisfaction also depended on forces beyond their immediate control. Job satisfaction in law enforcement is directly related to perceptions that individual behavior affects the outcome of events.[7] In most instances, the agent initially experiences satisfaction by apprehending the illegal alien, but this satisfaction is diluted since the agent rarely learns the outcome of the arrest. Unlike most criminal cases, INS agents rarely testified during the administrative deportation hearing. In other law enforcement agencies, the agents are key witnesses, and play an integral part in any prosecutions. Participating in the disposition of a case permits the agent to maintain a connection with the criminal justice process. Furthermore, INS administrative judges often permit the clear majority of illegal aliens to leave the US voluntarily, even though the alien can easily abscond after leaving the courtroom. Sometimes, agents perceive the futility of their arrests when they recapture the alien that failed to depart the US.

The processing of illegal aliens is similar to others processed in the criminal justice system. A major criticism of the criminal justice system is that it facilitates "revolving door justice." Police officers commonly cite cases where the arrested person is released before their paperwork is completed. Agents similarly viewed the INS judicial process as revolving door justice because most illegal aliens simply abscond after they are processed. Current DHS enforcement policies have also exacerbated the enormous backlog of immigration cases, which according the American Immigration Council undermines justice.[8] Due to a shortage of immigration judges, and underfunding of immigration courts, there are backlogs of up to a year and a half. Although CBP and ICE increased spending from 2003 through 2015 from $9.1 billion to $18.7 billion, backlogs increased 163% during this same period, but court spending increased only 74%, from $199 million to $347.2 million.

Federal criminal investigators consider themselves "law enforcers," and hold the same public perception about police officers. Since most of their work involves enforcement, immigration agents share this perception. Agents also believe that illegal aliens are a serious problem, and that their agency should investigate criminal aliens, instead of concentrating on low-level visa abusers. The General Investigations Unit concentrated on the established INS priority, but had the lowest relative status. It appears that the agency itself considered that unit low in the hierarchy, since it usually placed former border patrol agents, or former police officers in the CIN (criminal) Section. Among agents, the ASU had the highest relative status, followed by the CIN Section. INS would assign their best personnel to apprehending low level visa abusers if that were the agency priority. Actually, locating and apprehending the low-level visa abuser is another example of Hughes' definition of dirty work. Officers in Special Investigations, or the ASU measured their higher status in terms of their distance from that "dirty work," where higher status is indirectly related to the amount of dirty work performed.

Agents stated that the federal promotion freeze contributed to their low morale, and this illustrates the direct relationship between incentives, productivity and morale.[9] Career oriented individuals will not be receptive to requests to be more productive if they believe they are in a dead-end job. Morale is also lowered by organizational policies that prevent involvement in more complex work. Managers that carefully screen casework to deter desk audits are an example of this policy. On the surface, it appears that the organizational strategies were meant to encourage officers to leave the agency. Perhaps such a strategy encourages the removal of individuals that are independent thinkers, or who resist conformity, or it simply satisfies the need to reduce the size of the federal work force. Regardless of intent, most of the agents stated that they would leave the agency if they could. For criminal investigators, this usually means transferring to another federal law enforcement agency.

The FBI is often considered the most prestigious criminal investigative agency in the law enforcement hierarchy. This perception was highlighted during the 2016 Presidential campaign, when Director Comey issued conflicting edicts about the Hillary Clinton email controversy. One of the reasons for this popular perception, is that the agency takes great care in maintaining its public image. Agents believed that their prestige could be enhanced if the INS made similar efforts to maintain a good public image. At the time, DEA and the Secret Service also held significant claims to the top of the law enforcement hierarchy. The INA offers its agents a rather limited number of comparatively significant crimes to investigate. For the most part, criminal enforcement of the INA focuses on smuggling illegal aliens, and visa fraud. Even with this limited role, INS preferred to concentrate on the administrative enforcement of the INA. INS spent most of its enforcement resources on locating and apprehending illegal aliens in the work place, but agents considered criminal investigations preferable to administrative work. For example, ASU investigators considered administrative enforcement dirty work. Manning considers paperwork a kind of dirty work because it is beyond the code of the street. This is the police officers view of what real police work involves.[10] Agents considered tasks not directly related to criminal investigation as dirty work. They consider an officer's record of successful prosecutions to be a true indicator of high prestige in the hierarchy of tasks.

Two important features common among GS-1811 investigators involve their preference for an informal basis of evaluation, and deference to other investigators' judgments about priorities.[11] Investigators considered both these factors central to the successful completion of their tasks. Basically, INS managers conflicted with investigators regarding perceptions of task and goals. INS measured productivity in terms of statistics, number of cases completed, and preferred quantity over quality. Investigators preferred to be evaluated informally, and considered such evaluations to be more accurate. Agencies that have a clear enforcement mandate are more aware of the importance of this informal evaluation. Such law enforcement agencies pay lip service to the traditional formal evaluation found in other bureaucracies. The tendency of INS managers to evaluate investigators based on formal criteria illustrates a reluctance to surrender to personal knowledge.

> . . . defined as knowledge possessed by individual officers . . . a source of power and independence . . . it creates dependence by the supervisors and administrators upon the lower participants . . . This control, discretion, and source of power gives the drug officer a great deal of power and shapes his role in an important fashion. [12]

At INS, ACIS investigators concentrated exclusively on locating and arresting illegal aliens. These investigators rely on techniques that are closest to the code of the street, and carry a minimum of case record information on suspects. Even though these factors exist, managers evaluate their productivity formally by focusing on the number of arrests they made. Such a method of evaluation further illustrates how INS avoids operators' accumulation of personal knowledge.

NOTES

1. Peter K. Manning, *The Narc's Game: Organizational and Informational Limits on Drug Law Enforcement*, (Massachusetts: MIT Press, 1980).

2. James Q., Wilson, *The Investigators: Managing FBI and Narcotics Agents*, (New York: Basic Books, Inc., 1978). pp. 16-17.

3. Charles Perrow, *Complex Organizations: A Critical Essay, 2nd edition*, (Illinois: Scott, Foresman and Company, 1979), p. 162.

4. Jerome H, Skolnick, *Justice Without Trial: Law Enforcement in Democratic Society*, (New York: John Wiley and Sons, 1966).

5. E. C. Hughes, *Men and Their Work*, (New York: The Free Press, 1958), pp. 49-53.

6. Michael Cutler, (March 11, 2004) Testimony before the Subcommittee on Immigration, Border Security and Claims. Retrieved from http://www.house.gov/judiciary/cutler031104.htm

7. David Lester and J. L. Genz, "Internal and External Locus of Control, Experience as a Police Officer, and Job Satisfaction in Municipal Police Officers," *Journal of Police Science and Administration*, 1978 6(4): 479-481.

8. American Immigration Council, "Factsheet: Empty Benches: Underfunding of Immigration Courts Undermines Justice," June 17, 2016. Accessed on October 10, 2016, https://www.americanimmigrationcouncil.org/research/empty-benches-underfunding-immigration-courts-undermines-justice

9. Edward W. Lehman, "Opportunity, Mobility and Satisfaction Within an Industrial Organization," *Social Forces*, 46: 492-501, 1968.

10. Manning, 1980, pp. 220-221.

11. Manning, 1980, pp. 224-228.

12. Manning, 1980, pp. 226-227.

Chapter Nine

The Illegal Alien

Characteristics of Interior Enforcement

THE ILLEGAL ALIEN PROBLEM

Congressional hearings,[1] studies,[2] research,[3] and media reports and debates,[4] document the impact of illegal aliens on society. Not all data relating to the size and impact of the illegal alien population are completely reliable, and estimates measuring the number of illegal aliens vary. Although critics admit that a significant problem exists, law enforcement agencies are often accused of overestimating the size, and impact on society, or creating the impression that the immigration problem is under control. The General Accounting Office recently audited the effectiveness of the Border Patrol along the southwest US border, and concluded that the Consequence Delivery System (CDS) relating to most effective and efficient efforts to deter illegal cross border activity

> did not account for an alien's apprehension history beyond one fiscal year and neither accounts for nor excludes apprehended aliens for whom there is no record of removal after apprehension and who may have remained in the United States without an opportunity to recidivate.[5]

In doing so, the agency creates the impression that the best practices are being employed to deal with underlying mission. However, such practices ignore the fact that recidivism increases when violators are not sanctioned. In the case of DACA, and DAPA, the administration essentially provided a *de facto* amnesty for millions of illegal aliens, and in doing so rewarded those who intentionally violated the law. For any reasonable person, the "consequences" of such a delivery system are inevitable.

Pro-immigrant activists claim that the impact is more positive than negative, that illegal aliens take jobs that others do not want, and that they are
more contributors than drainers on society. An economist indicates that the
impact of illegal aliens is significant on unskilled labor in the US, although
relatively small on the economy.[6] As with most illegal alien research, that
study dealt exclusively with Mexican illegal immigration. North and Houstoun[7] supplements this finding by indicating that the illegal alien population
represents a *subclass* in society that concomitantly prevents the lower classes
from advancing in the economic system.

Almost half of the annual population growth in the US comes from legal
and illegal immigration. According to one study, " . . . the growing number of
illegal immigrants may make it impossible to stabilize the US population."[8]
Later, I discuss the illegal alien problem as part of the general environment,
but one may conclude that it is not simply a Mexico-US problem.[9] In fact,
the problems surrounding the illegal alien in the US require a global view,
and suggest more diverse strategies than the history of immigration law
enforcement seems to offer. As I discuss in this study, the enforcement
strategy of the legacy INS was based on a border patrol model of enforcement. The legacy agency focused on apprehending as many illegal entrants
as it could, while ignoring those who successfully eluded the process. Once
inside the US, the illegal alien was viewed as an undocumented worker, and
the impact status was minimally labeled by most. The view that the illegal
alien is powerless needs to be reexamined considering recent events. Prior to
the terrorist attacks on 911, it seemed inevitable that some form of amnesty
was in the making. Although advocates for amnesty rely on the perception of
the powerless undocumented worker, others point out that this so-called
powerless group is no longer living in the shadows. They have begun to
speak out, and protest their plight.[10]

The 911 attacks also forced policy makers to consider other problems
relating to the illegal alien, including terrorism and criminal aliens. Although
polls suggest that voters are opposed to the fact that there are millions of
illegal aliens in the US, most lawmakers do not propose strict interior enforcement.[11] Although the legacy INS investigators might be content with
the new attention to immigration enforcement, they might be surprised that
very little is being done about interior enforcement of the INA. Even after the
transition to ICE, the traditional policies governing interior enforcement continued. On October 23, 2003, ICE agents apprehended 245 Wal-Mart stores
low-level undocumented workers in *Operation Rollback*, and although they
were from 18 foreign countries most of them were from Mexico. If they did
not have a criminal record, they were released with notices to appear later
before immigration judges.[12] Such policies rarely work in deterring illegal
immigration, since the law-breakers simply abscond after they are released.

The traditional border patrol approach to immigration law enforcement evolved into various strategies such as *Operation Gatekeeper* in California, *Hold the Line, Rio Grande*, in Texas and New Mexico, and *Safeguard* in Arizona, as well as initiatives along the northern US border. The border patrol concentrated their efforts in areas known to be high traffic entry points. In response to these strategies, the illegal entrants began entering through more dangerous mountain, and desert areas. During a twelve-month period ending September 30, 2003, 151 illegal aliens died attempting to cross over into the US from Mexico, and others increased that number to 205 to include the bodies found by other law enforcement. [13]

Estimates notwithstanding, it is assumed that the number of illegal aliens in the US is significant. It is equally important to evaluate how the control agency defined the illegal alien problem through the perceptions of the control agents.

THE ILLEGAL ALIEN IN NEW YORK: A SAMPLE

The findings in the NYDO sample [14] are more relevant to the period in which they were collected (late 1970 through 1980), and represent interior enforcement activity that predates the passage of IRCA. Except for the apprehension statistics on Mexico, there is a remarkable similarity between the NYDO sample, and the more current data on illegal aliens inside the US. In addition to the NYDO sample, estimates of the current illegal alien population are presented for comparison. There was a steady increase in apprehensions in the NYDO, and this trend continued until the 911 attacks.

There was a significant difference [15] between the percentage of Mexican nationals in the NYDO sample (11.5%) and what the agency reported nationally as the estimated number of illegal aliens inside the US. Before 1980, INS used ACIS as the main strategy in locating and apprehending illegal aliens inside the US. About 26% of the New York Investigations Unit was assigned to ACIS operations in 1977. In that year, the Investigations program nationwide located 204,193 deportable aliens, and 184,401 of these were located by ACIS. This was a 36% increase over the previous fiscal year. [16] During that same year, the border patrol located 838,022 deportable aliens. The data for the NYDO sample is derived from Form I-213, Record of Deportable Alien, from October 1977 through September 1978. The total number of apprehensions in the NYDO during the fiscal year in which the sample was collected was 10,843. The NYDO has jurisdiction over the five boroughs of New York City (Queens, Brooklyn, Staten Island, Bronx, and Manhattan), Long Island, and parts of upstate New York. Of the 10,843 deportable aliens located, 67% were employed. INS traditionally viewed the illegal alien problem as primarily made up of illegal border-crossers from Mexico. As with the sample, current data indicates that most illegal aliens in the US are still from Mexico, and that they are males.

As previously stated, although many in the NYDO sample were from Mexico, the size of that cohort is far less than expected compared to national data, and suggests that the illegal alien population inside the US is more diverse. The demographics of the NYDO sample will differ from the southwestern US. where the border patrol makes almost all the apprehensions. In the NYDO sample, there were almost twice as many persons from the Caribbean Islands (Haiti-7.5%; Dominican Republic-8.3%; Trinidad and Tobago-1.4%; Jamica-4.7%) than from Mexico. At the time, such statistics suggest that the INS enforcement strategy placed a lower priority on other-than-Mexico illegal immigration.

Official statistics on apprehended aliens will reflect the priorities of the control agency. During most of its existence, these priorities were border patrol activity along the southwest border of the US. A breakdown of deportable aliens located by agency program revealed some interesting data. In 2001, the investigations program located 41% fewer deportable aliens than it did in 1977 when the ACIS program was in full operation. However, the number of interior apprehensions continued to rise from a low of 64,819 in 1991 when ACIS was replaced with other strategies such as worksite enforcement, to 121,273 apprehensions in 2001. The ratio of investigations program apprehensions to border patrol apprehensions continued to increase from 5.4% in 1991 to 10.1% of all apprehensions in 2002. It should be noted that border patrol positions are usually increased annually, while the investigations program tends to remain the same in size. In 2002, 34% of the legacy INS workforce consisted of border patrol officers, while only 9% were special agents, or interior enforcement. After the passage of IRCA, INS implemented worksite enforcement with the belief that focusing on employers would deter illegal aliens from entering the US. With agency estimates of over 7 million illegal aliens inside the US, and 1,062,279 deportable aliens located in 2002, one might reasonably conclude that this strategy was not working.

The Obama Administration policies dramatically reduced both interior, and border enforcement of the immigration laws. The reductions in apprehensions clearly reflect the juxtaposition of policy, and enforcement. From 2008 through the latest available data in 2014, there was an overall reduction of alien apprehensions in all enforcement programs. During this period, CBP reduced apprehensions by 35%, ICE HIS by 63%, and ICE ERO by 27%. If we look at the data from 2005 when HIS had a peak apprehension total of 102,034 aliens, the decrease through 2014 is 89%.[17]

Traditionally, the illegal alien population is largely made up of males, although legal immigrant populations have been younger, and more heavily female than the total US population.[18] As more and more individuals legalize

Table 9.1. Deportable Aliens Located by INS Program[1].

Year	Total Located	Located by Border patrol	Located by Investigations/ ICE	Investigations/ ICE Percentage of Total
1977	1,042,215	838,022	204,193	19.6
1991	1,197,875	1,132,933	64,819	5.4
1992	1,258,481	1,199,560	58,317	4.6
1993	1,327,261	1,263,490	60,761	4.6
1994	1,094,719	1,031,668	61,973	5.7
1995	1,394,554	1,324,202	70,352	5.0
1996	1,649,986	1,549,876	100,110	6.1
1997	1,536,520	1,412,953	123,567	8.0
1998	1,679,439	1,555,776	123,663	7.4
1999	1,714,035	1,579,010	135,025	7.9
2000	1,814,729	1,676,438	138,291	7.6
2001	1,387,486	1,266,213	121,273	8.7
2002	1,062,279	955,310	106,969	10.1
2008	1,043,799	723,865	31,123 HIS/288,811 ERO	2.98/27.7
2009	889,203	556,032	21,251/311,920	2.39/35.1
2010	796,587	463,382	18,290/314,915	2.30/39.5
2011	678,606	340,252	16,261/322,093	2.40/47.5
2012	671,327	364,768	15,937/290,622	2.37/43.3
2013	662,483	420,789	11,996/229,698	1.81/34.7
2014	679,996	486,651	11,626/181,719	1.71/26.7

1. INS Statistical Yearbooks, 1977, 2002, 2002, and 2014. Removals and Returns.
Source: DHS.GOV, Accessed on October 16, 2016, https://www.dhs.gov/news/2015/07/
21/written-testimony-ice-director-senate-committee-judiciary-hearing-titled-
%E2%80%9Coversight

their status, and develop networks in the wider community, it is expected that the female proportion of the illegal alien population will also increase in size.[19] The NYDO sample showed that more males (64.8%) were apprehended than females, and this was a significant difference. In the NYDO sample, most of the apprehended aliens were between 15 and 44 years (85.7%) and there was a significant difference between the age groups apprehended.

Regarding time in the US, many illegal aliens were apprehended during the first year. The distribution appears to be bimodal, in that just as many are apprehended after five years as are in the first year after entry. These statistics only reflect apprehended aliens in the NYDO sample, and there is no information about those aliens that elude apprehension altogether.

Most of the apprehensions in the NYDO sample were tourists, and those who entered without inspection. Many of the apprehended aliens entered the New York area through major ports of entry (International Airports) since the possession of a tourist visa indicates that INS approved an initial legal entry. The significant number of entries without inspection supports the priority of INS to apprehend that cohort of violators. INS grants most apprehended aliens voluntary departure. If an alien leaves the US under voluntary departure there is no punishment imposed, and the alien can make an application for readmission anytime thereafter.

Along the southwest border, most illegal aliens enter the US with the help of a smuggler, or *coyote*. Data from the Legalized Population Survey (LPS), and Mexican Migration Project (MMP71) indicate that 68% of IRCA applicants usually entered the US with the help of a smuggler, or some other illegal entry method.[20] 19% of the sample entered as tourists.

There is a significant difference between those earning above and below the minimum wage, for apprehended aliens from Mexico and other countries. Apprehended aliens in the NYDO sample with two or more years in the US earned above the minimum wage (60.9%), while those with less than two years in the US (35.6%) earned less than the minimum wage. The minimum wage in 1977 was $2.30, and in 1978 was $2.65. Today, we may assume that most of the illegal aliens working in the US earn more than the minimum wage, especially with the lax interior enforcement policies in place.

After processing a deportable alien, the recommendations an agent can make are often shaped by agency policies. Recommendations often depend on whether the deportable alien will show up for future deportation proceedings, or whether the alien poses a risk to the community if released. In the case of deportable aliens, the presumption is that most are high-flight risks, however because the violation of law is considered administrative, the bond is often low, or absent (similar to being released on their own recognizance). Generally, the basis of the recommendation for illegal aliens is often considered less serious than other violations. After 1987, the Federal Sentencing Guidelines Act increased penalties for criminal aliens with prior deportations for aggravated felonies.[21]

Although not statistically significant, those in the NYDO sample with criminal convictions, or pending criminal cases generally had a higher bond than those without a criminal record. It is also important to point out that the higher rate of arrest warrants for Mexican nationals does not necessarily indicate a bias against Mexicans. I would suggest that the large number of arrest warrants issued on Mexican nationals was because those apprehended entered the US without inspection (EWI), a criminal charge though routinely declined prosecution by a standard waiver.

The NYDO sample showed that more Mexican nationals were issued arrest warrants after being apprehended (78%) than any other group of apprehended aliens. Only 29% of all other deportable aliens were issued warrants of arrest. 12% of the sample were designated Western Hemisphere Temporary Restraining Order (WHTRO) receiving employment authorization, and could remain in the US indefinitely. 4% of the sample was classified as *Rearrests*, who had arrest warrants issued prior to their apprehension. 19% were issued Orders to Show Cause (OSC), and 34% of all the apprehended aliens in the sample were issued OSC with Warrant of Arrest. 11% of the NYDO sample had criminal records and this included both convictions and pending criminal cases. It should be noted that the criminal record is a crude indicator of actual criminal activity since they are based on self-reports of the apprehended alien before criminal record checks are completed, and probably underestimate actual criminal activity. All apprehended aliens were fingerprinted in the NYDO sample, but the results of the fingerprinting may take several months. This is usually sometime after the alien is processed, and a disposition in made. The best predictors of criminal activity in the NYDO sample were the amount of time the alien was in the US, age, and gender. Of those apprehended aliens with criminal records, there were more males (89%) than females. 76% of the apprehended aliens with criminal records were between the ages of 17 and 35 years of age. In addition, the enforcement priorities concentrated on illegal aliens employed in the community. Therefore, career offenders, and professional criminals might not be well represented in this population.

As expected, there was a significant difference regarding the amount of bond between males and females in the NYDO sample. Males received higher bonds than females, and this could be explained by the fact that there was less jail space allocated for females. In addition, it might be that agents were more reluctant to detain females because of the possible public reaction, or negative media attention that could result. This corresponds to national arrest data based on gender. More males get arrested than females, and females are more likely to get an order to show cause, or receive the benefits of the WHTRO. The average bond for Mexico was $3,006, compared to $1,118 for all other apprehended aliens.

Single aliens had significantly higher bonds than those that were married. Those aliens in the NYDO sample that were married (35%) were less likely to receive arrest warrants than those who were not (44%). Tourists were more likely to receive an order to show cause without an arrest warrant (19%), and those who entered without inspection (EWI) were more likely to receive an arrest warrant (66%) than the rest of the apprehended aliens in the NYDO. Similarly, EWI's were less likely to receive voluntary departure

(5%) than the rest of the sample (14%). Regarding employment, more service employees were arrested and issued warrants than either professional, or self-employed apprehended aliens. At the time, this finding supports the tradition-al INS policy of focusing on low-level visa abusers. Also, service workers have significantly higher bonds than either professionals, or those classified as self-employed. Overall, those apprehended aliens from Asia, Eastern Europe, and the Middle East were more likely to receive an Order to Show Cause compared with those apprehended aliens from Mexico who were more likely to receive and Order to Show Cause with a Warrant of Arrest. Those apprehended aliens from Western Europe, and the Middle East were more likely to receive Voluntary Departure as a disposition. Those from the Carib-bean were more likely to receive the WHTRO disposition.

The amount of time an apprehended alien is in the US is negatively correlated with the amount of bond received. That is, the longer the appre-hended alien resides in the US before apprehension, the less likely it is that the alien will be detained if arrested by INS. It is obvious that the longer the apprehended alien resides in the US, the more likelihood exists that the alien will be able to acquire some equity that will prevent deportation.

It should be noted that both DACA, and DAPA, as well as the Enforce-ment Priority Program have created a *de facto* amnesty for most of the illegal aliens currently residing in the US. Thus, the above data might offer some insights into the demographics of that population.

CRIMINAL ALIENS IN THE US

Early editions of the INS Statistical Yearbook routinely listed the principal activities and accomplishments of the border patrol. In 1997, the agency began reporting the principal activities and accomplishments of the investi-gations program, signaling a renewed emphasis on criminal aliens. IRCA included a priority on locating, and removing criminal aliens, and IIRIRA allowed for expedited removals of such aliens. The investigators were as-signed to process the now deportable criminal aliens.

Throughout this study, the legacy INS investigators expressed a prefer-ence for working criminal cases, even though most of their work was admin-istrative in nature. As previously indicated, locating and apprehending an illegal alien is an administrative function, although there are instances when a criminal prosecution might be initiated. Agents might be content working on the location of criminal aliens for deportation, but there were limitations due to agency policies, and lack of resources. Recent immigration legislation attempted to focus on removing criminal aliens from the US. Although the legacy INS investigators migrated to DHS on March 1, 2003, most of their workforce continued to work on immigration related matters. The transition to a unified workforce continued, but resistance was expected from former customs agents.

There was a steady increase in Institutional Apprehensions by the investigations program until 2001. Thereafter, there was a decrease in apprehensions, attributed most likely to the transition to the DHS. In 1999, the General Accounting Office (GAO) revisited the factors summarized in a previous finding in 1997 that INS "needed to improve its efforts to identify potentially deportable criminal aliens in federal and state prisons and complete Institutional Hearing Program (IHP) for these aliens before they were released."[22] The GAO report found that INS failed to have records on 36% of the released inmates who could potentially be deportable aliens. In looking at the available data, especially from the Federal Justice Statistics Resource Center (FJSRC)[23] and other sources including Schuck and Williams's[24] analysis on the criminal alien removal system it is suggested that far more criminal aliens than that are not removed. Schuck and Williams concluded that over 90% of the removable criminal aliens in the US go undetected, or are not removed. The reasons for the failure of INS to remove criminal aliens became apparent. INS initiated the IHP, now designated through a Corrective Action Memorandum Institutional Removal Program (IRP), but did not have the manpower to complete the task. The Alien Criminal Apprehension Program (ACAP) also commenced to assist local law enforcement, and remove criminal aliens. In the ACAP, investigators were supposed to respond to reports by local law enforcement regarding aliens in custody. The shortage of investigators made these programs difficult to implement. Also, some local jurisdictions routinely refuse to refer persons suspected of being illegal aliens to the federal immigration complex. At the time, ICE was transitioning, and cross training through its management division, and the role of the special agents to remove criminal aliens was moving to a proposed new classification of immigration agent, and Detention Enforcement Officer.[25] As with any transition, it is suspected that even more of the criminal alien population slipped through the cracks. Before the new agents were in place, it was rumored that the investigations program cut back on the IRP significantly, focusing on more relevant priorities, such as terrorism.

To better understand the magnitude, and shape of the criminal alien population, I decided to use official statistics from DHS supplemented with FJSRC data, especially Study Number 2598[26], Survey of Inmates in State/Federal Correctional Facilities (SISCF), that provided the current data on foreign-born inmates. In 1996, INS processed 65,411 foreign born nationals in institutions throughout the US. This was approximately 6.2% of the total inmate population represented in the SISCF. In that sample, I found that 9.8% were foreign born, indicating that INS may have missed at least 3.6% of that sample based on the DHS data of aliens processed in institutions. Many inmates either refuse to answer questions about their alienage, or give false information to case managers to avoid being deported from the US. As such, it is very likely that such surveys will underestimate the number of foreign-born inmates. As expected, Mexico is the largest contributor to the illegal alien population, and the foreign born criminal population. 43.5% of the foreign-born inmates of the national sample and 87.9% of the aliens processed by INS in jails, and prisons were from Mexico. Since DHS began interior enforcement of the immigration laws there has been a consistent decrease from year to year in the removal of criminal aliens. In January 2004, DHS removed 14,638 aliens from the US. 6,277 of these aliens were criminal aliens, and this was a 12% decrease from the previous year. In September 2003, DHS removed 13,462 aliens from the US, and 5,598 of these aliens were criminals, a 5% decrease from the previous year. [27]

The SISCF includes data for inmates in State and Federal facilities in one file. The data was collected from a universe of 1,409 state prisons, and 127 federally owned and operated facilities. The sample design for both surveys was a stratified two-stage selection that first selected prisons, and then inmates in sampled prisons. The total sample size was 18,326 with 14,285 inmates in State Facilities, and 4,041 inmates in Federal Facilities. The approximate size of the total population was 1,053,451 as of June 30, 1996. The SPSS file generated for this data was recoded primarily to analyze the foreign-born population, and countries were recoded into regions as follows: Other Western Hemisphere, Mexico, Africa, Europe, Asia, Middle East, Oceania, and West Indies. SISCF data reflects that 45.9% of the inmates were in Federal prisons, while 54.1% were in State facilities, and most inmates were in custody for drug offenses (41.4%). 24.6% of the foreign-born inmates were violent offenders, and 20.1% were in custody for public-order offenses. In 2000, most foreign-born federal inmates were in custody for drug (55%), and immigration (36%) convictions, with a steady significant increase in these types of convictions since 1985.

Mexico continued to be the largest contributor of criminal aliens in the foreign-born inmate population. Between 1992 and 2003, INS located 897,706 criminal aliens in institutions and 81.1% of that total was from Mexico. The next largest contributor of criminal aliens comes from other Western Hemisphere countries (9.1%) and the West Indies (5.2%).

REPEAT OFFENDERS

A serious problem confronting the criminal justice system today is the increase in the number of repeat offenders. Recidivism may be defined as a return to criminality after being sentenced for an offense. An offender usually commits another crime after being released from prison. For example, in a study of prisoners released in 15 states in 1994, 67.5% became repeat offenders within 3 years of their release. [28]

In the SISCF sample a significant number of foreign-born are repeat offenders (46.7%). Although 70.5% of the US born inmates are repeat offenders, there are more first-time offenders among the foreign-born inmates (52.8%) than the US born inmates (29%). The fact that US born inmates are returned to the community after they are released, and the foreign born are deported may explain the higher number of native-born recidivists. If this were the case, it would be a strong recommendation for DHS to increase the effectiveness of the IRP. By removing criminal aliens after they complete their sentences we can reduce the recidivist crime rate (repeat offenders) significantly. As a result of the Enforcement Priority Program, DHS now releases some apprehended aliens with criminal records that do not fall within the parameters of the priority program.

Most foreign-born inmates are in custody for drug offenses (41.4%). 24.6% of the foreign-born inmates are classified as violent offenders, and Mexico contributes the highest number of violent offenders by count (179). 40.1% of the violent offenders were from Mexico, although more Mexicans (within the region) were in custody for drug offenses (42.5%). Asia contributed more violent offenders as total percent (31.5%). More Mexicans are in state (56.5%) than federal prisons, as is the case with foreign-born inmates from Europe. Although the modal sentence length is 5-10 years, most Mexicans are serving sentences of 1-3 years (28.7%), and significantly less time than other inmates. These differences were found to be significant.

ICE: THE NEW INS & HOMELAND SECURITY

The transition to DHS merged immigration and customs special agents into one agency. The Office of Personnel Management (OPM) showed 18,509 employees in ICE, and 21,874 in the Bureau of Customs and Border Patrol (CBP), which combines border patrol agents, and INS inspectors with Customs Inspectors. The mission of this new agency is to prevent terrorism, and remove criminal aliens. The political climate, and ongoing debate surrounding illegal aliens will continue to cause problems in developing a sound immigration policy. The history of immigration enforcement is clearly one that focuses on border patrol activity, and can be summarily classified as Mexican immigration control. CBP will most likely continue to be concerned with locating, and apprehending illegal border crossers, mostly Mexicans. The CBP may also continue to exert more power in the overall enforcement policies. Combining former immigration special agents with customs special agents might have initiated the boost interior immigration enforcement needed. However, the transition forced a blend between rival agencies, and created different morale problems among the participants. Although the legacy INS relied on the border patrol for its enforcement strategies, investigating immigration law violations inside the US requires a different strategy. The creation of the Critical Incident Response Team (CIRT) within ICE, added to the enforcement identity long suppressed within the legacy INS. By publishing a Ten Most Wanted Alien List that mirrors the well-known FBI Ten Most Wanted List, ICE attempted to create a positive enforcement identity. The customs agents had higher-grade levels than the immigration agents, and customs was a stronger agency in the criminal justice hierarchy. This contributed to morale problems for the legacy INS, but most of the morale issues surrounded the implementation of agency policies.

It appears that the Obama administration, through DHS, did not prioritize interior enforcement, or rationalized its policies based on prosecutorial discretion, and lack of resources. The perception of the illegal alien as poor, hard-working, and simply without proper documentation, will continue to obfuscate the problem, making solutions problematic. Even the USA Patriot Act minimized the problem of illegal aliens living in the US, and viewed immigration as a service for admitting aliens, coupled with political confusion about the seriousness of the problem.[29] Legislators avoid the use of the term amnesty in any immigration law reform, but policies suggest the opposite. Depending on who is in power will determine whether amnesty will be considered in new legislation, or cloaked as a guest worker program. The small number of agents allocated for locating and apprehending the millions of illegal aliens in the US serves as reminder that removing them would be difficult. Historically, the standard solution was to grant amnesty, even though most responsible scholars agree that this is not a good idea. Mainly because it rewards rule breaking, and creates an endless cycle of such behavior.

According to Vaughn, DHS agents encountered 722,000 deportable aliens in 2013, and many were released in what is referred to as *catch and release*. Most of the deportable aliens came to the attention of ICE after they were arrested by local police. This process resulted in immigration charges on only 195,000 (25%), and 68,000 (35% of all criminal aliens encountered) aliens with criminal convictions were released. Vaughn further reported that interior enforcement declined 40% since 2011 because of the enforcement priority program. In addition, 870,000 deportable aliens that were ordered removed, remain in the US.[30]

CONCLUDING STATEMENT

If we observe the ongoing processes involved in social interaction, we may better understand why they occur. In the global environment, relationships between operators, the political structure, and the other parts of the general environment can explain the course of immigration enforcement. It appeared that loosely coupled agencies such as the legacy INS were resistant to change.[31] The 911 terrorist attacks contributed to the dismantling of that agency, and even though the effects of 911 were global, it took another 18 months before DHS-ICE took over the enforcement of the immigration laws. There are high expectations about immigration reform, but very little has changed regarding perceptions about the way immigration laws should be enforced. Unable, or unwilling to pass legislation regarding the immigration problem, President Obama implemented his plans through executive orders, and the policies that followed. These plans were essentially ideologically based, and paid scant attention to the rule of law. The hope and change mantra of his campaign rhetoric left immigration policies in complete disarray, and failed to establish any semblance of a meaningful reform of immigration law.

We can also gain a better understanding of how deviance is defined by focusing on the concept of *power*. A relationship exists between the deviant, and those who label them. Power is the ability to influence the behavior of others in accordance with the intentions of the one who wields the power.[32] It is also the potential ability of one person to induce forces on another toward change.[33] Power is also

> . . . the probability that one actor within a social relationship will be in a position to carry out his will despite resistance, regardless of the basis on which this probability rests.[34]

In civil societies, coercive power, especially the use of force, is the least acceptable method to achieve an outcome. Such coercion leads to decreased attraction, and high resistance of the coerced toward the one coercing.[35] Weber's rational-legal legitimation serves as the basis for power in most large-scale organizations. This power revolves around a set of logical rules that the members in the organization accept as plausible. The findings illustrated that the control agents strongly disagreed with agency policies, but they followed them even when the policies contradicted perceived mission goals. Investigators accepted the legal system, and the legitimate right of those empowered to administer it. Etzioni characterizes the *involvement* of the actor in the organization as being *committed,* or *alienated*, and the agents were, more or less, alienated. The control agent's view from the bottom up reflected a perceived sense of powerlessness.

> An actor who exercises power, and an actor subject to this power, who responds to this subjection with either more or less alienation or more or less commitment.[36]

Although coercive force is the least acceptable method of achieving an outcome in a democratic society, one should not underestimate the clear message underlying the potential use of force. Control agencies are especially protective of their internal machinations. Agents may be fully aware of what is going on inside their agency, and disagree with policies that seem to be counterproductive, but they rarely make their disagreements public. Even though whistleblower rules exist, it is unusual for a law enforcement officer to come forward and publicly confront perceived wrongdoings. It does occur, but less than it should. The government has the capacity to employ all three types of power, but in civil society most compliance rests on a blend of utilitarian (job security, employee benefits, compensation, and status), and normative (intrinsic rewards such as interesting work, identification with goals, and making a contribution to society).[37] The normative power of the agency has eroded, as reflected in the low morale of agents who essentially continue to perceive their goals as contradicted by the agency's policies. Although the official mission statements and policies appear to merge, the implementation of these official strategies are quite the opposite.

On the other hand, whenever lethal force is used, the user will undoubtedly be subject to intense scrutiny. Examples of the use of lethal force by control agencies include the Waco, Texas incident involving David Koresh and the Branch Davidians, and the actions of a white separatist, Randy Weaver, at Ruby Ridge, that led to the killing of his wife and son, and a U. S. Marshal. Both incidents resulted in official critiques of the agencies involved.[38] At the legacy INS, lethal force was rarely used, since the population is controlled through administrative processes. On the other hand, illegal aliens die attempting to enter the US illegally. This creates sympathy for their plight, and further directs criticism at enforcement strategies such as *Operation Gatekeeper*[39] that attempted to restrict illegal alien traffic in high impact areas. As expected, the illegal aliens simply avoided those areas, choosing even more dangerous routes over deserts that cause loss of life due to dehydration, and exposure to the elements. If the strategy is to deter, such enforcement strategies seem pointless, and inhumane. Solutions to the illegal alien problem are far more complex than this. Enhancing border security should be a priority, but history reminds us that certain legislation and enforcement strategies may also strengthen the nefarious efforts of those whose business it is to circumvent these laws. The war on drugs which created the cartels, and how prohibition did the same for the *mafia,* serve as examples of how criminalizing behavior may increase deviance.

Perhaps the hesitancy to rebel against perceived contradictions stems from the societal prerequisite to conform to legitimate authority. When the boundaries of legitimacy are breached, the community may decide that new leadership is needed. A stark difference between the presidential candidates in 2016 regarding immigration enforcement may reflect this process. Mrs.

Clinton promoted a liberal immigration policy, which would allow the millions of illegal aliens currently in the US to remain here, and eventually become citizens. The justification for such a strategy is typically based on humanitarian grounds, since the long-term costs of such a policy could be catastrophic with regard to entitlement programs.[40] More importantly, rewarding someone for breaking the rules will only send the message that such behavior is appropriate. The only way this could be achieved would be through an amnesty bill, regardless of what the proponents of such a strategy call it. The same strategy was implemented under President Reagan with IRCA, and the result is what we currently have in the US. Instead of halting illegal entries, amnesty encouraged more of the same behavior, and instead of several million illegal aliens we may now have up to 20 million illegal aliens waiting for another IRCA. The decades old position that only 11 million illegal aliens are in the US fails to recognize the reality of migration patterns, and surely does not consider the impact of President Obama's executive orders that encouraged massive illegal entries. Among other factors, immigration may be one of the main reasons Mrs. Clinton lost the election.

Schur refers to the relationships between deviants, and those that label them, as *stigma contests*.[41] The state labels real, imagined individuals, or groups that threaten the established order, as deviants. Illegal aliens are placed at the lower end of the continuum of deviantness because the state does not perceive them as a serious threat to the social system. Illegal immigration is tolerated, and even encouraged by the state because illegal aliens provide a source of cheap labor. However, they are not permitted total access to the social system, since complete access might contribute to economic instability. Perhaps, this explains the preference to concentrate on border, over interior enforcement. If the border patrol made one million or more apprehensions annually, does this mean that just as many eluded detections? The *dark figure*[42] in criminology suggests that possibility. A significant number of aliens enter the US legally with temporary visas, and then overstay their time becoming illegal aliens. Most of the overstay aliens do so intentionally, and use the liberal temporary visa approval process to do so. It is difficult to estimate the number of illegal aliens that successfully elude apprehension, but current polices will not stem the tide of illegal aliens flowing into the US. It is possible to seal the border, but doing so would cause extreme hardship for international commerce, and tourism.

Similarly, DEA has admitted that attempts to prevent drug trafficking are not very successful. Gordon states that the so-called *war on drugs* is viewed as a complete failure[43], including tens of thousands of lives lost, and human rights violations. Mexico is considered the main source of worldwide illegal drugs, and the drug cartels continue to flourish there despite the arrest of high-level cartel members. The US government continues to support this war on drugs, both with financial and technical assistance. Gordon further explains that the drug war has a direct connection to the proliferation of gangs in the US, who act as part of the cartel's drug distribution network, as well as the proliferation of firearms on both sides of the southwest US border.

The enormous cost of the war on drugs with clearly little success to date, and the proliferation of drugs including an apparent national fascination with the legalization of marijuana, perhaps one of the most dangerous drugs of all, gives one pause when considering solutions to crime prevention. Michael Levine, a former undercover DEA agent, describes the organizational ineptitude of the DEA, and reading his account[44] of Operation Trifecta suggested a parallel to the INS debacle. It seems that those at the top levels of the enforcement agencies are more concerned with their personal success than with successfully implementing an agency mission. Even the FBI under Director Comey became embroiled in a political controversy surrounding whether to indict Mrs. Clinton over her use of a private server. Politics and law enforcement go hand in hand, but politics based on greed and self-preservation can only be an impediment to good law enforcement. The examples of managerial obstruction to the efforts of INS agents to conduct investigations mirror this process.

Legislators also attempted to deal with the illegal alien problem by removing the main lure of illegal aliens to the US—jobs. To do this effectively, the agency would have to strictly enforce job site investigations, which creates even more problems than locating and apprehending illegal aliens inside the US. Violations of such laws could result in punishing employers with fines, criminal prosecution, and even detaining those who hired illegal aliens. It seemed like a good idea, but it was difficult to implement. The problem in enforcing the immigration laws at job sites is that employers are not experts at document fraud, and they often accept any documentation offered by the alien. Although most could become proficient in determining alien eligibility for lawful employment, there does not seem to be much interest in doing so. If businesses hire accountants to prepare tax returns to comply with the tax laws, they could also hire immigration consultants to monitor a firm's compliance with immigration laws. Such consultants would have to be monitored, but accountants are monitored as well. One of the most productive strategies used by the legacy INS to locate and apprehend illegal aliens employed in the community was the ACIS unit. Unfortunately, the agency chose to stop this type of enforcement, most likely as a result of pressure from various interest groups, or ideological concerns. When in full operation, ACIS was very effective in locating and apprehending illegal aliens, and the investigators assigned to those units experienced higher morale.

Stigma contests evolve between aliens, the control agency, as well as other parts of the general environment. Legal and social groups, including immigration lawyers, religious and human interest groups, and others develop a vested interest in advocating on behalf of illegal aliens. We know that organizations create networks that perpetuate their existence, and the immigration enforcement environment is no exception. On the surface, illegal aliens appear to be a powerless group living in fear of deportation. However, their relationship to other parts of the social structure contributes to the overall perception. Businessmen view the illegal alien as a source of cheap labor, while other interest groups view that population as an unlimited client pool. Since immigrants are potential voters, politicians push for amnesty and *a path to citizenship* thinking that the new citizens will vote for them. The plight of the illegal alien serves as the *raison d'être* for these advocates. Immigration lawyers, and the enormous industry of immigration consultants have a limitless pool of clients at their disposal. In the final analysis, the powerlessness of illegal aliens is reversed by their position in these stigma contests. Some of the recommendations in the *Final Report of the Select Committee on Immigration and Refugee Policy*[45] supported this view. For example, the recommendation to give amnesty to illegal aliens in the US clearly reflected this pattern. We now see illegal aliens congregate on street corners as so-called day laborers.[46] They can do so in plain view of the authorities, and an immigration agent could easily articulate probable cause to question their right to be in the US. Every immigration officer has that authority under the law, but policies and sanctuary cities prevent them from doing so. In addition, illegal aliens are destigmatized by institutional changes such as the availability of identification cards for access to city services,[47] in-state tuition benefits for illegal alien college students,[48] and eligibility for health care[49] to cite a few.

Critics referred to the legacy INS as an ineffective, corrupt, weak, and overburdened bureaucratic *nightmare*.[50] On behalf of the real policy makers, the agency did an excellent job in accomplishing their goals by allowing a marginal class of individuals to become entrenched in the social system of the US. This same characterization can be applied to the DHS. This arrangement offers sending countries a *release valve* for their overburdened populations, and facilitates the greedy businesses that profit from employing illegal aliens. Admittedly, this eases the domestic problems of Mexico, a country that also has large oil and natural gas reserves, and provides a source of cheap labor for businesses in the US. Such policies will perpetuate the status of the illegal alien, denying them full participation in the social system. As previously indicated, the illegal alien also serves as a convenient scapegoat for the problems of our society, the effects of which create an organizational environment in which agents, and their managers are in continuous conflict. The legacy INS continued in a downward spiral as agents became more and more frustrated with their inability to complete their mission, and this morale problem carried over to the DHS-ICE. Morale in a public-sector agency is problematic. It is difficult to accommodate the needs of employees when agencies are driven by politics, and policies can make adherence to statutes a contradiction, in some instances.

Although it was based on guesswork and poor estimates, legislators passed the 1986 Immigration Act, which offered amnesty to millions of illegal aliens. Some consider the implementation of an effective interior enforcement strategy a drastic measure, likening agents to the *Gestapo,* and fearing the creation of a police state. To deal with such fears, legislators decided to grant amnesty, believing such a policy would solve the immigration problem. However, granting amnesty to economic refugees can have a negative impact on the economy, since the new legal aliens will assumedly exacerbate taxed entitlement programs. Amnesty also creates problems for future interior enforcement measures by creating another subclass with equities. Merely proposing amnesty increases surreptitious entries into the US, because the border crosser hopes to take advantage of expected amnesty legislation. It will also increase the demand for fraudulent documents to support claims of required residence in the US, mandated by any amnesty legislation.

In January 2004, President Bush recommended a new guest worker program, and clearly stated that he was opposed to amnesty "because it encourages the violation of our laws and perpetuates illegal immigration." According to this plan, willing workers, and employers will unite to form a unique relationship based on mutual needs. The foreign workers, mostly Mexicans, will return "permanently" to their homeland after they finish their work in the US. These workers will receive credit for retirement in their home countries as an enticement to return home. An important provision of this new plan included reducing the cost of remittances, and President Bush indicated that such costs have already been reduced by 60%. The plan will be enhanced with the continuation of the North American Fair Trade Agreement (NAFTA), and both the US and then President Vicente Fox of Mexico supported the provisions of the plan.[51] It did not seem to be well thought out, nor did it address the immediate problems regarding the interior enforcement issues. Morgan recommended against such plans that mirror the Bracero programs of the past because they fail to consider border control, and working conditions of migrants. Both need to be in place for such programs to work.[52] Others believed the President had "taken on one of our thorniest problems . . . articulating a conservative case for change . . . accepting the reality of the market-driven migrant flow."[53] Both presidential candidates in the 2016 election were reportedly opposed to the Trans Pacific Partnership (TPP), and suggest that it was detrimental to American workers.[54] TPP is arguably NAFTA on steroids, and feeds into the global capitalist's policies regarding immigration.

In some instances, labeling theory suggests that identifying an individual as a deviant may lead to a pattern of *secondary deviance,* a condition thrust upon the individual in this case either by the control agency, which seeks to control, or the deviant that comes to identify with the label. Comparing Lemert's[55] concepts of primary and secondary deviance, Clinard referred to this as the irony of social control[56]. The act of labeling an individual creates a set of expectations that the individual is expected to fulfill. In some cases, it might deter further deviant acts, or cause the deviant to stop being a deviant. In terms of labeling illegal aliens as deviants, our tolerance for ethnic diversity prevents labeling them as such. Citizens seem to acknowledge their presence as part of the social milieu, and the flow of illegal aliens into the US continues unabated. The label illegal alien creates an environment in which everyone understands the expectations of the other. The control agency parses the label even further to clarify its mission. By issuing an enforcement priorities memorandum,[57] DHS specified three categories of illegal aliens as priorities within the general concerns of national security, border security, and public safety. The underlying strategy was to implement these priorities at the earliest point in the process, and placed most of the discretion in the hands of the control agents. Of course, this discretion was rigidly tempered by approval from the top down. Utilizing the legal construct of prosecutorial discretion, the agency created an enforcement strategy that targeted only a small portion of the illegal alien population, and even that cohort was subject to interpretation. Some even consider the current enforcement policies nothing more than a *de facto* amnesty.[58] In fact, unless the agent follows the imputed priorities of the *de facto* amnesty that agent can expect disciplinary action.[59] As such, the control agent has very little discretion in completing tasks.

The DHS has carefully avoided dealing with the illegal alien problem by limiting its priorities to terrorism, and criminal aliens. Except for those "defined by the agency" as a threat to society, it chooses to ignore the millions of illegal aliens inside the US. Even in this exclusive mission, DHS appears incompetent in attempting to implement the policy. Because of sanctuary city policies, law enforcement agencies throughout the US are not permitted to enforce immigration laws, and ICE ignores any referrals unless they fit into the self-defined categories.

Insiders have characterized ICE in its early development as a hostile takeover by the Customs Service, however it appears that the transition normalized. It may be that the higher-grade customs agents did not consider the lower grade legacy INS agents their equals, but this does not seem to be endemic, according to SAC Ficke. At this time, most of the legacy agents have retired, and the newly hired agents will be trained by the agency to conform to stated policies. For all practical purposes, the legacy INS interior enforcement border patrol strategies were abandoned. All these considerations will continue to obscure the fundamental issue of a viable interior immigration enforcement strategy.

Official policies continue to ignore the problem, and most of the participants in the total environment of the illegal alien remain in limbo. Citizens
and lawful resident aliens of the US compete with illegal aliens who are
willing to take low paying jobs. A large segment of the legal population
might be attracted to the jobs, if wages and working conditions were acceptable. Historically, illegal aliens remain silent on low wages or inferior working conditions, because doing so threatened detection and deportation, but
recently it seems that they are becoming more brazen in this regard. As a
result of institutional proclamations from state authorities to intentionally
ignore immigration laws, and provide sanctuary for millions of law breakers
it appears that the illegal alien population is far from powerless.

The weak interior enforcement of the immigration laws benefits the sending countries in the short term by relieving population demands. However,
the brain drain impacts on the long-term growth of these sending countries.
Furthermore, the sending countries defer correcting the problems that cause
the migration flow in the first place. Advocates of increased immigration
maintain that the US lags behind other countries in attracting the "best and
brightest," and that current immigration laws should increase the admission
of skilled and educated immigrants.[60] Often, these "best and brightest" permanently emigrate to the host countries, contributing to the conditions in
their country of origin that force them to leave in the first place. The recommendations to increase immigration of the special skills classes, which includes a preference for mostly younger rather than older immigrants, reflects
a selfish ideology that ignores the needs of the poor developing countries
providing these best and brightest candidates. Ecologically, such a policy
promotes academic wastelands in the sending countries. Some in the US are
concerned about losing immigrants due to the economy, and recognize the
impact of brain drain policies.[61] Some legislators consider ways of keeping
undocumented aliens in the US such as granting permanent visas to them if
they graduate from college.[62] Such policies would further contribute to the
brain drain, encourage illegal immigration, and essentially contradict the
intent of the laws regarding study abroad, which promote returning to the
country of origin with the knowledge gained. Perhaps the advocates of increased immigration make their claims at the behest of globalists, and the
real intent is to obtain special needed skills at lower wages. The H1 visa
programs facilitate this brain drain scenario, but even in a more sinister way.
They create a cohort of dependent intending migrants who are locked in a
limbo state in which they can remain only if they agree to a form of contract
slavery. Their working conditions are often not the same as legal residents in
the same positions. Often, policies to implement these special labor certification visas pay scant attention to the integrity of the visa application process.
One might also suggest that brain drain policies are a form of intellectual
colonialism. In terms of national security, it is imperative that control agen-

cies pay careful attention to potential fraud, and the ever-growing threat of terrorism.

Undoubtedly, this understanding between nations does little to address issues of corruption and inequality. The current situation increases poverty, lack of jobs, overpopulation, and corruption in the sending countries, and the illegal alien population in the US continues to grow. How much more illegal immigration the US can absorb is not known, but the presence of millions of illegal aliens undoubtedly impacts on the availability of services to the general population. The greed of business owners that want cheap labor lowers the overall standard of living in the host country. The decisions to increase international migration based on the policies of the globalists contribute to a symbiotic relationship. This relationship increases the brain drain from countries that will lose the individuals who might solve the problems causing the brain drain.

Perhaps the illegal alien is a symptom of global capitalism. The debate between the globalists and the nativists continues to grow, and the migration of millions of people on the planet is part of that process. Immigration enforcement can be placed on a continuum that runs from open borders through closed borders. It is not practical to view this macrosociological process in terms of one issue, such as immigration enforcement. Immigration matters are closely tied to macro-level processes, and the solutions to any problems resulting from the world market interactions must be addressed in the same manner. In discussing Brexit, or the United Kingdom's (UK) decision to separate from the European Union (EU), Bennett[63] suggests that a confederation with mutually beneficial agreements would create a group of nations in which migration would be facilitated, and welcomed. He indicates that if the UK were to separate from the EU, and subsequently create a confederation with countries including Australia, New Zealand, and the US, including access to NAFTA, the outcome would be beneficial to all parties concerned. According to Bennett, immigration and open borders contributed to the UK Brexit movement in which the UK could not deport criminal aliens (unless they committed serious crimes—similar to the Priority Enforcement Program in DHS ICE), nor could it even investigate the sham marriages so often perpetrated in immigration applications, since it was in the EU, and part of the European Court of Human Rights (ECHR). The failure to address such obvious deviant acts necessarily contributes to a response by those in the population who are directly impacted by them. That response may boil over into a demand for change that will not be ignored, or quashed by those in power.

In 1974, I was sworn in as a criminal investigator in a small room on the top floor of 20 West Broadway, just a block away from the tragedy that occurred in New York City on 911. I was proud that I had achieved becoming a federal agent, and I continue to hold the belief that law enforcement is a noble profession that provides for the public safety. After leaving INS, I transferred to Federal Parole where I eventually was promoted to Senior Federal Parole Officer in the Special Offender Unit which included supervising organized crime and other violent predatory offenders. Although the agency maintained a dual mandate including rehabilitation and public safety, the Special Offender Unit concentrated on the latter part of the mission. I worked with the FBI, other federal agencies, and local police to supervise these career offenders. I remember one high ranking member of the mafia telling me that when he was in prison, he heard rumors from other inmates that I was the toughest parole officer in the system. I found this interesting, since my self-perception was that I held parolees accountable, but was fair in the way I treated them. My first meeting with a parolee involved explaining the conditions of release, and telling the parolee that that there was zero tolerance for any new criminal behavior. The parolees seemed to understand this simple rule, and the integrity of the criminal justice system is based on the understanding that the rule of law is sacrosanct. Parolees, especially career offenders, will attempt to negotiate a supervision plan by testing how the parole officer stands up to intimidation. If the parole officer seems weak, or easily intimidated, the parolee is then in control of the relationship. It is imperative that the officer not fall prey to this technique. The law-abiding public expects the police to enforce the laws, and when this expectation is lost there are consequences. In my opinion, Donald Trump won the 2016 presidential election because many saw a breakdown in this process. In this case, ignoring the rule of law regarding illegal aliens sends a strong message, and an obvious outcome.

Highlighting issues and concerns that contribute to dysfunction in a law enforcement agency may suggest solutions to the overall immigration problem, and hopefully contribute to the study of law enforcement as well. One tenet of sociology points to what happens when a significant number of people fail to follow the rules in the social structure. Significant rule breaking by large numbers of people may initiate changing the rules. On the other hand, ignoring rule breakers, or continuing to forgive them, only contributes to confusion, implicitly rewards such behavior, and sends the message that normlessness is acceptable. The result is *anomie*. The success of a tertiary deviant revolution is relative to the gravity of the deviance, and whether most participants in the environment can adapt to it. Because of the 2016 election, it appears that the movement to normalize the deviantness of illegal aliens has failed to convince most Americans, who decided that border security and immigration reform are still relevant. If we realize that the illegal alien problem is caused by macro level variables, the solution to the problem necessitates a global plan. If sovereignty seems to get in the way, the global capitalists may be able to resolve some of these issues by working on the negatives associated with global capitalism. Globalists should consider what Etzioni suggested in his compliance theory,[64] a cooperation within the global community, including all the stakeholders, not just those in power.

The script for this book began in the shadow of the World Trade Center, and the denouement unravels with the election of Donald Trump as President of the US. Mr. Trump enters office with a Republican majority in both houses of Congress. He promised to enforce the laws of the US, and received the endorsement of both the Customs Border Patrol union, as well as ICE agents. Solving the illegal alien problem will not be an easy task, especially regarding certain local politicians who have stated that they intend to continue to provide sanctuary to millions of illegal aliens.[65] However, it is a violation of law to harbor illegal aliens (8 USC 1324), and it is also illegal for any government entity or official to prohibit, or restrict sending information to ICE about the immigration status of any individual (8 USC 1373). It is unlikely that the new US Attorney General will prosecute local politicians under these laws, but the underlying principles of the rule of law are in jeopardy if sanctuary cities are not brought under control. It is also unlikely that there will be mass deportations, and the newly elected President indicated that he will continue the basic provisions of Obama's enforcement priority program which concentrates on the removal of criminal illegal aliens. Since the late Leonard Chapman was Commissioner of the INS, the enforcement of the immigration laws continued to deteriorate, due to inconsistent policies and weak leadership. Politics, and political correctness got in the way of intelligent law enforcement, placing the public safety at ever increasing risk. With this new administration, our leaders could move to correct the malfeasance and ineptitude that obstructed efforts to enforce the law. It is imperative that President Trump refresh his administration, and appoint new leadership that will enforce the rule of law, and support the faithful completion of the respective missions of all law enforcement agencies. Comprehensive immigration reform is not as complicated as one might think. Most of the provisions of the current INA provide a good foundation to implement the immigration mandate. The main problem is that critical sections of the law are not being enforced. President Trump's clarion call to *build the wall* is more a symbolic reference to the vulnerability of the southwest border, and will be less effective than restoring the rule of law, coupled with the necessary resources and support to do so.

NOTES

1. Committee on the Judiciary. (1979). *U. S. Immigration Law and Policy: 1952-1979,* Washington, DC: U. S. Government Printing Office.

———. (1977a). *Illegal aliens: Analysis and Background,* Washington, DC: U. S. Government Printing Office.

———. (1977b). Illegal aliens and Alien Labor: A Bibliography and Compilation of Background Materials, 1970-June 1977, Washington, DC: U. S. Government Printing Office.

Select Committee on Population. (1978). *Legal and Illegal Immigration to the US,* Washington, DC: U. S. Government Printing Office.

2. North, David S. (1978). Illegal aliens: Final Report Outlining a Rationale for and a Preliminary Design of a Study of the Magnitude, Distribution, flow Characteristics and Impacts of Illegal aliens in the US, Washington, DC: Linton and Company.

———. and Marion F. Houstoun. (1976). The Characteristics and Role of Illegal Aliens in the US Labor Market: An Exploratory Study, Washington, DC: Linton and Company.

3. Keely, Charles B. (1977). "Counting the Uncountable: Estimates of Undocumented Aliens in the US". *Population and Development Review.* 3(4): 473-481.Bustamante, Jorge. (1973). "The Historical Context of Undocumented Mexican Migration to the US". *Aztlan,* 3(2): 257-281.

Bustamante, Jorge A., (1972). "The Wetback as Deviant: An Application of Labeling Theory," American *Journal of Sociology,* 77(4): 706-718.

Schroeder, Richard C. (1976). *Illegal Immigration,* Editorial Research Reports, 2 (Dec. 10): 22.

Samora, Julian (1971). *Los Mojados: The Wetback Story,* Indiana: University of Notre Dame Press.

4. Simon, Julian. (July 10, 1980). Immigrants, Especially Illegals, Raise U. S. Incomes, Newsday.Weissinger, George J. (July 26, 1980). "Assessing Aliens Impact,*" Newsday,* Letters to the Editor.

5. US General Accounting Office, "Border Patrol Action Needed to Improve Oversight of Post Apprehension Consequences," GAO-17-66, Accessed January 22, 2017, http://www.gao.gov/products/GAO-17-66

6. King, Allan. (1979). The Effect of Illegal aliens on Employment in the US, Texas: University of Texas at Austin.

7. North, David S., Marion F. Houstoun, and Washington, DC. Linton and Co. 1976. "The Characteristics and Role of Illegal Aliens in the U.S. Labor Market: An Exploratory Study." *ERIC*, EBSCO*host* (Accessed October 1, 2016).

8. Behrens, Steve, ed. (1978). *Questions and Answers on U. S. Immigration and Population,* Washington, DC: Zero Population Growth.

9. Weissinger, George. (2003). The Illegal Alien Problem: Enforcing the Immigration Laws. Immigration-usa.com, Accessed June 16, 2016, http://www.immigration-usa.com/george_weissinger.html

10. Skerry, Peter, (August 12, 2001), "Why Amnesty is the wrong way to go," Washington Post, p. B1.

11. Camorata, S.A., R. Beck, & J Gimpel (December 17, 2002). Elite v. Public Opinion: An Examination of Divergent Views on Immigration. Paper presented at the National Press Club. Washington D.C. CIS.org, Accessed June 16, 2016, http://www.cis.org/articles/2002/elitepublic.html

12. Greenhouse, Steven. (October 24, 2003). Wal-Mart Raids by US Aimed at Illegal Immigrants. New York Times, NYTimes.com, Accessed June 16, 2016, http://www.nytimes.com/2003/10/24/national/24IMMI.html

13. Riley, Michael. "A grim gamble," *Denver Post,* October 19, 2003.

14. All reported differences were significant using Chi-square analysis for both the NYDO sample and the FJSRC data analysis.

15. Chi-square=552.89, df=1, p<0.01.

16. INS Statistical Yearbook, 1977.

17. DHS Statistical Table 35, Aliens apprehended by program and border patrol sector, investigations special agents in charge (SAC) jurisdiction, and area of responsibility: fiscal years 2005-2015.

18. Triennial Comprehensive Report on Immigration, p. 16.

19. The Mexican Migration Project and Latin American Migration Project offer databases that can test the hypotheses suggested here.

20. "The Mexican Migration Project (MMP) is a collaborative research project based at the Princeton University and the University of Guadalajara", Accessed June 16, 2016, http://mmp.opr.princeton.edu/databases/citations-en.aspx

21. Aggravated felonies included violent drug trafficking, felony property offenses, or smuggling more than six aliens. U.S.S.G. App. C, Nos. 193, 196, 375, 450, 524; in BJS, NCJ 191745, p. 8.

22. Criminal Aliens: INS' Efforts to Identify and Remove Imprisoned Aliens Need to Be Improved (GAO/TGGD-99-47)

23. Survey of Inmates in State and Federal Correctional Facilities-1997, Source at: http://webapp.icpsr.umich.edu/cocoon/NACJD-STUDY/02598.xml

24. Schuck, Peter H. and John Williams, (Spring, 1999). "Removing Criminal Aliens: The pitfalls and promises of federalism." Harvard Journal of Law and Public Policy. Cambridge: MA, pp. 367-463.

25. USDOJ Annual Reports, "Corrective Action Report: Efforts to Identify and Remove Criminal Aliens." (12/2/02)

26. U.S. Dept. of Justice, Bureau of Justice Statistics, and U.S. Dept. of Justice, Federal Bureau of Prisons. SURVEY OF INMATES IN STATE AND FEDERAL CORRECTIONAL FACILITIES, 1997 [Computer file]. Compiled by U.S. Dept. of Commerce, Bureau of the Census. ICPSR ed. Ann Arbor, MI: Inter-university Consortium for Political and Social Research [producer and distributor], 2001.

27. DHS Monthly Statistical Reports, DHS Website, Accessed June 16, 2016, http://uscis.gov/graphics/shared/aboutus/statistics/msrsep03/REMOVAL.HTM

28. Lanagan, Patrick A., David J. Levin. (June 2002). Recidivism of Prisoners Released in 1994. NCJ 193427. US Department of Justice, Office of Justice Programs, Bureau of Justice Statistics. Washington, DC. Accessed June 16, 2016, http://www.ojp.usdoj.gov/bjs/

29. Jenks, Rosemary, *The USA Patriot Act of 2001: A Summary of the Anti-Terrorism Law's Immigration-Related Problems,* Washington, DC: Center for Immigration Studies, December 2001. CIS.org, Accessed June 16, 2016, http://www.cis.org/articles/2001/back1501.html

30. Jessica Vaughn, "Catch and Release," Center for Immigration Studies, Accessed October 11, 2016, http://cis.org/catch-and-release.

31. Hall, Richard H. (1977). *Organizations: Structure and Process,* New Jersey: Prentice-Hall.

32. Goldhamer and Shils, 1939.

33. Winch, 1962.

34. Weber, Max. (1947). The Theory of Social and Economic Organization, New York: The Free Press.

35. French and Raven, 1959.

36. Etzioni, Amitai. (1970). "Compliance Theory," in *The Sociology of Organizations: Basic Studies,* ed. By Oscar Grusky and George Miller, New York: The Free Press, p. 103.

37. Fred C. Lunenburg, "Compliance Theory and Organizational Effectiveness," *International Journal of Scholarly Academic Intellectual Diversity* 14, no. 1 (2012).

38. Johnston, David. (September 9, 1995). "Informer Says Siege Figure Pressed Gun Sale," *New York Times,* p. 8.

39. The National Border Patrol Strategy. Retrieved from http://www.immigration.gov/graphics/exec/shared/lawenf/bpatrol/strategy.htm

40. Rector, Robert, "Amnesty Would Cost Taxpayers Trillions, National Academy of Sciences Report Indicates," The Daily Signal, November 4, 2916, Accessed on November 30, 2916 at http://dailysignal.com/2016/11/04/amnesty-would-cost-taxpayers-trillions-national-academy-of-sciences-report-indicates/

41. Schur, Edwin M. (1980). The Politics of Deviance: Stigma Contests and the Uses of Power, New Jersey: Prentice Hall, Inc.

42. Sagarin, Edward. 1976. "The impact of crime (Book Review)." *American Journal of Sociology* 81, 1223. *Book Review Digest Retrospective: 1903-1982 (H.W. Wilson),* EBSCO*host* (accessed October 4, 2016).

43. Rebecca Gordon, "The US's War on Drugs' Has Spiraled Dangerously Out of Control," *The Nation,* March 23, 2015, https://www.thenation.com/article/can-you-say-blowback-spanish-failed-war-drugs-mexico-and-united-states/ (Accessed on October 3, 2016)

44. Levine, Michael. *Deep Cover: The Inside Story of How DEA Infighting, Incompetence, and Subterfuge Lost US the Biggest Battle of the Drug War.* Book Baby, 1990.

45. Congress of the U.S., Washington, DC, Select Commission on Immigration and Refugee Policy. 1981. "U.S. Immigration Policy and the National Interest. The Final Report and Recommendations of the Select Commission on Immigration and Refugee Policy with Supplemental Views by Commissioners." *ERIC*, EBSCO*host* (Accessed October 1, 2016).

46. Ordóñez, Juan Thomas. "Introduction." In *Jornalero: Being a Day Laborer in the USA*, 1-20. University of California Press, 2015. http://www.jstor.org/stable/10.1525/j.ctt14btfzf.6.

47. NYC IDNYC, "Idnyc," ed. IDNYC (New York, NY: New York City 2014). https://www1.nyc.gov/site/idnyc/about/about.page (Accessed on October 8, 2016)

48. National Conference of State Legislatures, "Undocumented Student Tuition: Overview," (2015).

49. Louise Radnofsky, "Illegal Immigrants Get Public Health Care, Despite Federal Policy," *Wall Street Journal*, March 24, 2016.

50. Kelly, Orr. (June 22, 1981). "The Great American Immigration Nightmare," *U. S. News and World Report*, pp. 27-32.

51. Associated Press, *Text of Bush, Fox Comments*, The Guardian Unlimited, 1/12/2004, http://www.guardian.co.uk/worldlatest/story/0,1280,-3617017,00.html

52. Morgan, Kristi L.1. 2004. "Evaluating Guest Worker Programs in the U.S.: A Comparison of the Bracero Program and President Bush's Proposed Immigration Reform Plan." *Berkeley La Raza Law Journal* 15, no. 2: 125-144. *Legal Source*, EBSCO*host* (accessed October 1, 2016).

53. Jacoby, Tamar, (1/12/2004). *America as a beacon: American Conservatism*, The Wall Street Journal Online, http://online.wsj.com/article/0,,SB107386487358072700,00.html

54. "2016 presidential candidates on the Trans-Pacific Partnership trade deal," Accessed on September 16, 2016 at https://ballotpedia.org/2016_presidential_candidates_on_the_Trans-Pacific_Partnership_trade_deal

55. Edwin M. Lemert, *Social Pathology* (NY: McGraw Hill, 1951).

56. Marshall Clinard and Robert F. Meier, Sociology of Deviant Behavior (Boston, MA: Cengage, 2016), 43.

57. Jeh Charles Johnson, "Policies for the Apprehension, Detention and Removal of Undocumented Immigrants," ed. DHS Homeland Security (2014).

58. Dan Stein, "DHS's Priority Enforcement Program More Like "Pretend Enforcement Program," Says Fair," (FAIR, 2015). Accessed on October 6, 2016 at http://www.fairus.org/news/dhs-s-priority-enforcement-program-more-like-pretend-enforcement-program-says-fair

59. Jeff Sessions, "Sessions to Ice Director: Tell Me Why You're Suspending Agent for Upholding   the   Law,"   http://www.sessions.senate.gov/public/index.cfm/news-releases?ID=edfd60df-ba3e-e501-845e-ff41ea971c18.

60. Gafner, Chris, and Stephen Yale-Loehr. 2010. "ATTRACTING THE BEST AND THE BRIGHTEST: A CRITIQUE OF THE CURRENT U.S. IMMIGRATION SYSTEM." *Fordham Urban Law Journal* 38, no. 1: 183-215. *Academic Search Complete*, EBSCO*host* (accessed September 26, 2016).

61. Wadhwa, Vivek. "A Reverse Brain Drain." *Issues in Science & Technology* 25, no. 3 (Spring2009 2009): 45-52. *Professional Development Collection*, EBSCO*host* (accessed September 26, 2016).

62. Noyes, Andrew. "Committee Revives Debate Over Green Card Allocation." *CongressDaily*, June 12, 2008., 7, *MasterFILE Complete*, EBSCO*host* (accessed September 26, 2016).

63. Bennett, James. 2014. "After the Brexit." *New Criterion* 32, no. 5: 40. *MasterFILE Complete*, EBSCO*host* (accessed October 3, 2016).

64. James L. Curtis, n.d. "The Moral Dimension (Book)." *Studies in Comparative International Development* 24, no. 4: 87. *SocINDEX with Full Text*, EBSCO*host* (accessed October 9, 2016).

65. Johnson, Gene, "Sanctuary Cities vow to protect immigrants from Trump plan," CNSNews.com, November 15, 2016, Accessed on November 20, 2016, http://www.cnsnews.com/news/article/sanctuary-cities-vow-protect-immigrants-trump-plan.

Discussion Questions

Chapter One

1. Both the legacy INS and DHS have mission statements. What is the difference between service and enforcement as it relates to the Immigration and Nationality Act (INA)?
2. What is the difference between a special agent (criminal investigator), and a border patrol agent? Discuss the way INS/DHS allocates resources and priorities about each function?
3. What is the sociological definition of deviance as applied to the illegal alien?

Chapter Two

1. Provide a brief historical review of immigration legislation in the US.
2. What is meant by enforcement as a reaction to crisis?
3. How did the 911 terrorist attacks impact on immigration enforcement?
4. What is the difference between legislation and executive orders? Briefly discuss President Obama's executive orders regarding DACA, and DAPA, and the Supreme Court decisions that resulted from them.

Chapter Three

1. Discuss the application of norms as rules in use, and the interpretive framework in the analysis of immigration enforcement.
2. What are the external relations that interact with the legacy INS, and DHS, and how do they effect the enforcement of the immigration laws?
3. Discuss how morale effects the way an organization operates.

Chapter Four

1. Discuss the different methodologies employed in this study. How does participant observation differ from other methods of analysis?
2. How important are official statistics in criminological research, and what are the concerns in interpreting them?
3. How do focused interviews with elites compare with random surveys?
4. What are verbal cues, and how do they impact on interview responses?

Chapter Five

1. What are the basic investigator tasks regarding casework, and how do these tasks compare with police patrol functions?
2. How do investigator's perceptions of task compare with the agency's policies in the legacy INS/DHS?
3. Discuss criminal prosecutions compared with administrative law enforcement in the legacy INS/DHS.

Chapter Six

1. Discuss the investigator's perceptions of status and morale, and the hierarchy in law enforcement.
2. Discuss the relationship between field agents and their supervisors.
3. What factors determine morale in a law enforcement agency?

Chapter Seven

1. What role does the head of a law enforcement agency play in running an agency? Where do agency policies come from? Do policies accurately describe what an agency does, or should do, in terms of its mission statement?
2. Discuss the debate on whether illegal aliens are drainers, or contributors to society?
3. What is the relationship between the US Attorney's Office and the INS/DHS enforcement branches?

Chapter Eight

1. What are the morale problems that surfaced in the legacy INS, and were they resolved in the DHS-ICE?
2. Characterize the relationship between upper-management and field agents in the legacy INS, and the DHS-ICE.

3. How do notions about professionalization impact on morale in an organization like the INS/DHS?

Chapter Nine

1. What is meant by the illegal alien problem?
2. Compare the immigration problem in the US with the immigration problem in Europe, with special reference to what happened in the UK with Brexit.
3. What is the difference between President Trump and President Obama regarding immigration matters? Which strategies do you think will work under the Trump Administration?

References

"2016 presidential candidates on the Trans-Pacific Partnership trade deal," Accessed on September 16, 2016, https://ballotpedia.org/2016_presidential_candidates_on_the_Trans-Pacific_Partnership_trade_deal198-220.

Aldrich, Howard E. (1979). Organizations and Environments, New Jersey: Prentice-Hall, Inc., p. 77.

Allan Silver, "The Demand for Order in Civil Society: A Review of Some Themes in the History of Urban Crime, Police, and Riot," in David Bordua, *The Police: Six Sociological Essays*, New York: John Wiley and Sons, Inc. (1967) 3.

American Immigration Council, "Factsheet: Empty Benches: Underfunding of Immigration Courts Undermines Justice," June 17, 2016. Accessed on October 10, 2016, https://www.americanimmigrationcouncil.org/research/empty-benches-underfunding-immigration-courts-undermines-justice

Associated Press, *Text of Bush, Fox Comments*, The Guardian Unlimited, 1/12/2004, http://www.guardian.co.uk/worldlatest/story/0,1280,-3617017,00.html

Becker, Howard, (1989). "Moral Entrepreneurs: The Creation and Enforcement of Deviant Categories," in Delos H. Kelly, *Deviant Behavior: A Text Reader in the Sociology of Deviance,* edited by Delos H. Kelly, 24. New York: St. Martin's Press.

Becker, Howard. (1989). "Moral Entrepreneurs: The Creation and Enforcement of Deviant Categories," in Delos H. Kelly, Deviant Behavior: A Text Reader in the Sociology of Deviance, New York: St. Martin's Press, p. 24.

Behrens, Steve, ed. (1978). *Questions and Answers on U. S. Immigration and Population,* Washington, DC: Zero Population Growth.

Bennett, James. 2014. "After the Brexit." *New Criterion* 32, no. 5: 40. *MasterFILE Complete,* EDSCO*host* (accessed October 3, 2016).

Bent, Alan E. (1974). The Politics of Law Enforcement: Conflict and Power in Urban Communities, Massachusetts: D. C. Heath and Company, p. 1.

Bertness, Glenn A., *Acting Associate Commissioner, INS, Remarks Concerning Department of Justice Authorization--INS,* before Committee on the Judiciary, Subcommittee on Immigration, Refugees, and International Law, US Senate, April 1, 1981, pp. 1-2.

BJS, "Aggravated felonies included violent drug trafficking, felony property offenses, or smuggling more than six aliens," U.S.S.G. App. C, Nos. 193, 196, 375, 450, 524; in NCJ 191745, p. 8.

Blau, Peter M., and M. W. Meyer. (1971). *Bureaucracy in Modern Society*, New York: Random House, p. 23.

Blau, Peter, M., *On The Nature of Organizations*, New York: John Wiley and Sons, Inc., p. 29.

Bob Price, Breitbart.com, "ICE Agent shot and killed himself on Friday just blocks from his lower Manhattan office," (May 9, 2016) Accessed on June 23, 2016, http://www.breitbart.com/texas/2016/05/09/ice-agent-shoots-blocks-new-york-city-office/

Boss, R. Wayne, "It Doesn't Matter If You Win or Lose, Unless You're Losing: Organizational Change in a Law Enforcement Agency," Journal of Applied Behavioral Science, April 1979 15: 198-220.

Brandon Darby, *Breitbart*, "Retribution: Border patrol Agent Suffers After Blowing Whistle To Congress," (April 18, 2016) Accessed on July 5, 2016, http://www.breitbart.com/texas/2016/04/18/retribution-border-patrol-agent-suffers-blowing-whistle-congress/

Branigin, William. (Dec. 22, 1998). INS Reviews DWI Deportations; Texas Offices' Program Angers Immigrants' Rights Groups, The Washington Post, p. A21.

Bustamante, Jorge A. (1972). "The Wetback as Deviant: An Application of Labeling Theory," American Journal of Sociology, 77(4):716.

Bustamante, Jorge A., "The Wetback as Deviant: An Application of Labeling Theory," *American Journal of Sociology,* 77(4) (1972): 716.

Bustamante, Jorge. (1973). "The Historical Context of Undocumented Mexican Migration to the US". *Aztlan,* 3(2): 257-281.

Byron York, "Why didn't Obama and the Dems pass immigration reform whey they could have in 2009," Washington Examiner, (September 9, 2014), Accessed June 20, 2016, http://washingtonexaminer.com.

C. B. Macpherson, ed., "Introduction," in Thomas Hobbes, *Leviathan,* Maryland: Penguin Books, (1968) 53.

C. Wright Mills, *The Sociological Imagination,* (1959), New York: Oxford University Press.

Camorata, S.A., R. Beck, & J Gimpel (December 17, 2002). Elite v. Public Opinion: An Examination of Divergent Views on Immigration. Paper presented at the National Press Club. Washington D.C. CIS.org, Accessed June 16, 2016, http://www.cis.org/articles/2002/elitepublic.html

Castillo, Leonel, and Others, "New Immigrants," interview by Public Broadcasting System, New York: PBS, 1979.

Central Broadcasting System. (August 28, 1977). Undocumented Aliens, New York: CBS, Inc.

Chapman, Leonard F. Jr. (1975). "A Look at Illegal Immigration: Causes and Impact on the US," *San Diego Law Review*, Volume 13: 34.

CIS.org, Accessed June 16, 2016, http://cis.org/Sanctuary-Cities-Map

City of New Orleans website, Accessed June 16, 2016, http://www.nola.gov/nopd/nopd-con-sent-decree/

Clinard, Marshall and Robert F. Meier, Sociology of Deviant Behavior (Boston, MA: Cengage, 2016), 43.

Comey, James M., FBI.gov, "Testimony: FBI Budget Requests for Fiscal Year 2016," (March 12, 2015) Accessed on June 23, 2016) https://www.fbi.gov/news/testimony/fbi-budget-re-quest-for-fiscal-year-2016

Committee on the Judiciary. (1979). *U. S. Immigration Law and Policy: 1952-1979,* Washington, DC: U. S. Government Printing Office, p. 66.

Comptroller General, Report to the Congress of the US, Prospects Dim for Effectively Enforc-ing Immigration Laws, Washington, DC: U. S. Government Printing Office, 1980, p 24.

Congress of the U.S., Washington, DC, Select Commission on Immigration and Refugee Poli-cy. 1981. "U.S. Immigration Policy and the National Interest. The Final Report and Recom-mendations of the Select Commission on Immigration and Refugee Policy with Supplemen-tal Views by Commissioners." *ERIC*, EBSCO*host* (Accessed October 1, 2016).

Cornelius, Wayne A., "Methodological concerns about research on illegal aliens parallel the methodological concerns in this study." in *Interviewing Illegal aliens: Methodological Re-flections Based on Fieldwork in Mexico and the U. S., International Migration Review,* 16(2): 378-411.

Crewdson, John M., "Legalized Status for Most Aliens in U. S. Proposed," *New York Times,* (Dec. 5, 1980), A20.

Criminal Aliens: INS' Efforts to Identify and Remove Imprisoned Aliens Need to Be Improved (GAO/TGGD-99-47)

Curtis, James L. n.d. "The Moral Dimension (Book)." *Studies in Comparative International Development* 24, no. 4: 87. *SocINDEX with Full Text*, EBSCO*host* (accessed October 9, 2016).

Cutler, Michael, (March 11, 2004) Testimony before the Subcommittee on Immigration, Border Security and Claims. Retrieved from http://www.house.gov/judiciary/cutler031104.htm

Davies, I. R., "A study of colour grouping in three languages: A test of the linguistic relativity hypothesis," *British Journal of Psychology 89*(3) (1998): 433.

Department of Justice, "Organized Crime Drug Enforcement Task Forces," Accessed on June 23, 2016, https://www.justice.gov/criminal/organized-crime-drug-enforcement-task-forces

Dexter, Lewis A., *Elite and Specialized Interviewing,* Ohio: Northwestern University Press, (1970) 5.

DHS Budget data, Annual Yearbook 2015.

DHS Monthly Statistical Reports, DHS Website, Accessed June 16, 2016.

DHS Statistical Table 35, Aliens apprehended by program and border patrol sector, investigations special agents in charge (SAC) jurisdiction, and area of responsibility: fiscal years 2005-2015.

DHS website, "Executive Actions on Immigration," Accessed June 20, 2016, https://www.uscis.gov/immigrationaction

DHS website, "Who We Are,", Accessed June16, 2016 https://www.ice.gov/

DHS website, Accessed June 16, 2016, http://www.immigration.gov/graphics/shared/aboutus/statistics/legishist/act140.htm

DHS website, Accessed June 16, 2016, https://e-verify.uscis.gov/esp/media/resourcesContents/Glossary/glossary.htm#i

DHS website, *History of ICE,* Accessed June 16, 2016, https://www.ice.gov/history

DHS, "Budget-in-Brief: Fiscal Year 2015," Accessed on July 7, 2016, https://www.dhs.gov/sites/default/files/publications/FY15BIB.pdf

DHS, "Consideration of Deferred Action for Childhood Arrivals (DACA)," Accessed on June 24, 2016, https://www.uscis.gov/humanitarian/consideration-deferred-action-childhood-arrivals-daca#guidelines

DHS, "Department of Homeland Security 2015 Federal Employee Viewpoint Survey Results," Accessed on June 28, 2016, https://www.dhs.gov/sites/default/files/publications/2015_FEVS_AES_Department_of_Homeland_Security.pdf

DHS, "Jeh Johnson," Accessed on July 9, 2016, https://www.dhs.gov/person/jeh-johnson

DHS, "Late Twentieth Century," Accessed on July 18, 2016, https://www.uscis.gov/history-and-genealogy/our-history/agency-history/late-twentieth-century

DHS, "Office of Legislative Affairs," Accessed on July 20, 2016, https://www.dhs.gov/about-office-legislative-affairs

DHS, "Our Mission," Accessed on June 30, 2016, https://www.dhs.gov/our-mission

DHS, "Policies for the Apprehension, Detention and Removal of Undocumented Immigrants," (November 20, 2014) Accessed on July 5, 2016, https://www.dhs.gov/sites/default/files/publications/14_1120_memo_prosecutorial_discretion.pdf

DHS, "Written Testimony of ICE Director Sarah Saldana," Accessed on June 30, 2016, https://www.dhs.gov/news/2016/03/15/written-testimony-ice-director-senate-committee-homeland-security-and-governmental

Dinan, Stephen, "Immigration agents sue to stop Obama's non-deportation policy," The Washington Times, (August 23, 2012) Accessed on June 23, 2016, http://www.washingtontimes.com/news/2012/aug/23/immigration-agents-sue-stop-obamas-non-deportation/#pagebreak

Dougherty, Jon, (2003). "Border Militia Critic gets cold feet." World Net Daily. Retrieved from

Dow, Mark. (October 21, 2003). *Scarface and Mariel's Forgotten Prisoners,* Miami, FL: Miami Herald. Retrieved from http://www.cubanet.org/CNews/y03/oct03/22e9.htm

Edelman, Murray, "Power and Symbol in Administrative Regulation," in Social Problems and Public Policy: *Inequality and Justice*, ed., by L. Rainwater, Chicago: Aldine Publishing Company, p. 317.

Etzioni, Amitai. (1970). "Compliance Theory," in *The Sociology of Organizations: Basic Studies,* ed. By Oscar Grusky and George Miller, New York: The Free Press, p. 103.

FAIRUS.org, Accessed June 16, 2016, http://www.fairus.org/DocServer/research-pub/Use_of_Illegal-Alien.pdf

Farnsworth, Elizabeth. (April 1, 1997) Real Audio Interview, Newsmaker, Interview with INS Commissioner Doris Meissner.

Fragomen, Austin T., Jr. (1973). The Illegal alien: Criminal or Economic Refugee, New York: Center for Migration Studies.

J. French and B. Raven, "The Bases of Social Power," in Studies in Social Power, edited by D. Cartwright (MI: Institute for Social Research, 1959), 150-167.

Freund, Julien, The Sociology of Max Weber, New York: Pantheon Books, p. 89.

Friedson, Eliot and J. Lorber, editors. (1972). Medical Men and Their Work: A Sociological Reader, New York: Aldine-Atherton, Inc., 185.

Frontline, "Waco: The Inside Story," Accessed on July 28, 2016, http://www.pbs.org/wgbh/pages/frontline/waco/timeline.html

Gafner, Chris, and Stephen Yale-Loehr. "Attracting the best and the brightest: a critique of the current U.S. immigration system." *Fordham Urban Law Journal* 38, no. 1 (November 2010): 183-215. *Legal Source*, EBSCO*host* (accessed July 18, 2016).

GlobalSecurity.org, "Mariel Boatlift," Accessed June 16, 2016, http://www.globalsecurity.org/military/ops/mariel-boatlift.htm

Goldhamer, Herbert and E. A. Shils, "Types of Power and Status," *American Journal of Sociology*, Vol 45, (September 1939): 171-182.

Gordon, Rebecca, "The US's War on Drugs' Has Spiraled Dangerously Out of Control," *The Nation,* March 23, 2015, https://www.thenation.com/article/can-you-say-blowback-spanish-failed-war-drugs-mexico-and-united-states/ (Accessed on October 3, 2016)

Graham, Otis, "Illegal Immigration and the New Restrictionism," *The Center Magazine,* (1979), 12(3) 54-64.

Greenhouse, Steven. (October 24, 2003). Wal-Mart Raids by US Aimed at Illegal Immigrants. New York Times, NYTimes.com, Accessed June 16, 2016, http://www.nytimes.com/2003/10/24/national/24IMMI.html

Hageman, M. J. C. (1977). "Occupational Stress of Law Enforcement Officers and Marital and Familial Relationships," Doctoral Dissertation, Pullman, Washington: Washington State University.

Hall, R., "Organizations: Structure and Process, 2nd ed.," NJ: Prentice Hall, (1977) 303-312.

Hall, Richard H. (1977). *Organizations: Structure and Process,* New Jersey: Prentice-Hall.

Halsell, Grace, *The Illegals,* (New York: Stein and Day, 1978) 5.

Hawkins, Richard and Gary Tiedeman, *The Creation of Deviance: Interpersonal and Organizational Determinants,* (Ohio: Merrill Publishing Company, 1975), 24-25.

Hawkins, Richard, and Gary Tiedeman. (1975). The Creation of Deviance: Interpersonal and Organizational Determinants, Ohio: Merrill Publishing Company.

Hayward, John, "DHS Whistleblower: PC killed investigation that might have stopped San Bernardino Attack," Breitbart, (December 11, 2015), Accessed June 21, 2016, http://www.breitbart.com/big-government/2015/12/11/dhs-whistleblower-philip-haney-p-c-killed-investigation-might-stopped-san-bernardino-attack/

Hewlett, Sylvia Ann, *Coping with Illegal Immigrants,* Foreign Affairs, (Winter 1981-1982) 358-378.

Huffington Post," Over Half the States Are Suing Obama For Immigration Actions," Accessed June 20, 2016. http://www.huffingtonpost.com/2015/01/26/states-lawsuit-immigration_n_6550840.html

Hughes, Brittany M., CNSnews.com, "ICE Director: Agents Risk 'Termination' For not Enforcing Obama's Immigration Policy, (April 14, 2005) Accessed on June 23, 2016, http://www.cnsnews.com/news/article/brittany-m-hughes/ice-director-agents-risk-termination-not-enforcing-obama-s

Hughes, E. C., *Men and Their Work,* New York: The Free Press, 1958, pp. 49-53.

ICE, "U.S. Immigration and Customs Enforcement Strategic Plan 2016-2020," Accessed on June 28, 2016, https://www.ice.gov/sites/default/files/documents/Document/2016/strategic-plan-2020.PDF

INS Statistical Yearbooks, 1977, 2001, and 2002.

INS, *INS Annual Report*, (1978)

Ismail, Maimunah, Mageswari Kunasegaran, and Roziah Mohd Rasdi. 2014. "Evidence of Reverse Brain Drain in Selected Asian Countries: Human Resource Management Lessons for Malaysia." *Organizations & Markets in Emerging Economies* 5, no. 1: 31-48. *Business Source Complete*, EBSCO*host* (accessed July 18, 2016).

Jacoby, Tamar, (1/12/2004). *America as a Beacon: American Conservatism*, The Wall Street Journal Online, http://online.wsj.com/article/0,,SB107386487358072700,00.html

Jenkins, Sheriff Charles, Frederick County, Maryland, House website, (April 19, 2016), Accessed on June 22, 2016, https://judiciary.house.gov/wp-content/uploads/2016/04/Judicial-Testimony-2016-Sheriff-CJ.pdf

Jenks, Rosemary, *The USA Patriot Act of 2001: A Summary of the Anti-Terrorism Law's Immigration-Related Problems*, Washington, DC: Center for Immigration Studies, December 2001. CIS.org, Accessed June 16, 2016, http://www.cis.org/articles/2001/back1501.html

Johnson, Grassley Comment on DHS Inspector General Report Revealing Lack of Cooperation Between DHS Entities in Aftermath of San Bernardino Terror Attack, Accessed June 17, 2016, https://www.hsgac.senate.gov/media/majority-media/johnson-grassley-comment-on-dhs-inspector-general-report-revealing-lack-of-cooperation-between-dhs-entities-in-aftermath-of-san-bernardino-terror-attack

Johnson, Jeh Charles, "Policies for the Apprehension, Detention and Removal of Undocumented Immigrants," ed. DHS Homeland Security (2014).

Johnston, David, "Border Crossings Near Old Record; U. S. to Crack Down," *New York Times* (February 9, 1992), 1, 34.

Johnston, David. (September 9, 1995). "Informer Says Siege Figure Pressed Gun Sale," *New York Times,* p. 8.

JudicialWatch.org, Accessed June 16, 2016, http://www.judicialwatch.org/blog/2016/04/obama-allots-19-mil-to-register-immigrant-voters/

Judiciary.house.gov, "Goodlatte and Gowdy demand answers on DOJ's efforts to coerce New Orleans to adopt sanctuary policies, Accessed on June 16, 2016, https://judiciary.house.gov/press-release/goodlatte-gowdy-demand-answers-dojs-efforts-coerce-new-orleans-adopt-sanctuary-policies/.

Keely, Charles B. (1977). "Counting the Uncountable: Estimates of Undocumented Aliens in the US". *Population and Development Review.* 3(4): 473-481.

Keely, Charles B., P. J. Elwell, et al., (1978). Profiles of Undocumented Aliens in New York City: Haitian and Dominicans, New York: Center for Migration Studies.

Kevin, J., (n.d). "Border Patrol Catches, then Releases, Illegals." *USA Today*.

King, Allan. (1979). *The Effect of Illegal aliens on Employment in the US*, Texas: University of Texas at Austin.

Kitsuse, John, and A. V. Cicourel. (1963). "A Note on the Use of Official Statistics," Social Problems, 11: 131-139.

Kyl, Statement by Senator Jon, Arizona. (12/12/2004) Senate Subcommittee on Immigration, Washington, D.C. Senator Kyl was responding to Steven Law, the Deputy Labor Secretary's comments.

Lambert, David H., "Target-Adjudications Backlog," *INS Reporter,* (Spring 1978), Washington, DC: INS, 53.

Lanagan, Patrick A., David J. Levin. (June 2002). Recidivism of Prisoners Released in 1994. NCJ 193427. US Department of Justice, Office of Justice Programs, Bureau of Justice Statistics. Washington, DC. Accessed June 16, 2016,

Lehman, Edward W., "Opportunity, Mobility and Satisfaction Within an Industrial Organization," *Social Forces,* 1968. 46: 492-501.

Lemert, Edwin M., *Social Pathology* (NY: McGraw Hill, 1951).

Lester, David, and J. L. Genz, "Internal and External Locus of Control, Experience as a Police Officer, and Job Satisfaction in Municipal Police Officers," *Journal of Police Science and Administration,* 1978. 6(4): 479-481.

Lester, Marilyn, "Generating Newsworthiness: The Interpretive Construction of Public Events," American Sociological Review, 45(December): 984-994.

Lunenburg, Fred C., "Compliance Theory and Organizational Effectiveness," *International Journal of Scholarly Academic Intellectual Diversity 14,* no. 1 (2012).

Manning, Peter K. (1980). The Narc's Game: Organizational and Informational Limits on Drug Law Enforcement, Massachusetts: MIT Press.

Manning, Peter K., *Police Work: The Social Organization of Policing* (Massachusetts: MIT Press, 1977), 5.

Martin Ficke, Interview by George Weissinger, New York, NY, April 29, 2004.

Matter of USINS and AFGE Local 1917, New York: General Services Administration.

Meissner, Doris, PBS Newshour, "Politics," (April 1, 1997), Accessed on June 24, 2016, http://www.pbs.org/newshour/bb/law-jan-june97-meissner_4-1/

Michael Cutler, Frontpage magazine, "Terror Investigation Obstructer Nominated for Secretary's Award for Valor: DHS manager gets honored for thwarting the San Bernardino Investigation," (June 27, 2016) Accessed on June 27, 2016, http://www.frontpagemag.com/fpm/263313/terror-investigation-obstructer-nominated-michael-cutler

Miller, S. M., "The Participant Observer and *Over Rapport,*" *American Sociological Review.* (1952) 17: 97-99.

Mintz, Morton and Jerry Cohen, Power, Inc.: Public and Private Rulers and How to Make Them Accountable, New York: The Viking Press, p. 329.

Morgan, Kristi L.1. 2004. "Evaluating Guest Worker Programs in the U.S.: A Comparison of the Bracero Program and President Bush's Proposed Immigration Reform Plan." *Berkeley La Raza Law Journal* 15, no. 2: 125-144. *Legal Source,* EBSCO*host* (accessed October 1, 2016).

Muller, Thomas, "Missing the Boat on Immigration," *Newsday,* (June 18, 1995), A39.

National Conference of State Legislatures, "Undocumented Student Tuition: Overview," (2015).

Neff, James, (June 17, 1981). "1500 Aliens Arrested Every Day in 12 Mile Border Stretch," *Staten Island Advance,* p. 1.

Neiderhoffer, Arthur. (1967). Behind the Shield: The Police in Urban Society, New York: Doubleday, p.58.

Niederhoffer, Arthur, *A Study of Police Cynicism,* New York: New York University, Ph. D. Dissertation, 1963.

Noah, Timothy, (March 14, 2002). INS Approves Student Visas for 911 terrorists six months after they toppled the World Trade Center. Retrieved from

North, David S. (1978). Illegal aliens: Final Report Outlining a Rationale for and a Preliminary Design of a Study of the Magnitude, Distribution, flow Characteristics and Impacts of Illegal aliens in the US, Washington, DC: Linton and Company.

North, David S., "A Tenuous Connection: Immigration Research and Policy Making," in *The Problem of the Undocumented Worker, ed.,* by R. S. Landmann, (1979) New Mexico: Latin American Institute, p. 21.

North, David S., and Marion F. Houstoun, "The Characteristics and Role of Illegal Aliens in the US Labor Market: An Exploratory Study," (1976) Washington, DC: Linton and Company.

North, David S., Marion F. Houstoun, and Washington, DC. Linton and Co. 1976. "The Characteristics and Role of Illegal Aliens in the U.S. Labor Market: An Exploratory Study." *ERIC,* EBSCO*host* (Accessed October 1, 2016).

Norwichbulletin.com, Accessed June 16, 2016, http://www.norwichbulletin.com/article/20160411/NEWS/160419919

Noyes, Andrew. "Committee Revives Debate Over Green Card Allocation." *CongressDaily,* June 12, 2008., 7, *MasterFILE Complete,* EBSCO*host* (accessed September 26, 2016).

NY Times.com, Accessed June 16, 2016, http://www.nytimes.com/2015/12/05/us/tashfeen-malik-islamic-state.html?_r=0

NYC IDNYC, "Idnyc," ed. IDNYC (New York, NY: New York City 2014). https://www1.nyc.gov/site/idnyc/about/about.page (Accessed on October 8, 2016)

O'Brien, John T. (1978). Public Attitudes Toward Police, Journal of Police Science and Administration, 6: 303-310.

OPM.gov, "Classification & Qualifications: General Schedule Qualification Standards," Accessed on June 27, 2016, https://www.opm.gov/policy-data-oversight/classification-qualifications/general-schedule-qualification-standards/1800/criminal-investigation-series-1811/

Ordóñez, Juan Thomas. "Introduction." In *Jornalero: Being a Day Laborer in the USA*, 1-20. University of California Press, 2015. http://www.jstor.org/stable/10.1525/j.ctt14btfzf.6.

Orr, Kelly, (June 22, 1981). "The Great American Immigration Nightmare," *U. S. News and World Report*, pp. 27-32.

Ostrow, Ronald J., "Bush Signs Law Boosting Immigration Quotas by 40%," *Los Angeles Times*, (Nov. 30, 1990), 39.

Perrow, Charles, *Complex Organizations: A Critical Essay, 2nd edition*, Illinois: Scott, Foresman and Company, 1979, p. 162.

Peter M Blau, *On the Nature of Organizations*, (New York: John Wiley and Sons, Inc., 1974), 15.

Procon.org, Accessed June 16, 2016, http://immigration.procon.org/view.answers.php?questionID=000757

Quinney, Richard, and John Wildeman, The Problem of Crime: A Peace and Social Justice Perspective, California: Mayfield Publishing Company, pp. 48-49.

Radnofsky, Louise, "Illegal Immigrants Get Public Health Care, Despite Federal Policy," *Wall Street Journal*, March 24, 2016.

Reiss, Albert J., and D. J. Bordua. (1967). "Environment and Organization: A Perspective on the Police," in David Bordua, The Police: Six Sociological Essays, pp. 25-26.

Reiss, Albert J., Jr. (1971). The Police and the Public, New Haven: Yale University Press, p. 173.

Richard, W. C. and R. D. Fell. (1975). "Health Factors in Police Job Stress," in W. H. Kroes, and J. J. Hurrell, editors, Job Stress and the Police Officer: Identifying Stress Reduction Techniques, Proceedings of Symposium, Washington, DC: U. S. Government Printing Office.

Riley, Michael. "A grim gamble," *Denver Post*, October 19, 2003.

Sagarin, Edward. 1976. "The impact of crime (Book Review)." *American Journal of Sociology* 81, 1223. *Book Review Digest Retrospective: 1903-1982 (H.W. Wilson)*, EBSCO*host* (accessed October 4, 2016).

Samora, Julian (1971). *Los Mojados: The Wetback Story*, Indiana: University of Notre Dame Press.

Schaefer, Roger, "Law Enforcer, Peace Keeper, Servicer: Role Alternatives for Policemen," *Journal of Police Science and Administration*, 1978. 6:324-335.

Schaefer, Roger, (1978). "Law Enforcer, Peace Keeper, Servicer: Role Alternatives for Policemen," *Journal of Police Science and Administration*. 6: 324-335.

Schaeffer, Joe, *Newsmax*, "Paperwork Hampers Border patrol as Illegals Flood Into US," (June 9, 2014), Accessed on July 6, 2016, http://www.newsmax.com/Newsfront/Henry-Cuellar-Texas-border-paperwork/2014/06/09/id/576016/

Schneider, J. W. and J. I. Kitsuse, *Studies in The Sociology of Social Problems* (1984).

Schroeder, Richard C. (1976). *Illegal Immigration*, Editorial Research Reports, 2 (Dec. 10): 22.

Schuck, Peter H. and John Williams, (Spring, 1999). "Removing Criminal Aliens: The pitfalls and promises of federalism." Harvard Journal of Law and Public Policy. Cambridge: MA, pp. 367-463.

Schur, Edwin M. (1980). The Politics of Deviance: Stigma Contests and the Uses of Power, New Jersey: Prentice Hall, Inc.

Schur, Edwin M., Interpreting Deviance: A Sociological Introduction, New York: Harper and Row, p. 370.

Select Committee on Population. (1978). *Legal and Illegal Immigration to the US*, Washington, DC: U. S. Government Printing Office.

Senate.gov, Accessed June 16, 2016, https://www.judiciary.senate.gov/imo/media/doc/05-19-16%20Homan%20Testimony.pdf

Senate.gov, Accessed June 16, 2016, https://www.judiciary.senate.gov/imo/media/doc/07-21-15%20Steinle%20Testimony.pdf

Seper, Jerry n.d., "Border patrol Union Survey finds job discontent," *Washington Times*, The (DC), n.d. *Regional Business News*, EBSCO host (accessed June 29, 2016).

Sessions, Jeff, "Sessions to Ice Director: Tell Me Why You're Suspending Agent for Upholding the Law," http://www.sessions.senate.gov/public/index.cfm/news-releases?ID=edfd60df-ba3e-e501-845e-ff41ea971c18.

Seymour, Whitney North, (1975). US Attorney: An Inside View of Justice in America Under the Nixon Administration, New York: William Morrow and Company, Inc., pp. 47-48.

Silver, Isidore, ed., (1974). The Crime Control Establishment, New Jersey: Prentice-Hall, Inc., p. 1.

Simon, Julian. (July 10, 1980). Immigrants, Especially Illegals, Raise U. S. Incomes, Newsday.

Sirica, Jack, "Audit Finds Immigration-Law Backlash," *Newsday*, (March 30, 1990) 15

Skerry, Peter, (August 12, 2001), "Why Amnesty is the wrong way to go," Washington Post, p. B1.

Skolnick, Jerome H. (1966). Justice Without Trial: Law Enforcement in Democratic Society, New York: John Wiley and Sons, p. 228.

Smith III, T. J., "The Media Elite Revisited. (Cover story)," *National Review, 45*(12), (1993): 34-37.

Snyder, Russell, "Bush Signs Sweeping Immigration Bill," *United Press International* (November 30, 1990).

Sofer, Eugene, "Illegal Immigration: Background to the Current Debate," (1980) *CONEG Policy Research Center, Inc.*

Stein, Dan, "DHS's Priority Enforcement Program More Like "Pretend Enforcement Program," Says Fair," (FAIR, 2015). Accessed on October 6, 2016 at http://www.fairus.org/news/dhs-s-priority-enforcement-program-more-like-pretend-enforcement-program-says-fair

Survey of Inmates in State and Federal Correctional Facilities-1997, Source at: http://webapp.icpsr.umich.edu/cocoon/NACJD-STUDY/02598.xml U.S. Dept. of Justice, Bureau of Justice Statistics, and U.S. Dept. of Justice, Federal Bureau of Prisons. SURVEY OF INMATES IN STATE AND FEDERAL CORRECTIONAL FACILITIES, 1997 [Computer file]. Compiled by U.S. Dept. of Commerce, Bureau of the Census. ICPSR ed. Ann Arbor, MI: Inter-university Consortium for Political and Social Research [producer and distributor], 2001.

Sutter, D., "Mechanisms of Liberal Bias in the News Media versus the Academy," *Independent Review, 16*(3), (2012): 399-415.

The Green Line Podcast, Episode 68: Blue Plate Special, starts at 34:00 minutes, (March 11, 2016) Accessed on July 5, 2016, http://www.bpunion.org/index.php/newsroom/the-green-line-podcast

Toch, Hans. (1978). "Police Morale: Living with Discontent," Journal of Police Science and Administration. 6:249-252.

Triennial Comprehensive Report on Immigration, p. 16.

United States Code Annotated, (St. Paul, Minnesota: West Publishing Company, 1976), Section 1551.

United States Commission on Civil Rights, *A Study of Federal Immigration Policies and Practices In southern California*, Washington, DC: U. S. Government Printing Office, p. 15.

United States Congress, Department of State, Justice, and Commerce, The Judiciary, and Related Agencies Appropriations for 1981, Hearings Before a Subcommittee of the Committee on Appropriations House of Representatives, 96th Congress, 2nd Session, Washington, DC: U. S. Government Printing Office, p. 538.

US General Accounting Office, "Briefing Report to the Honorable Alfonse M. D'Amato US Senate, Criminal Aliens: INS' Investigative Efforts in the New York City Area," (March, 1986) Maryland: U. S. General Accounting Office, GAO/GGD-86-58BR.

US General Accounting Office, "Criminal Aliens: INS' Efforts to Identify and Remove Imprisoned Aliens Continue to Need Improvement." (February 1999). GAO/T-GGD-99-47.

USAtoday.com, Accessed June 16, 2016, http://www.usatoday.com/story/news/nation/2016/06/13/orlando-shooting-what-we-know/85815500/

USDOJ Annual Reports, "Corrective Action Report: Efforts to Identify and Remove Criminal Aliens." (12/2/02)

USINS, "The Triennial Comprehensive Report on Immigration," (May 1999), Accessed June 16, 2016, https://www.uscis.gov/sites/default/files/USCIS/Resources/Reports%20and%20Studies/tri3fullreport.pdf

Van Maanen, John, "The Asshole," in Peter K. Manning and J. Van Maanen, *Policing: A View from the Street,* California: Goodyear Publishing Company, 1978, pp. 221-223.

Vaughn, Jessica, "Catch and Release," CIS, (March 2014), Accessed on June 22, 2016, http://cis.org/catch-and-release

Vladtepesblog.com, Accessed June 16, 2016, http://vladtepesblog.com/2015/12/16/dhs-whistleblower-philip-haney-in-open-letter-to-congress-no-confidence-in-administrations-vetting-process/

Vold, George B., and T. J. Bernard, *Theoretical Criminology, 3rd Edition* (New York: Oxford University Press, 1986), 146-150. Emile Durkheim considered crime a normal, inevitable and integral part of all societies. *The Rules of Sociological Method,* tr. by Sarah Solovay, and J. Mueller, ed. By G. E. G. Catlin, (New York: The Free Press, 1965).

Wadhia, S. S., "The History of Prosecutorial Discretion in Immigration Law." *American University Law Review, 64*(5) (2015). 1285-1302.

Wadhwa, Vivek. "A Reverse Brain Drain." *Issues in Science & Technology* 25, no. 3 (Spring2009 2009): 45-52. *Professional Development Collection,* EBSCO*host* (accessed September 26, 2016).

WallStreetJournal.com, Accessed June 16, 2016, http://www.wsj.com/articles/SB122721278056345271

Walrod, T. H. (1978). "Causes of Stress to Police Officers Detailed," National Sheriff, 30 (October) 12-29.

Weber, Max. (1947). *The Theory of Social and Economic Organization,* New York: The Free Press.

Weissinger, George J. (July 26, 1980). "Assessing Aliens Impact,*"* *Newsday,* Letters to the Editor.

Weissinger, George J., "Release of Iranians Brings Protest from INS Investigators," (1980). New York: *Federal Law Enforcement Officers Association Newsletter.*

Weissinger, George. (2003). The Illegal Alien Problem: Enforcing the Immigration Laws. Immigration-usa.com, Accessed June 16, 2016, http://www.immigration-usa.com/george_weissinger.html

Whitehead, John T. (1989). Burnout in Probation and Corrections, New York: Praeger Publishers.

Wilson, James Q. (1968). Varieties of Police Behavior: The Management of Law and Order in Eight Communities, Massachusetts: Harvard University Press.

Wilson, James Q. (1978). *The Investigators: Managing FBI and Narcotics Agents,* New York: Basic Books, Inc., p. 7.

Zimmerman, Malia and M. Dean. "Feds Blocked from Person of Interest after San Bernardino Attack," Foxnews.com, 2016, March 15. http://www.foxnews.com/politics/2016/03/15/feds-blocked-from-person-interest-after-san-bernardino-attack-lawmakers-told.html.

Index